MIRACLES & MURDERS

Miracles & Murders

An Introductory Anthology
of Breton Ballads

by
Mary-Ann Constantine & Éva Guillorel

With a foreword by
David Atkinson

Oxford University Press, Great Clarendon Street, Oxford OX2 6DP

First edition published in 2017

British Library Cataloguing in Publication Data
Data available

Library of Congress Cataloging in Publication Data
Data available

Typeset by Mach 3 Solutions Ltd, Stroud
Printed in Great Britain by CPI Antony Rowe, Chippenham, Wiltshire

ISBN 978-0-19-726619-9

For Donatien Laurent and Fañch Postic

Foreword by David Atkinson

The Breton *gwerz* has long been perceived to be at the forefront of the Romantic quest for the 'voice of the people', and English-speaking ballad scholars have probably been more aware of the controversy surrounding Hersart de La Villemarqué's *Barzaz-Breiz* than of the actual ballads, or *gwerziou*, themselves, if only because of the language barrier and limited access to recordings. Yet those who have been fortunate enough to enjoy some introduction to the substance of the Breton ballads have never failed to be fascinated and moved by the strange world they evoke. Strange, that is, to scholars most familiar with (and in some ways unhappily constrained by the authority of) F. J. Child's standard edition of *The English and Scottish Popular Ballads*.

As with the English-language ballads, the 'discovery', the collecting, editing and publishing of the Breton ballads was driven by a desire to rediscover the 'ancient' poetry of a nation or a people. That is especially true of narrative poetry that shades over into song, for song is often thought of as touching on the origins of language and as being somehow primitive, and narrative evokes the notion of long-standing story and myth. The idea no doubt reaches back to Homer, as well as to the early modern and Enlightenment 'discovery' of the cultures of indigenous peoples and consequent 'invention' of oral tradition, and it looks forward to the new impetus given to similar ideas by the Parry–Lord theory of oral literature.

La Villemarqué and the *Barzaz-Breiz*, and his 'nemesis', François-Marie Luzel, stand as parallels to Thomas Percy and his enemies, particularly Joseph Ritson and to some extent Child himself. Yet Child was absolutely indebted to Percy's *Reliques of Ancient English Poetry*, which, after all, inspired the whole Romantic-era interest in ballads right across Europe. The Breton *gwerziou*, though, are really quite unlike the English-language ballads. A guiding principle for Child was the identification of international parallels to the ballads he chose to print, and although he actually located rather few Breton analogues, the famous 'three hundred and five' of the Child canon probably still tend to suggest that there are more similarities than is actually the case. That is because the canon as it stands gives undue prominence to certain fantastical, supernatural ballads (the shape-shifting women, the fairy ride, the unexplained deaths, the flyting contests with the devil) at the expense of the printed ballads of England and Scotland.

For it is the printed ballads that were a constant presence in Britain from early modern times to the end of the 19th century, and it is in that respect that the English-language and Breton ballad traditions differ most markedly. While printed songs in English are absolutely intertwined with the ballads and folk songs collected directly from singers (and no one is suggesting that oral transmission did not take place), in Brittany the printed ballads or *feuilles volantes* (often 'news' ballads, which invite comparison with their counterparts in English and other languages such as German) are largely distinct from the collected *gwerziou*.

A corollary of this difference is the overwhelming sense of place evident in the Breton ballads. People are named, places are named and one feels the stories could not have happened anywhere else. 'Gwerz Penmarc'h' belongs to that particular commune on the far north-west coast of France and to nowhere else. In contrast, the action of a ballad such as 'Lord Thomas and Fair Eleanor' (Child 73) could take place more or less anywhere in a stylised 'ballad world'. Even seemingly localised pieces such as English broadside 'tragedies' with various county names attached to them are actually quite generic. There are some local, historical songs in English, but they mostly lack the legendary quality of the Breton *gwerziou*. The Breton ballads are rooted in a culture of Catholic legend, belief and practice, which is also made manifest in the churchyards of Breton villages and in the *pardons*, or local saints' festivals. The English-language ballads, in contrast, belong to a post-Reformation culture or *habitus* which embodies aspects of conventional moral teaching but rarely reverts to overtly religious themes. That is an important point of difference, which should not be allowed to mask an underlying similarity, that these are works of imaginative literature in either language and they should not be read simplistically as expressions of 'belief'.

Nevertheless, there is in the corpus of Breton narrative song a feeling of coherence that is lacking from, say, the Child canon, or even the corpus of English and Scottish folk songs as established by the collectors of the late 19th and early 20th centuries. There is a sense that it is possible to tell the whole story of the *gwerziou*, or at least to introduce a non-Breton-speaking audience to it in a rounded manner, as this volume does triumphantly. Undoubtedly, that characteristic derives from the history of the *gwerziou* and their distance from print, their relative continuity of common themes and of storytelling mode, and their relative isolation from foreign influences on account of their linguistic integrity (though French influences are certainly there, and the point should not be exaggerated). In comparison, the English-language ballad corpus feels amorphous.

The traditions of scholarship, however, are strikingly similar. It is not fashionable to praise either Percy or La Villemarqué. It is more in vogue to laud the condition of 'scientific folklore' (as if there could ever be such a thing) to which Luzel aspired, and certainly the ethnographic turn which gives space to singers and communities is to be welcomed. Modern technology has made ballad melodies more accessible, too, and there is no doubt that however intriguing the ballad is as literature, the tunes are also part of the aesthetic pull. It is a particular strength of this collection that the accompanying CD will allow readers to discover the sounds of the *gwerziou* in a variety of styles, dialects and contexts. An important strand in modern scholarship is that it should be self-reflexive, and in that regard it is as well to admit that the aesthetics of balladry are what draw in most scholars in the first place.

For the Breton corpus, the literary aesthetics are particularly memorable, adventures expounded often incrementally within a simple, emphatic verse form. Here are things such as the wax child of Tréguier (no. 20), the dead children concealed in an overgrown well (no. 17), the little book at the bottom of the sea, written with the Saviour's blood (no. 3), Catherin An Troadec, her cheeks eaten away by fish (no. 26), seven salted hearts in a broken pot (no. 14), the unfathomable cruelty of Mari Tili (no. 18). For all the Breton exceptionalism, however, there are themes that resonate right across European balladry: crime and justice; motherhood and infanticide; seductions and thwarted lovers; family and other rivalries; war, plague, famine.

It is natural to want to know how old such things are, and in Brittany it is even harder to tell than in England or Scotland. Of course, that is what the 19th-century collectors wanted to know, too, and on occasion they sought to imply that things were really very old indeed. The Breton ballads do have some occasional connections with things Celtic and with 'medieval' romance, just as some of the Child ballads have some relationships with romance. On the whole, though, it is probable that the majority of these ballads are later, and that is where they are best situated. Nevertheless, the idea of 'reliques of ancient poetry' is part of the cultural heritage of both ballad areas.

These few comparative remarks are intended simply to whet the appetite, to excite the reader familiar with the English-language ballads to go and explore another body of narrative song, here made accessible in a very fine set of translations – indeed, the first translations to make the original *gwerz* materials accessible to an English-speaking audience – and a set of recordings that are a delight to the ear. Becker and Le Gurun write, 'La Gwerz est la complainte tragique, épique, héroïque ou homérique de la littérature bretonne.'[1] If that is not enough to inspire further discovery, I don't know what is!

David Atkinson
Honorary Research Fellow,
Elphinstone Institute, University of Aberdeen

1   Roland Becker and Laure Le Gurun, *La Musique Bretonne* (Spézet: Coop Breizh, 1994), p. 9.

Contents

List of Maps and Plates

Maps

Plates

Black-and-white plates are between pages 112 and 113

Preface

One of the most insistent themes of the ballads included in this volume is that of the journey. People set off with certain intentions: to pay homage to a local saint, undertake a pilgrimage to save a soul, join the army, meet a sweetheart, draw water from a well. And surprising things happen as a result. Academics often find that their own journeys, usually to conferences, also cause things to happen, though they are (most of the time) less bloody and less tragic than the outcomes of many of these songs. The eclectic, invigorating environment of the International Ballad Conference (IBC) provided the authors of this volume, based in different countries, with the chance to meet and exchange ideas on several occasions, and there have been other equally stimulating opportunities besides.

Both of us had independently harboured the idea of bringing the *gwerz* (narrative song) tradition of Brittany to a wider, Anglophone audience. Indeed, part of the research for this volume was undertaken many years ago, in the course of a British Academy Postdoctoral Fellowship (1996–1999) and a Leverhulme Special Research Fellowhip (2000–2002) held by Mary-Ann Constantine. When Éva Guillorel was awarded a British Academy Newton International Fellowship, and learned of the possibility of publishing a monograph through the scheme, the idea of a collaborative project on the Breton ballads seemed like the perfect proposal. Both authors studied the *gwerziou* for their doctoral dissertations, and have published widely in French and English on them since. Our academic interests in the songs are helpfully complementary, with Guillorel trained as an ethnologist and historian of the early modern period, and Constantine as a literary critic. Pooling our knowledge and our expertise has enabled us to cover a wide range of song texts from various different perspectives. We are both, therefore, very grateful to Barbara Hillers and David Hopkin for initially recommending our idea, and to Brigid Hamilton-Jones and the publications team at the British Academy for their support for us both, and for the subject, over many years.

Books like this involve a great deal of external expertise, and in producing this volume we are very grateful to David Parsons, who has supplied us with maps and advice on place-names, and to Robert Bouthillier, for his painstaking transcriptions of the ballad tunes. We were especially pleased when David Atkinson (another IBC veteran) agreed to write a foreword. Both he and Oliver Padel, our insightful peer reviewer, made thoughtful suggestions after reading our initial draft, and have much improved the end result. Elizabeth Stone has been a careful and skilful editor, and we are most grateful for her help.

We owe a great deal too to the Dastum Centre, and its vast repository of Breton song texts and tunes: it is thanks to the Centre, and in particular to Gaétan Crespel, Gwenn Drapier and Vincent

Morel, that readers of this anthology will be able to hear some of the pieces for themselves on the accompanying CD. We are also much indebted to Véronique Brémon and Marie-Rose Prigent (CRBC) as well as the Austrian Academy of Sciences for help arranging permissions, Guy de La Villemarqué, Philippe-Étienne and Naïk Raviart and to all the collectors and singers involved in the initial recordings, including Daniel Giraudon, Michel Colleu, Jo Guilleux, Loeiz Le Bras, Roland Laigo, Claudine Mazéas, Jean-Yves Monnat, Nicole Pochic, René Richard, Pierre-Yves Pétillon and Ifig Troadeg. The CD was compiled and produced by Dastum (September 2016); it was mixed and mastered at Studio du Faune with the assistance of Vincent Morel.

Our respective institutions, the University of Caen and the University of Wales Centre for Advanced Welsh and Celtic Studies, have also been very supportive. The expertise of staff and librarians at the Centre de recherche bretonne et celtique (CRBC) at the Université de Bretagne Occidentale in Brest has been a mainstay of our research for several decades now. Two of its members, now retired, have had a powerful impact on academic interest in Breton popular culture over that time, and we are indebted intellectually and personally to them both. We would like this book to stand as a gesture of thanks and homage to Fañch Postic (until recently in charge of the Centre de recherche et de documentation de la littérature orale at the Manoir de Kernault, Mellac) and to Donatien Laurent (former director of the CRBC) – tenacious, inquisitive, witty and affectionate champions of a rich and under-appreciated culture. *Deoc'h ho-taou, trugarez vras a greiz kalon.*

Mary-Ann Constantine and Éva Guillorel

Introduction

It is the stranger details that stick in the mind: corpses on a beach being 'eaten by yellow crabs'; a penitent soul huddled in a cold field 'between the horses' feet'; a red-eyed fiend clinging to the burning spire of Quimper cathedral, boiling lead dripping down on terrified spectators. The world of the Breton *gwerz* is peculiar and tormented; it dramatises events that are shocking or sorrowful, retaining all the while a kind of dignified restraint. It brings the past alive in familiar, highly specific landscapes – *this* road, *that* cottage, *that* church, still there, still bearing witness. Events and characters in these songs may be intensely local but the stories, and the manner of telling them, speak compellingly beyond the immediate borders of language, time and place.

Our aim in this volume is to make the Breton-language ballad tradition better known. One of the richest and most unusual bodies of song in Europe, it received some attention for a period in the mid-19th century, when the first enthusiastic collectors of the 'voices of the people' began engaging with folk song and other 'national' traditions. The earliest published collection, Théodore Hersart de La Villemarqué's *Barzaz-Breiz* of 1839, offered the French-speaking public a literary and highly mediated version of the tradition which made some astonishing claims for the ballads' antiquity. The controversy that followed gave Breton ballads a certain notoriety, but despite more 'scientific' collections appearing later in the century, and work in the field continuing to this day, knowledge of the actual songs has remained restricted, especially in the anglophone world.[1]

This is not particularly surprising. The literatures of the Celtic languages are poorly known in the English-speaking world; even rich written literary traditions such as Irish and Welsh still have little place in the study of 'British' literature, and a language like Breton, with a flourishing oral tradition but a relatively sparse written record and few translations, is especially hard to access. We hope, though, to show in our collection of ballads just how much this material has to offer, not only for the scholar of comparative folk song, but for the Celtic linguist looking for new texts, the historian interested in how memories of past events are preserved and constructed in oral genres, the ethnomusicologist exploring performance contexts, and any reader with an appetite for dramatic stories and striking detail.

Breton is a Celtic language currently spoken by some 170,000 people in the far north-western corner of France. It belongs to the Brittonic branch of Celtic, and is thus a sister language to Welsh

---

1   For the best studies on the context and content of the *Barzaz-Breiz*, see Donatien Laurent, *Aux sources du Barzaz-Breiz: La mémoire d'un peuple* (Douarnenez: ArMen, 1989) and Nelly Blanchard, *Barzaz-Breiz. Une fiction pour s'inventer* (Rennes: Presses universitaires de Rennes, 2006).

and Cornish (Irish, Scots Gaelic and Manx form the Goidelic branch, and are more distantly related). The Brittonic languages (along with Cumbric in the north-west of Britain) would once have been part of a single more or less intelligible west-coast linguistic continuum, rather like the Scandinavian languages today. Modern surviving Brittonic languages (basically Welsh and Breton, with Cornish as a recently revived addition) share many important features of vocabulary and syntax but have been much influenced by their more powerful neighbours, English and French, and are no longer mutually comprehensible at any sustained level of conversation.[2]

The last decades of the 20th century saw a dramatic collapse in the numbers of people speaking Breton. Just after the Second World War, however, there were still over a million speakers in the western part of the country known as *Breiz-Izel* (Basse-Bretagne, Lower Brittany). Within *Breiz-Izel*, Breton is traditionally divided into four distinct dialect areas linked to the four bishoprics (though in truth the nature and range of linguistic variety is much more complex): *Leon* (Léon), *Treger* (Trégor), *Kerne* (Cornouaille) and *Gwened* (Vannetais).[3] The linguistic border dividing Upper and Lower Brittany (see Map 1) is centuries old, and has shifted relatively little; the fact that important cities such as Rennes and Nantes have always stood outside the Breton-speaking zone has had an impact on the social status and uses (and non-uses) of Breton, for example in matters of jurisdiction, education and printing.[4] Though printed texts (often religious tracts) did circulate among the Breton-speaking population,[5] Breton was and has remained very much the spoken language of a rural community used to receiving its written infrastructure through French (and, earlier, Latin). And although in the long term this has not helped the survival of the language, it may well be that the inventiveness and variety of Breton oral literary forms and musical traditions are a result of this sociolinguistic situation.[6]

The mid-19th century flowering of interest in the Breton song tradition stimulated by the romanticised versions of the *Barzaz-Breiz* led to more reliable collections, many with translations into French. Research into individual ballads, ballad clusters and singers' repertoires has also grown substantially over the past century and a half, and, as new methodologies have developed in disciplines previously resistant to orality, *gwerziou* are now no longer only the preserve of folklorists.[7] Many of these works appeared in local antiquarian journals or short-lived periodicals,

2   Martin J. Ball and James Fife (eds), *The Celtic Languages* (London: Taylor & Francis, 1993). For a wide-ranging introduction to Breton language and literature see Jean Balcou and Yves Le Gallo (eds), *Histoire littéraire et culturelle de la Bretagne*, 3 vols (Brest, Paris and Geneva: Champion, Slatkine, 1987). For broad historical context see Sharif Gemie, *Brittany 1750–1950: The Invisible Nation* (Cardiff: University of Wales Press, 2007) and Gwenno Piette, *Brittany: A Concise History* (Cardiff: University of Wales Press, 2008).

3   The form and orthography of Breton place names is a politically sensitive subject; please see our Editorial Policy, which follows this Introduction.

4   Fañch Broudic, *La pratique du breton de l'Ancien Régime à nos jours* (Rennes: Presses universitaires de Rennes, 1995); Fañch Broudic, *Parler breton au XXIe siècle* (Brest: Emgleo Breiz, 2009); Caroline Brett examines the use (and non-use) of Breton in the Middle Ages in 'Breton Latin literature as Evidence for Literature in the Vernacular AD 800–1300', *Cambrian Medieval Celtic Studies,* 18 (1989), 1–25.

5   Yves Le Berre, *La littérature de langue bretonne. Livres et brochures entre 1790 et 1918* (Brest: Ar Skol Vrezoneg, Emgleo Breiz, 1994); Yves Le Berre, *Qu'est-ce que la littérature bretonne? Essais de critique littéraire XVe–XXe siècle* (Rennes: Presses universitaires de Rennes, 2006).

6   Association Buhez (ed.), *Parlons du breton* (Rennes: Ouest-France, 2001).

7   Historians, for example, have increasingly explored the possibilities of the *gwerz*: see Alain Croix, *La Bretagne aux 16e et 17e siècles: La vie, la mort, la foi* (Paris: Maloine, 1981); Michel Nassiet, 'La littérature orale bretonne et l'histoire', *Annales de Bretagne et des Pays de*

and remain difficult to track down. English-language translations and discussions of the tradition remain both restricted and rare.[8]

The selection of ballads in this volume aims to offer a flavour of the great richness and diversity of the *gwerz* tradition in terms of form, narrative content and music. It contains ballads from different dialectal regions, and from different periods of collection, from the earliest 19th-century manuscripts to the most recent field recordings. The Breton texts are accompanied by English translations, which attempt (although folk songs are always remarkably resistant to capture in another language) to preserve something of the poetry and beauty of the originals, while remaining close enough to the texture and idioms of the Breton to offer a guide to those interested in the language. They are accompanied by brief commentaries which, often through comparison with other versions, explore the dramatic force of each song, its narrative technique and its historical context, summarising previous scholarship and providing references for further reading. These short case studies also provide, where known, details of the singers and the circumstances under which the songs were collected or performed. The accompanying CD offers a selection of ballads taken from field recordings. Actual voices, the human presence required for all oral tradition to survive, need not be entirely lost from the experience; these recordings, we hope, will allow listeners to appreciate some of the melodies, and the wide range of singing styles, intonations and dialects encompassed by the *gwerziou*.

I: Song collecting in Brittany: from the early 19th century to the present day

France came relatively late to the Europe-wide 'rediscovery' of popular traditions in the Romantic period.[9] Long after the 1760s, when the Ossianic poems of James Macpherson, the ballads of Thomas Percy and the enthusiastic responses of J. G. Herder had stirred imaginations with the creative, historical – and political – possibilities of folk song as the 'voice of the people', the more classically-inclined French began to search among their own vernacular traditions for potentially ancient narrative songs. An initial call by scholars, notably Pierre-Antoine La Place in 1785, for more research into narrative song-cycles or 'romances' produced few results.[10] Focus shifted to Brittany, where the presence of a Celtic language (which could be associated with France's

---

l'Ouest, 106 (1999), 35–64. Éva Guillorel, *La Complainte et la Plainte: Chanson, justice, cultures en Bretagne, XVIᵉ–XVIIIᵉ siècles* (Rennes and Brest: Presses universitaires de Rennes, Centre de recherche bretonne et celtique, Dastum, 2010).

8   Modern English translations include nine pieces in Mary-Ann Constantine, *Breton Ballads* (Aberystwyth: Cambrian Medieval Celtic Studies, 1996) and a few examples in Mary-Ann Constantine and Gerald Porter, *Fragments and Meaning in Traditional Song: from the Blues to the Baltic* (Oxford: Oxford University Press, 2003) and Natalie Franz, *Breton Song Traditions and the Case of the Gwerzioù: Women's Voices, Women's Lives* (Rennes: Tir, 2011).

9   Fañch Postic (ed.), *La Bretagne et la littérature orale en Europe* (Mellac and Brest: Centre de recherche bretonne et celtique, Centre de recherche et de documentation sur la littérature orale, Centre international de rencontres des cultures de tradition orale, 1995). For a wider view see the ambitious online project directed by Joep Leerssen, *Encyclopedia of Romantic Nationalism in Europe*: http://romanticnationalism.net.

10   Paul Bénichou, *Nerval et la chanson folklorique* (Paris: José Corti, 1970), p. 47.

ancestral Gauls) seemed to assure the cultural antiquity and continuity necessary for the survival of epic folk poetry.[11] In 1794, the Lorient-born Jacques Cambry, Commissioner for Science and Arts in the Revolutionary government, undertook a journey through Brittany. His principal aim was to survey the property confiscated from the nobility and the clergy, but his account of the tour, published as *Voyage dans le Finistère* (1797–8), included ethnographical description of the 'customs and manners' of the people, and made some note of the folk tales and songs he encountered on his travels.[12] The keynote in that respect, however, was disappointment:

> Les grands morceaux de l'antiquité se sont perdus à la chûte des Bardes: quelques recherches que j'aie faites, je n'ai pu trouver dans la mémoire ou dans les manuscrits des tems passés, ces chants majestueux qui conduisoient nos pères à la victoire, ces hymnes sublimes, chantés au milieu des combats, sur l'Océan, sur les rivages de la mer, entonnés par un peuple invincible, et dont l'effet étoit semblable à celui du tonnerre ou des mers en fureurs, au rapport des écrivains grecs et romains. La poésie a dû s'anéantir en Bretagne ...[13]

> [The great songs of antiquity have perished with the fall of the Bards; no matter how much I searched, neither memory nor ancient manuscripts could furnish me with those majestic songs which led our fathers to victory, those sublime hymns, sung in the midst of combat, on the Ocean, at the sea's edge, chanted by an invincible people, the effect of which was like thunder or like the raging seas, as the Greek and Roman authors tell us. Poetry must have died out altogether in Brittany ...]

Cambry would go on to be a founding member (and first president) of the Académie Celtique in 1805, and it is clear from this quotation that, like other antiquarians who saw popular tradition as a potential time capsule, his gaze was fixed on the deep past.[14] As would often prove the case, too clear a sense of the kind of song that *ought* to exist in Brittany – be it Gaulish war chant, or medieval Breton *lai* – rendered the actual tradition inadequate, if not inaudible.

   The first collections of Breton traditional song did not really begin, then, until the first decades of the 19th century; and they were relatively restricted in scope. An early enthusiast was the Morlaix printer Alexandre Lédan, whose notebook of traditional songs dates from 1815, but who preferred to publish and sell mainly 'feuilles volantes', the more sensational printed broadside ballads.[15] Other private collections were left by a small network of aristocratic amateurs (at least two of them women), who collected songs from the rural communities in the vicinity of

11   Bernard Tanguy, *Aux origines du nationalisme breton* (Paris: Union générale d'éditions, 1977).
12   Fañch Postic, 'Écrire "l'histoire de l'imagination": Cambry face au paysan breton', in Anne de Mathan (ed.), *Jacques Cambry (1749–1807): Un Breton des Lumières au service de la construction nationale* (Brest: Centre de recherche bretonne et celtique, 2008), pp. 73–83.
13   Jacques Cambry, *Voyage dans le Finistère, ou Etat de ce département en 1794 et 1795* (Paris, 1797–98), vol. I, p. 189.
14   Nicole Belmont (ed.), *Aux sources de l'ethnologie française. L'académie celtique* (Paris: Comité des travaux scientifiques et historiques, 1995).
15   Hervé Peaudecerf, 'Alexandre-Louis-Marie Lédan (1777–1855): Un imprimeur breton au XIXe siècle (1805–1855)', unpublished doctoral thesis, 3 vols (Université de Rennes, 2002).

their manors. Aymar de Blois de La Calande, Barbe-Émilie de Saint-Prix and Ursule Feydeau de Vaugien all left manuscripts containing song texts taken down from local people. Although in 1828 Aymar de Blois published a groundbreaking study of the *gwerz* of the 'Heiress of Keroulas' (no. 13), linking it to the marriage of Marie de Keroulas with François du Chastel in 1565, none of this group seems to have had the intention of making their song collections public.[16]

In 1834 the author Émile Souvestre, a native of Morlaix, published an article in the influential Paris-based journal *Revue des Deux Mondes* entitled 'Poésies populaires de la Basse-Bretagne'.[17] This was the first comprehensive discussion of Breton oral tradition, and for many it came as a revelation; indeed, Souvestre's various articles on Breton life and customs, which appeared in the *Revue des Deux Mondes* and the *Revue de Bretagne*, and were brought together in 1836 as *Les Derniers Bretons*, played an important role in countering the prevalent idea of Brittany as an uncultured, superstitious society with an ugly, awkward language. Along with other French-language works such as Auguste Brizeux's poetic collection *Marie* (1840), Souvestre's highly romanticised accounts of peasant life effectively reversed the polarities of the primitivism which still coloured perceptions of all the Celtic-speaking countries at this time.[18] Just as the Ossianic poems of Macpherson had invested a long-despised Scots Gaelic culture with the glamour of the antique, so too did the works of these French-language romantic writers claim a special place for Brittany, and especially its song traditions, within France as a whole. During the first half of the 19th century Brittany would, in short, become France's mysterious other: a repository for all things attractively irrational, ancient and wild, securely contained within the framework of a modern, enlightened state.[19]

La Villemarqué and the **Barzaz-Breiz** *(1839)*

It was this changing cultural environment that made possible the success of Brittany's most influential collection of folk songs, the *Barzaz-Breiz*, published in two volumes in Paris in 1839.[20] Its author, a 24-year-old viscount, Théodore Hersart de La Villemarqué, came from Nizon, near

---

16   Patrick Malrieu, *Histoire de la chanson populaire bretonne* (Rennes: Dastum, Skol, 1983); Donatien Laurent, Fañch Postic and Pierre Prat, *Les passeurs de mémoire* (Mellac: Association du manoir de Kernault, 1996); Donatien Laurent, 'Aymar I de Blois (1760–1852) et "L'héritière de Keroulas"', in Gwennolé Le Menn and Jean-Yves Le Moign (eds), *Bretagne et pays celtiques. Langues, histoire, civilisation. Mélanges offerts à la mémoire de Léon Fleuriot* (Saint-Brieuc and Rennes: Skol, Presses universitaires de Rennes, 1992), pp. 415–43; Yvon Le Rol, 'La langue des "gwerzioù" à travers l'étude des manuscrits inédits de Mme de Saint-Prix (1789–1869)', unpublished doctoral thesis (Université de Rennes, 2013), 229–44: https://tel.archives-ouvertes.fr/tel-00854190.

17   Émile Souvestre, 'Poésies populaires de la Basse-Bretagne', *Revue des deux mondes* (1 December 1834), 489–537. See Fañch Postic, 'Le rôle d'Émile Souvestre dans le développement du mouvement d'intérêt pour les traditions orales', in Bärbel Plötner-Le Lay and Nelly Blanchard (eds), *Émile Souvestre: Écrivain breton porté par l'utopie sociale* (Brest: Centre de recherche bretonne et celtique, 2007), pp. 117–36.

18   For the changing fortunes of the Celtic countries in the Romantic period see Patrick Sims-Williams, 'The visionary Celt: the construction of an "ethnic preconception"', *Cambrian Medieval Celtic Studies*, 11 (1986), 71–96; Patrick Sims-Williams, 'Celtomania and Celtoscepticism', *Cambrian Medieval Celtic Studies*, 36 (1998), 1–36; Terence Brown (ed.), *Celticism* (Amsterdam and Atlanta: Rodopi, 1996).

19   For the 'invention' of Romantic Brittany in the works of authors such as Brizeux, Balzac, Chateaubriand and Renan see Heather Williams, *Postcolonial Brittany: Literature between Languages* (Bern: Peter Lang, 2007).

20   Théodore Hersart de La Villemarqué, *Barzas-Breiz. Chants populaires de la Bretagne* (Paris, 1839). The commonly used spelling *Barzaz-Breiz* comes from the modification of the title in subsequent editions.

Quimperlé, in the Breton-speaking region of Cornouaille; he was the youngest child of Ursule de Vaugien, who had herself noted down songs from labourers and servants on their estate, as well as from itinerant pedlars who called at the manor. From 1833 La Villemarqué attended classes at the École des Chartes in Paris, and it was in the imaginative space between his home territory of Nizon (where he, too, had begun noting down pieces from local singers) and this metropolitan climate of literary salons and new publications, combined with the energetic intellectual revival of interest in the Celtic and medieval past, that his ideas for the collection crystallised.[21]

One particular stimulus was the *Recherches sur les ouvrages des bardes de la Bretagne Armoricaine*, published in 1815 by the abbé Gervais de La Rue, a work which had suggested the possibility of a lost or undiscovered literature in Breton corresponding to the famed Breton *lais* cited in the middle-French romances of Chrétien de Troyes and Marie de France.[22] La Rue had urged further research into manuscript sources, and as a student La Villemarqué had taken this seriously enough to undertake more than one expedition into the Breton hinterland in search of ancient texts.[23] A journey to south Wales in 1838 (at which, during an elaborate *eisteddfod* ceremony in Abergavenny, he was made a Welsh Bard) was also partly undertaken with the aim of finding manuscripts.[24] What emerged, however, from this intense period of engagement with the earliest literatures of France and the Celtic countries was not in fact a lost medieval text, but a collection bearing the subtitle 'Chants populaires de la Basse-Bretagne'. Contemporary Breton oral tradition could, it seemed, be the key to the missing material.

The *Barzaz-Breiz* offered its readers a selection of 30 or so ballads (titled '*Gwerzéennou*', 'Chants historiques'), most of them located in historical periods and events, and presented in chronological order from the earliest time of the Bards up to the revolution of 1789. These were followed by a number of more lyrical love songs ('*Sounennou*', 'Chants d'amour') and a handful of religious pieces. It had facing-page translations into French and detailed historical commentaries, which often stressed the protagonists' attachment to their native land and language, and their resistance to the French. It was a huge success. Critical responses were enthusiastic, and throughout the 19th century selections from the work were translated into several languages, including three into English.[25] The writer George Sand was delighted by the 'diamonds' of the *Barzaz-Breiz* and

21   Francis Gourvil, *Théodore-Claude-Henri Hersart de La Villemarqué (1815–1895) et le 'Barzaz-Breiz' (1839–1845–1867)* (Rennes: Oberthur, 1960); Laurent, *Aux sources du Barzaz-Breiz*, pp. 20–41; Michael Glencross, *Reconstructing Camelot: French Romantic Medievalism and the Arthurian Tradition* (Cambridge: Brewer, 1995), pp. 130–43.

22   Gwenaël Le Duc, 'Les lais de Marie de France', *Regards étonnés: De l'expression de l'altérité … à la construction de l'idéntité. Mélanges offerts au professeur Gaël Milin* (Brest: Centre de recherche bretonne et celtique, 2002), 299–316.

23   Francis Gourvil, '"Voleur sans le savoir": Prosper Mérimée et Gwenc'hlan en 1835', *Nouvelle Revue de Bretagne* (1949/2), 104–15; (1949/3), 211–23; (1949/4), 299–306.

24   Fañch Postic, 'Premiers échanges interceltiques: Le voyage de La Villemarqué au pays de Galles', *Armen*, 125 (2001), 34–43; Mary-Ann Constantine, '"Impertinent structures": a Breton's Adventures in Neo-Gothic Wales', *Studies in Travel Writing*, 18 (2014), 134–47; and for a detailed discussion of La Villemarqué's complex relationship with Wales and Welsh see Mary-Ann Constantine, *The Truth Against the World: Iolo Morganwg and Romantic Forgery* (Cardiff: University of Wales Press, 2007), pp. 145–98.

25   Louisa Stuart Costello, *A Summer Amongst the Bocages and the Vines* (London: Richard Bentley, 1840); Tom Taylor, *Ballads and Songs of Brittany* (London: Macmillan and co, 1865); Henry Carrington, *Breton Ballads Translated from the Barzaz-Breiz* (Edinburgh: Turnbull and Spears, 1886). See the entertaining chapter by Jean-Yves Le Disez, 'Miss Costello, ou la Bretagne vue du *Barzaz-Breiz*' in his *Étrange Bretagne: Récits de voyageurs brittaniques en Bretagne (1830–1900)* (Rennes: Presses universitaires de Rennes, 2002), pp. 356–73.

found the collection 'plus complet, plus beau, plus parfait qu'aucun chef-d'œuvre sorti de l'esprit humain'.[26] A substantially expanded second edition in 1845 revised many of the texts and translations, strengthened its patriotic stance, and included over 30 new pieces; a third edition in 1867 added another three.

The *Barzaz-Breiz* became a new motivating force in the quest for traditional songs across France; it was taken as the model for an initiative led by the Ministry of Public Instruction, known as the 'Ampère-Fortoul Enquiry', which attempted a survey of popular song across all the French regions in the years 1840–50.[27] But the effects of the volume were felt particularly in Brittany, where a new generation of enthusiasts was inspired to go searching for further examples of these evocative survivals of the past. The findings of major collectors such as Jean-Marie de Penguern, Gabriel Milin, François-Marie Luzel and Anatole Le Braz would, in time, form the basis for a critique of the claims and the methodology of the *Barzaz-Breiz*, but the initial impulse was one of curiosity and excitement.[28]

Alongside the collecting and the publication of new songs came a wave of articles and essays from scholars such as Louis Le Guennec, Gaston de Carné and Arthur de La Borderie exploring their origins, authenticity and potential historical value. Folk song – oral, ephemeral and protean though it was – became the object of serious scholarly endeavour, with studies published in a range of academic journals which came into being around this time, such as the *Bulletin de la Société Archéologique du Finistère*, the *Revue de l'Histoire de l'Ouest* and the *Annales de Bretagne*.[29]

Inevitably, the body of evidence produced by dozens of new song collections showed the historical claims of the *Barzaz-Breiz* in a new light. In vain the new generation of collectors hunted for fragments relating to a supposedly 5th-century prophetic bard, Gwenc'hlan. Songs about Merlin, or the Breton prototype for the Arthurian Perceval, also proved elusive. Variants and fragments of the later songs suggested, as often as not, that names and locations had been misconstrued (wilfully or otherwise) to link local ballads to key events in Brittany's turbulent

26   'More complete, more beautiful and more perfect than any masterpiece yet sprung from the human mind.' George Sand, 'Les visions de la nuit dans les campagnes', *L'Illustration*, 504 (1852), 267–8.

27   Laurence Berthou-Bécam and Didier Bécam, *L'enquête Fortoul (1852–1876). Chansons populaires de Haute et Basse-Bretagne*, 2 vols (Paris and Rennes: Comité des travaux scientifiques et historiques, Dastum, 2010).

28   Nelly Blanchard (ed.), *Jean-Marie de Penguern (1807–1856): Collecteur et collectionneur breton* (Brest: Centre de recherche bretonne et celtique, 2008); Laurence Berthou-Bécam, 'Après Luzel et La Villemarqué … Gabriel Milin', *Musique Bretonne*, 139 (1996), 14–19; Françoise Morvan, *François-Marie Luzel: Enquête sur une experience de collectage folklorique en Bretagne au XIXᵉ siècle* (Rennes: Terre de Brume, Presses universitaires de Rennes, 1999); Alain Tanguy, 'Anatole Le Braz (1859–1926) et la tradition populaire en Bretagne – analyse de quatre carnets d'enquêtes inédits – (1890–1895)', unpublished doctoral thesis, 5 vols (Brest: Université Occidentale de Bretagne, 1997). Of these major collections much remained unpublished during the collectors' life-times, with the important exception of François-Marie Luzel, *Gwerziou-Breiz Izel: Chants et chansons populaires de la Basse-Bretagne. Gwerziou*, 2 vols (Lorient: Corfmat, 1868 and 1874) and François-Marie Luzel, *Soniou Breiz-Izel: Chants et chansons populaires de la Basse-Bretagne*, 2 vols (Paris: Bouillon, 1890). More recent publications include Gabriel Milin, *Gwerin*, vols 1–3 (Lesneven: Hor Yezh, 1961–2); Jean-Marie de Penguern, *Gwerin*, vols 4–6 and 8–10 (Lesneven: Hor Yezh, 1963–5 and 1997–8); *Dastumad Pennwern, Chants populaires bretons de la collection de Penguern* (Rennes: Dastum, 1983).

29   For example, an article published in 1888 by Gaston de Carné, based on a piece from the *Barzaz-Breiz*, resulted in a lively debate over several decades concerning the historicity of the events: see, e.g., Gaston Paris, 'L'élégie de Monsieur de Névet', *Revue de l'Histoire de l'Ouest*, 4 (1888), 5–28 ; Louis Le Guennec, '"L'élégie de Monsieur de Névet" et "Le Baron Huet"', *Bulletin de la Société Archéologique du Finistère*, 48 (1921), 112–21.

history. Breton ballad heroes were more likely to die for their sweetheart or their honour than for their country; nor, indeed, were all Breton ballad heroines as well behaved and as meekly long-suffering as the *Barzaz-Breiz* depicted them. La Villemarqué could quite readily be accused of having invented or heavily rewritten many of the songs, giving them an antique patina and 'celticising' them by replacing French loanwords with neologisms drawn from Welsh.[30]

Yet a great deal was at stake; anyone daring to criticise a book that had gained Breton culture so much prestige across France, and indeed across Europe, could (and would) be branded as 'unpatriotic'. In a pattern repeated all over Europe from Macpherson's *Ossian* to the Czech manuscripts of Dvůr Králové and the Finnish *Kalevala*, and from Antoine Fabre d'Olivet's Occitan troubadours to Iolo Morganwg's Welsh bards, this work of intense cultural significance and debatable authenticity left a legacy as complex and as damaging as it was inspiring.[31]

Luzel and the Gwerziou Breiz-Izel (1868)

The *Barzaz-Breiz* controversy (which is still capable of stirring strong opinions today) tends to be framed, not entirely helpfully, as a clash between La Villemarqué and Luzel. It is true that when the 'showdown' came, during the Celtic Congress at Saint-Brieuc in 1867, it was organised by a group of Luzel's supporters keen to bring La Villemarqué down in public. But in the brief, non-confrontational (and disingenuous) introduction to his own collection of ballads, *Gwerziou Breiz-Izel*, published the following year, Luzel contented himself with pointing out the very different aims of the two works. Whereas the *Barzaz-Breiz* was conceived as 'une œuvre plus littéraire qu'historique' which aimed to please its readership, his own more modest desire was to present the song texts:

> tels absolument que je les ai trouvés dans nos campagnes armoricaines, et qu'on peut les y retrouver encore; souvent incomplets, altérés, interpolés, irréguliers, bizarres; mélange singulier de beauté et de trivialités, de fautes de goût, de grossièretés qui sentent un peu leur barbarie, et poésie simple et naturelle, tendre et sentimentale, humaine toujours, et qui va droit au cœur, qui nous intéresse et nous émeut, par je ne sais quels secrets, quel mystère, bien mieux que la poésie d'art. C'est réellement le cœur du peuple breton qui bat en ces chants spontanés.[32]

---

30   Henri d'Arbois de Jubainville, 'Note sur une chanson bretonne intitulée *Le Retour d'Angleterre* et qu'on croit supposée', *Revue Archéologique*, 17 (1868), 227–40; François-Marie Luzel, *De l'authenticité des chants du Barzaz-Breiz* (Saint-Brieuc: Guyon, 1872); Gourvil, *Théodore-Claude-Henri Hersart de La Villemarqué*.

31   See Joep Leerssen, 'Ossian and the Rise of Literary Historicism' in Howard Gaskill (ed.), *The Reception of Ossian in Europe* (London: Thoemmes Continuum, 2004), pp. 109–25; Gaela Keryell, 'The *Kalevala* and the *Barzaz-Breiz*: The Relativity of the Concept of "Forgery"' in Anders Ahlqvist et al. (eds), *Celtica Helsingiensia*, 107 (Helsinki: Societas Scientiarum Fennica, 1996), pp. 57–103. Constantine, *The Truth Against the World* explores ideas of textual and oral authenticity in this period and discusses a number of other European forgery debates.

32   Luzel, *Gwerziou I*, p. iii.

[exactly as I found them in our Armorican countryside, and exactly as you may still find them there; often incomplete, altered, interrupted, irregular, bizarre; a strange mixture of the beautiful and the inconsequential, where errors of taste and crude vulgarities combine with a poetry both simple and natural, tender and full of feeling, a poetry which speaks directly to the heart, and which intrigues and moves us by I know not what secrets, what mystery, far more than the poetry of art. In these spontaneous songs the heart of the Breton people truly beats.]

The debate over the authenticity of the *Barzaz-Breiz* hinged on two different approaches to the editing of song texts. The differences are often framed as generational, with La Villemarqué following the more 'Romantic' criteria of an earlier period, and Luzel representing the modern 'scientific' approach. The former saw in the raw material of the song tradition degenerate forms of perfect originals recoverable through careful reconstitution. In a passage echoing Walter Scott's views on the 'perverted alchemy' of orality, La Villemarqué explains:

Pour avoir des textes aussi complets et aussi purs que possible, je me les suis fait répéter, souvent jusqu'à quinze et vingt fois par différentes personnes. Les versions les plus détaillées ont toujours fixé mon choix; car la pauvreté ne me semble pas le caractère des chants populaires originaux; je crois au contraire qu'ils sont riches et ornés dans le principe, et que le temps seul les dépouille.[33]

[In order to have texts that were as complete and as unadulterated as possible I had them repeated, sometimes up to fifteen or twenty times, by different people. I always chose the most detailed versions; spareness does not seem to me to be the true nature of folk songs in their original state; I believe, rather, that they are rich and intricate in essence, and that they are merely stripped down by the passage of time.]

The editor's task, therefore, was to recover that rich complexity of form. In the immediate archaeological context of Jean-François Champollion's work on the Rosetta Stone – the key to unlocking the secrets of the Egyptian hieroglyphs – it was not too difficult to believe that a part might give access to the whole, that a song fragment might be extrapolated to its original complete beauty.[34] Luzel, a generation later, adopted an approach far closer to the type of ethnographic methodology accepted as standard today, an approach which set aside interpretation of the texts in favour of their presentation in as 'natural' a state as possible, provenanced, with the name of the singer and the date of the recording.

But drawing a neat historical watershed between 'romantic' and 'scientific' approaches does not quite explain everything. By 1839 (and more so by the second and third editions of 1845 and 1867) La Villemarqué's heavily manipulated collection of songs entered a world of European

33 La Villemarqué, *Barzas-Breiz* (1839), p. iii. Scott famously described tradition as 'a sort of perverted alchemy, which converts gold to lead', *Quarterly Review*, 1 (1809), 30.
34 Blanchard, *Barzaz-Breiz. Une fiction pour s'inventer*, pp. 28–73. For an exploration of different notions of 'completeness' in songs see Constantine and Porter, *Fragments and Meaning in Traditional Song*.

letters which had been vexed by issues of textual presentation and the authenticity of oral material since at least the *Ossian* controversy over 70 years earlier.[35] France in the 1820s and 1830s was hardly innocent of such issues, which were aired over various literary hoaxes, the most relevant in this context being Prosper Mérimée's anonymously published collection of invented Serbo-Croat epic folk songs, *La Guzla,* in 1827.[36] It is hard to believe that, even for a fastidiously literary French readership, there were no acceptable editorial options beyond the Romantic paradigm of 'renovation' and the '*poésie d'art*'. Indeed, in his *Chants populaires de la Grèce moderne*, itself a model for the *Barzaz-Breiz*, Claude Fauriel had written at length and with some passion of a not dissimilar cultural situation – a modern, despised people, treated as the decayed remnant of a former glorious civilisation – but, apparently, had not felt the need to rework his actual texts to prove his point as La Villemarqué undoubtedly did with his.[37] Viewed in the broader European context, La Villemarqué's cavalier treatment of the *gwerz* tradition does look, at best, extremely belated.

The principal biography of La Villemarqué, published by Francis Gourvil in 1960, takes a more unforgiving stance on the question of fidelity to the tradition, and treats the *Barzaz-Breiz* as an extended 'imposture', whose texts – measured against the benchmark of Luzel's *Gwerziou* – range from tidied-up versions of actual songs to pieces wholly invented for the occasion. Donatien Laurent's rediscovery and publication of La Villemarqué's collecting notebooks, however, have allowed for a more nuanced understanding of the processes involved in creating the *Barzaz-Breiz*, and there have been some surprises, not least the discovery that one of the least plausible-looking pieces in the collection, the highly 'Celtic' and medieval *Merlin-Barde*, has an identifiable, oral, provenanced source.[38]

The differences between the collections of La Villemarqué and Luzel stem not only from methodology but from the very different sociocultural backgrounds of the two collectors, and their experiences in the field. Born into a farming family which gained material benefits during the period of the Revolution, a teacher and a convinced republican, Luzel collected almost exclusively in the northern Trégor region (the 'Attica' of Brittany, as he put it) and from a high proportion of women, many of them travelling beggars and artisans. La Villemarqué, an aristocrat, was from the south of Brittany, and collected from a higher proportion of men, some of them former Chouans who had fought against the French Republic in the 1790s. Unsurprisingly, the world views of the two collections do not exactly overlap.

35   Leerssen, 'Ossian and the rise of literary historicism', 116.

36   Ludmila Charles-Wurtz, 'Le lyrisme de *La Guzla*', in Antonia Fonyi (ed.), *Prosper Mérimée: Ecrivain, Archéologue, Historien* (Geneva: Droz, 1999), pp. 99–110.

37   Claude Fauriel, *Chants populaires de la Grèce moderne*, 2 vols (Paris: Didot, 1824–5).

38   For the extraordinary Merlin text (included in the 1845 edition) see Laurent, *Aux sources du Barzaz-Breiz*, 287–96; and the discussion in Mary-Ann Constantine, 'Neither flesh nor fowl: Merlin as bird-man in Breton folk tradition', *Arthurian Literature*, XXI (2004), 95–114.

A broadening repertoire: later collectors

No one collection or collector, then, could properly represent the dialectal, stylistic and narrative variety of the Breton ballad tradition, but Luzel's approach formed the model for various other song collections around the end of the 19th century. Though not all were published at the time, these collections helped to fill in some of the gaps in areas which had been previously little explored. The long-neglected Vannetais saw important work undertaken by Yves Le Diberder, Augustin Guillevic, François and Jean-Mathurin Cadic, Loeiz Herrieu, and other collectors, many of them involved with the church, who constitute what has been called the 'Vannetais school'.[39] Other 'priest-collectors' had a similar impact in Léon, grouped around the charismatic figure of Jean-Marie Perrot who, on the eve of the First World War, collected nearly a thousand Breton songs by organising a competition aimed at displaying the richness and variety of a hitherto little-explored tradition in the north-west.[40] At the same time, Anatole Le Braz continued to collect in the Trégor region, while Constance Le Mérer privately filled some 30 notebooks of songs from around Lannion – her collection has only recently been published, and is particularly valuable for its musical transcriptions, rarely noted down during this period.[41] Henri Guillerm collected and published songs in Cornouaille.[42]

Song collecting slowed down in the difficult period between the two world wars, with the exception of a valuable ethnographic enquiry launched in 1939 by the Musée des Arts et Traditions Populaires, but then interrupted by the Second World War.[43] From the late 1950s to the 1980s (partly in response to the rapid decline of the language itself), there was renewed interest in all aspects of Breton folk tradition. A series of high-quality recordings was made just after the war by Claudine Mazéas, and the work of ethnologists and researchers Donatien Laurent and Daniel Giraudon resulted in important collections and studies. Song collection was also carried out by practising performers such as Yann-Fañch Kemener, Ifig Troadeg and Jorj Belz in the context of a broader cultural revival which took singing and the social gatherings of the *fest-noz* very

39   Loeiz Herrieu, *Guerzenneu ha soñnenneu Bro-Guened. Chansons populaires du pays de Vannes* (Paris: Rouard, Lerolle, 1911); François Cadic, *Chansons populaires de Bretagne publiées dans la Paroisse bretonne de Paris (1899–1929)* (Rennes, Brest: Presses universitaires de Rennes, Dastum, Centre de recherche bretonne et celtique, 2010); Augustin Guillevic and Jean-Mathurin Cadic, *Chants et airs traditionnels du pays vannetais* (Pontivy and Vannes: Dastum Bro-Ereg, Archives départementales du Morbihan, 2007); Yves Le Diberder, *Chansons traditionnelles du pays vannetais (1910–1915)*, 2 vols (Vannes: Archives départementales du Morbihan, 2010); Jean-Louis Larboulette, *Chants traditionnels vannetais (1902–1905)* (Pontivy: Dastum Bro-Ereg, 2005); Mathurin Buléon, *Chansons traditionnelles du pays vannetais* (Vannes: Archives départementales du Morbihan, Dastum Bro-Ereg, 2012). Studies on this extremely fertile Vannetais fieldwork include Michel Oiry, 'L'école vannetaise (1825–1916) et les collectes d'Yves Le Diberder (1910–1916)' in Postic, *La Bretagne et la littérature orale en Europe*, pp. 177–89; and Fañch Postic, (ed.), *François Cadic (1864–1929), Un collecteur vannetais 'recteur' des Bretons de Paris* (Brest: Centre de recherche bretonne et celtique, 2012).

40   Éva Guillorel, *Barzaz Bro-Leon: Une expérience inédite de collecte en Bretagne* (Rennes and Brest: Presses universitaires de Rennes, Centre de recherche bretonne et celtique, 2012); Jean-Pierre Pichette (ed.), *L'apport des prêtres et des religieux au patrimoine des minorités: Parcours comparés Bretagne/Canada français*, special issue of *Port-Acadie. Revue internationale en études acadiennes*, 24–25–26 (2014).

41   Constance Le Mérer, *Une collecte de chants populaires dans le pays de Lannion*. Textes et musiques présentés par Bernard Lasbleiz & Daniel Giraudon (Lannion: Dastum Bro-Dreger, 2015).

42   Henri Guillerm, *Recueil de chants populaires bretons du pays de Cornouailles* (Rennes: François Simon, 1905).

43   Marie-Barbara Le Gonidec, *Les archives de la Mission de folklore musical en Basse-Bretagne de 1939 du Musée national des arts et traditions populaires* (Rennes and Paris: Dastum, Comité des travaux scientifiques et historiques, 2009).

much to its heart.[44] Organisations such as Dastum (the name means 'Collect') have both encouraged people to record songs and begun the complex task of coordinating and cataloguing sound recordings and text versions.[45] As a result, Brittany remains pre-eminent within France in the richness and variety of its song collections.

II: The nature of the *gwerz* tradition

What makes a *gwerz*? As with most areas of popular tradition issues of taxonomy are often more fluid on the ground than in the critical works devoted to them; different regions, individual singers and scholars have all shown differing perceptions of what kinds of song the word might or should cover. The word itself, a feminine noun in Breton (pl. *gwerziou*), derives from the Latin *versus* (a line of poetry or a poem) and appears in the earliest Breton-language dictionaries. In the *Catholicon* of Jehan Lagadeuc (1499) it is translated as '*vers*', '*petit vers*' or '*chanczon*', but also more specifically as a '*chanczon quo[n] cha[n]te aux enfans pour leur faire dormir*', '*cha[n]czon faicte sur le mort*' or '*chanczon vilaine*'.[46] In the Latin–French–Breton *Nomenclator* of Guillaume Quiquer of Roscoff (1633), and in the dictionary of the Jesuit missionary Julien Maunoir (1659), *gwerz* is simply associated with songs and verses. In Dom Le Pelletier's dictionary of 1716 the term seems also to cover a wide spectrum: '*vers, cantique, chanson, poëme*'.[47]

It is not until we reach the folklorists of the 19th century, however, that the term really enters academic discourse and more precise definitions are developed and contested. Émile Souvestre was the first to use '*gwerz*' in his 1834 article for the *Revue des Deux Mondes*, defining it as a 'grande complainte', or ballad, reflecting events of significance in the lives of the Breton peasantry (love, death, suffering and miracles).[48] As classification became increasingly important, the Breton song tradition (like many other folk song traditions) was perceived in terms of a major, and enduring, division between lyric and narrative genres. This was most influentially evoked by François-Marie Luzel, for whom the *gwerziou* were essentially in the latter category and included all kinds of '*[C]hants sombres, fantastiques, tragiques, racontant des apparitions surnaturelles, des assassinats, des infanticides, des duels à mort, des trahisons, des enlèvements et des violences de toute sorte*'.[49] The lyric songs, or *soniou*, '*plus tendres et plus humains*', included love songs, elegies, dance songs, games, and songs for children.[50]

---

44   Yann-Fañch Kemener, *Carnets de route. Kanaouennoù Kalon Vreizh, Chants profonds de Bretagne* (Morlaix: Skol Vreizh, 1996); Ifig Troadeg, *Carnets de route* (Lannion: Dastum Bro Dreger, 2005); Jorj Belz and Fañch Desbordes, *Sonamb get en Drouzerion. 100 sonenn a vro-Gwened*, 2 vols (Lesneven: Hor Yezh, 1985).

45   Since 1972 Dastum has assembled an oral archive of some 90,000 items, recorded from 5,000 informants by some 400 collectors, far exceeding anything comparable in the field of oral tradition in the rest of France. Many of these recordings are accessible through their data-base 'Archives du patrimoine oral': www.dastum.net. For more information see the introduction to our accompanying CD.

46   'A song sung to children to get them to sleep'; 'song about death'; 'common song': Jehan Lagadeuc, *Le Catholicon armoricain* [1499] (Mayenne: J. Floch, 1977), pp. 104–5.

47   For the lexicographical works of Quiquer, Le Maunoir and Le Pelletier see Guillorel, *La Complainte et la Plainte*, pp. 66–9.

48   Souvestre, 'Poésies populaires de la Basse-Bretagne'.

49   'Dark, fantastic and tragic songs telling of supernatural apparitions, murders, infanticides, duels to the death, betrayals, kidnappings and all manner of violent events', Luzel, *Gwerziou II* [1874] (1971), p. vi.

50   Luzel, *Gwerziou II* [1874] (1971), p. vi.

The borders between these two major types of song are necessarily more porous than such classifications allow, and even the small selection of ballads chosen for this volume bears witness to the variety of forms the *gwerz* can encompass. By the 20th century the quest for definitions had shifted to the singers themselves, with collectors and ethnographers discovering a repeated claim that the *gwerziou* were 'long songs' which 'told a true story' (or a story believed to be true).[51] That link between the *gwerz* and a particular conception of 'truth' can be found as far back as 1845, when La Villemarqué noted that when a Breton peasant wishes to praise an example of the genre 'il ne dit pas: *c'est beau*; il dit: *c'est vrai.*'[52] Singers have offered similar comments to later collectors, including Donatien Laurent, who notes:

> On comprend dès lors l'importance de ce type de chansons, censées porter la Vérité du groupe, dans une société orale où la parole a un prix très supérieur à celui qu'elle a dans nos civilisations de l'écrit. On comprend la responsabilité de l'auteur de la chanson – qui doit n'y mettre que ce qu'il sait être 'vrai' – comme celle du transmetteur qui, sous le contrôle de la communauté, doit rester fidèle à cette 'vérité'. Le sentiment de respect qui s'attache à de telles compositions les différencie d'emblée de tout ce qui est rumeur, bruit commun, légende ou récit en prose qui n'ont pas les mêmes prétentions.[53]

> [It is easy, then, to understand the importance of this type of song, believed to convey the Truth of the group in an oral society where the spoken word is valued far higher than in our writing-based culture. Easy, too, to grasp the burden of responsibility carried by the song's author – who may only include what he knows to be 'true' – as well as by the song-bearer who, under the watchful eye of the community, must remain faithful to this 'truth'. The sense of respect surrounding these sorts of compositions clearly marks them out from mere rumour, hearsay, legend or prose account, none of which makes the same kind of claim.]

The notion of the *gwerz* thus goes beyond mere formal characteristics to include other more indefinable elements, including a traditional sense of importance, lending it a kind of aura of solemnity. For the purposes of this volume, then, a brief synopsis of how we define the genre should give the reader some sense of where to situate these songs in a rich and often confusing field – one that could in its broadest manifestations include printed ballads, manuscript lyrics, hymns and many other types of song.

Our *gwerziou* are Breton-language songs collected from oral tradition, between the early decades of the 19th century and the present day. They are narrative songs, though their story-telling techniques are far from uniform and sometimes indirect. For reasons of space we have often chosen relatively succinct versions in this volume, but *gwerziou* may be very long, many

---

51   See Daniel Giraudon, 'Chansons de langue bretonne sur feuilles volantes et compositeurs populaires: Un chanteur-chansonnier du Trégor. Yann ar Gwenn', unpublished doctoral thesis (Brest: 1982), p. 19.
52   'He does not say *It's beautiful*; he says *It's true*', *Barzaz-Breiz 1845*, p. xxviii.
53   Donatien Laurent, 'Histoire et poésie chantée: l'exemple de la Bretagne', *Historiens-Géographes*, 318 (1988), 111; Kemener, *Carnets de route*, p. 19.

dozens of couplets in length, with some exceeding 80 couplets (the performance of such pieces may take well over half an hour). They are songs with a distinctive metrical pattern and lexis, different from the various dialectal forms of Breton used in everyday speech, but different, too, from the literary language.[54]

The stories they tell are serious, often tragic, and frequently relate to events which can be located in precise local and historical detail. There are also a number of songs drawing on more imaginative sources, often anchored in Christian miracle and legend. Though dating orally trans-mitted ballads is not possible in the way that one might date a literary text or a historical docu-ment, their narrative material is generally 'old', sometimes with strong medieval parallels, but by and large deriving from the 16th to the 18th centuries and reflecting Brittany under the *ancien régime*. The more commercial, and often more sensational, printed ballads (*feuilles volantes*), which flourished in the 19th century and have clear affinities with similar traditions across Europe, offer another fascinating repository of events and stories, but fall beyond the scope of this collection.[55]

From scraps and couplets scribbled in roughly bound notebooks to the latest digital tech-nology, the songs collected in Brittany over two centuries number in their thousands. For the first 70 or 80 years, of course, they are resolutely mute, but in 1900 the school teacher François Vallée recorded on wax cylinders the voice of one of Luzel and Le Braz's most significant informants, Marc'harit Fulup (Marguerite Philippe).[56] As different types of recording spread rapidly after the Second World War, so more and more actual performances could be captured along with contex-tual, conversational material adding depth and meaning to the songs. Above all, these recordings ensured that text and tunes were no longer recorded separately, with one or the other frequently ignored, as was particularly the case for the earlier period when words were privileged consider-ably above music (a gap partially filled by certain musicologists, such as Maurice Duhamel, who early in the 20th century deliberately set out to cover territories collected by Luzel).[57]

Shaping the repertoire

In assessing the nature of the repertoire that has come down to us, it is important to consider some of the inherent, often unconscious, biases of the collectors, which led them to seek out certain

54   Le Rol, *La langue des 'gwerziou'*.

55   Joseph Ollivier, *La chanson populaire sur feuilles volantes: Catalogue bibliographique* (Quimper: Le Goaziou, 1942); Daniel Giraudon, *Chansons populaires de Basse-Bretagne sur feuilles volantes* (Morlaix: Skol Vreizh, 1985). See also Patrick Malrieu's newly available and comprehensive catalogue for the Breton broadside ballads: http://www.kan.bzh.

56   For Breton/French personal names see our Editorial Policy below. A short recording of Marc'harit Fulup can be heard on the accompanying CD. François Vallée, 'Une exploration musicale en Basse-Bretagne! Les airs des Gwerziou de Luzel retrouvés et phonographiés', *Annales de Bretagne*, 16 (1/1900), 130–5; Bernard Lasbleiz, 'Marc'harit Fulup: Les enregistrements de François Vallée', *Musique bretonne*, 173 (2002) 33–5.

57   Maurice Duhamel, *Gwerziou ha soniou Breiz-Izel: Musiques bretonnes: Airs et variantes mélodiques des 'chants et chansons populaires de la Basse-Bretagne' publiés par F. M. Luzel et A. Le Braz* (Paris: Lerolle, 1913, repr. Dastum, 1997). Marthe Vasallo, *Les Chants du livre bleu. À travers les Musiques bretonnes de Maurice Duhamel* (Guimaëc: Son an Ero, 2015).

types of informants, and select certain types of song.[58] The *gwerziou* were undoubtedly the beneficiaries of a general Romantic-era interest in ballad-style narratives across Europe, and felt to be more 'noble' as a genre, and certainly linguistically 'purer' than the printed ballads. They seemed, too, to offer a direct window on to the past, and, as La Villemarqué discovered, could be readily adapted to suit a broader cultural agenda. There is, then, already a large element of prior selection in the song repertoire as it appears today, but not only because collectors focused on the more 'valuable' genres. Singers, too, might operate a form of self-censoring, withholding songs that felt awkward in particular social contexts, because of gender, politics or class (racy or scatological repertoires are inevitably under-represented).

A further selection process often takes place during publication – as when Luzel, republican by conviction, nevertheless held back from including anticlerical songs in his collection after receiving threats. The first volume of *Gwerziou* (1868) contained a ballad about the brutal activities of the bishop of Penarstank, a débauché and serial rapist; this was judged to be both obscene and anticlerical by some of the Trégor clergy, who attempted to block sales of the book. Preparing the second volume for publication some five years later, Luzel sought advice from the bishop of Saint-Brieuc, who made his feelings on the subject extremely clear:

> Vous interrogez ma conscience, elle vous répond: non! au nom du ciel, ne publiez pas ces pièces de
> poésie où le prêtre est livré à la malédiction et au mépris des honnêtes gens; où le poète le charge
> de crimes monstrueux dont la seule expression est une flétrissure pour l'âme des simples. Dans quel
> intérêt les publieriez-vous? Dans un intérêt moral? non évidemment. Dans un intérêt historique?
> Mais il faudrait d'abord prouver que ces légendes sont de l'histoire. [...] Dans un intérêt littéraire? je
> ne le vois pas. Je vous en prie, ne les publiez pas. Ceux qui à la rigueur peuvent être édités demandent
> au moins des points dans les endroits scabreux.[59]

> [You appeal to my conscience, and my conscience replies: no! In heaven's name, do not publish those
> pieces in which the priest is exposed to the curses and disdain of honest people; where the poet accuses
> him of crimes the very mention of which stains the souls of the innocent. To what end would you publish
> them? In the interests of morality? Of course not. In the interests of history? But you would first have to
> prove that these fables are historical. [...] In the interests of literature? Hardly. I beg of you, do not publish
> them. Those susceptible of being edited should at the very least substitute dots for the improper sections.]

Luzel accepted this position, which was also supported by his friend Ernest Renan and by several other important names in ethnographical research at the time.[60]

---

58   Guillorel, *La Complainte et la Plainte*, pp. 81–98.
59   Letter from Mgr David to François-Marie Luzel, 29 June 1873, Bibliothèque municipale de Rennes, fonds Ollivier, mns. 958, f°123r. Cited in Laurence Berthou-Bécam, 'Enquête officielle sur les poésies populaires de la France', unpublished doctoral thesis (Rennes, 1998), I, p. 346. Some of these 'suppressed' ballads have since been published in Bécam and Berthou-Bécam, *L'enquête Fortoul (1852–1876). Chansons populaires de Haute et Basse-Bretagne*, vol. 2, pp. 986–1005.
60   François-Marie Luzel, *Correspondance Luzel-Renan*. Texte établi et présenté par Françoise Morvan (Rennes: Presses universitaires de Rennes, Terre de Brume, 1995), pp. 145, 209 and 213.

Another factor shaping the tradition as we have it is the work of editing, of preparing songs for publication; even the most scrupulous of collectors tends to correct irregular lines, or alter occasional words to make the sense clearer. Musicians likewise often could not help but transpose awkward or 'barbarous'-sounding tunes to something more readily recognisable, as the collector Louis-Albert Bourgault-Ducoudray readily admitted:

> J'ai essuyé dans mon voyage bien des averses de fausses notes, bien des avalanches de voix calleuses et nasillardes. Les Bretons ont ceci de singulier, que pour eux, chanter du nez n'est point un défaut ; c'est, au contraire, une qualité indispensable pour que l'exécution soit véritablement fine et raffinée. Ce goût bizarre leur est commun avec les Orientaux. [...] Pas plus en Bretagne qu'en Orient, je n'ai pu me faire à ce genre de beauté.[61]

> [I have, along the way, wiped up whole showers of false notes, whole avalanches of harsh and nasal voices. The Bretons are odd in this respect, in that for them singing through the nose is not a fault; on the contrary, it is completely indispensible to a fine and polished performance. They share this peculiar taste with the Orientals. [...] Neither in the Orient, nor in Brittany have I been able to make much of this kind of beauty.]

Geographical bias also plays its part. Most collectors worked intensively in a fairly restricted area, usually around their home, where they had access to a known community and the support of family and friends; here, they could easily revisit their singers, and they were familiar with the local dialect. Penguern collected most of his songs in the Morlaix region; La Villemarqué drew on the area around his native Quimperlé. Dialect difference was also a reason for the relative lack of interest in songs from the Vannetais region, and it is striking how certain areas, especially Luzel's northern Trégor, remained consistently the focus of collection over successive generations – Ifig Troadeg recorded hundreds of songs in Luzel's home territory almost a 150 years later.

In addition to all this, certain types of singer tended to be privileged in the search for songs. There was a general presumption that the best singers would be rural, labouring-class, illiterate and female. Particular vocations – tailor, seamstress – were more readily visible and indeed more sociable than others: tailors would travel from farm to farm, bringing new songs and stories, as well as local news, with them. Professional beggars and 'hired pilgrims' such as Marc'harit Fulup (who would visit churches, pray and do penance on behalf of other people) moved in regular circuits and had access to a rich repertoire of traditional material. The end result of these different, often unconscious 'filters' was a relatively homogeneous published repertoire that did not reflect the variety of songs circulating among Breton-speakers at any given time.[62]

61   Louis Bourgault-Ducoudray, *Trente Mélodies populaires de Basse-Bretagne* (Paris, Brussels: Lemoine, 1885), p. 7.
62   Guillorel, *La Complainte et la Plainte*, pp. 87–97.

The 'matière' of the gwerziou: *from legends to local events*

The *gwerziou* offer a rich and distinctive body of material within the wider corpus of Breton popular literature. Like other narrative song traditions they draw on a wide range of sources, and share various themes and stylistic features with ballads and songs across Europe and (through migration and colonisation) well beyond. Donatien Laurent has outlined four main types of source material feeding into the ballad tradition: a strand of themes and motifs derived from a shared Celtic heritage (nos 2 and 3); Europe-wide texts in medieval Latin drawing on a widely dispersed body of Christian legend, such as the account of the crippled Saint Brigit (no. 7), the misadventures and miraculous rescue of travellers to Compostela (no. 5) and the story of the cock that crows after its death (no. 4); French-language sources (including printed broadsheets, discussed below); and finally, and by far the largest category, local events – shipwrecks, murders, family tragedies.[63] This rich and varied mix of raw material is then homogenised by the process of transmission; even songs with recognisably international themes adapt their material thoroughly to the form and style of the *gwerz*, creating a body of songs with a highly distinctive aesthetic.

When the Welsh scholar and clergyman Thomas Price visited Brittany in 1829 he was less than impressed by the songs he heard, finding them monotonous and musically uninteresting. His comments, though negative, are interestingly perceptive:

> if the tunes are short, the words seem interminable. When I had listened to this Chevy Chase style of singing for some time, I would occasionally ask if they had no other sort of song, and was always answered, that they had a great number; and, upon my requesting to be favoured with one, they would strike up Chevy Chase again with the greatest composure, always appearing to estimate the singing according to the merits of the words, the air being a very secondary consideration.[64]

Gwerziou do tend to be long, and (for those who understand them) rich in details – place names, personal names – which can help identify actual historical events behind the narrative. Characterisation is often marked and intensely local, and even ballads with international parallels feel deeply rooted in place. If a young girl encounters a mysterious rider at a well, the Breton version will tell us her family name and the name of her native parish, and often that of her murderer (such encounters rarely have a positive outcome). In these cases, local memory of a real event has usually been reshaped by the form and demands of the ballad genre.

These songs are indeed versions of history, but they need to be read in a particular way, embedded, ideally, in a context of other forms of documentation (parish registers, legal records or genealogies) and in as many different versions as possible. Case studies such as those of the

63   Donatien Laurent, 'Breton Orally Transmitted Folk Poetry', in Otto Holzapfel (ed.), *The European Medieval Ballad: A Symposium* (Odense: Odense University Press, 1978), pp. 16–25.
64   Jane Williams, *The Literary Remains of the Rev. Thomas Price, Carnhuanawc* (2 vols, Llandovery and London: W. Rees and Longman, 1855), I, p. 21. 'Chevy Chase' (Child no. 162) is an old and much-cited border ballad about a hunting party in the Cheviots. It is found in many early ballad collections, including the Pepys Collection and the *Reliques* of Thomas Percy.

murder of Loeiz Er Ravalleg (no. 31) or Lord Penanger (no. 23) show how these distinctive forms of memorialisation can enrich, and occasionally illuminate, our understanding of the past.[65] Their rich evocation of the details of everyday life offer a rare window onto aspects of prerevolutionary Brittany from a non-elite perspective. Again, one should note important regional differences; the dialect of the Vannetais in southern Brittany is notably closer to a French style of singing, far less detailed, more lyrical and often with much shorter songs. The detailed *gwerz* of the death of Toussaint de Kerguézec (no. 29) in Trégor becomes in its Vannetais version a brief, impersonal lyric about a young man out shooting ducks.[66] This brevity of form is another reason for the relatively poor representation of the Vannetais in 19th-century collections.[67]

The longevity and richness of the narrative song tradition in Breton are in no doubt, since a relatively short period of collecting – some two and half centuries – has resulted in hundreds of song types expressed through thousands of versions. And it remains, in spite of social change and a dramatic crash in the number of Breton speakers in the course of the 20th century, a living tradition. Several of the songs in this collection were widely collected in the 1970s and 1980s, and can still be heard in the traditional 'veillées' or evening social events, whose singers and audiences come from overlapping worlds of amateurs and professionals, some of whom will have learned their repertoire from family members, others from recordings. (In Brittany as elsewhere the notion of a 'pure' or 'authentic' song tradition preserved by indigenous tightly knit communities is not especially helpful.)

The similarly vexed question of origins and authorship has preoccupied many writers since the 19th century.[68] As elsewhere in Europe, many of the early Breton collectors subscribed to the Romantic-era concept of a folk repertoire exclusively composed and transmitted by an idealised peasant population. In reaction, the beginning of the 20th century saw the development of a theory that cast the 'people' as passive transmittors or imitators of poetry which originated at the higher end of society. Recent studies have concerned themselves more with questions of the interactions between the peasantry and the elite classes, often focusing on figures (such as clerics) who mediate between them. Discussion of the subject, however, is still often ideologically partisan – and reliable facts about the authors of *gwerziou* are extremely rare. We have some direct knowledge of songs composed by minor gentry or rural priests who acted as cultural intermediaries, speaking both French and Breton, and comfortable in oral and written milieux.[69] Other songs contain self-referential couplets claiming composition by artisans or farmers, and similar authors are mentioned in written archives, especially in the case of the lyrical *soniou* or defamatory songs.[70] Theories about the composition of these songs are often based solely on analysis of the

65   Donatien Laurent, 'La gwerz de Louis Le Ravallec', *Arts et Traditions Populaires*, 15 (1967), 19–79; Daniel Giraudon, 'Penanger et de La Lande, Gwerz tragique au XVIIᵉ siècle en Trégor', *Annales de Bretagne et des Pays de l'Ouest*, 112 (2005), 7–42.
66   Daniel Giraudon and Donatien Laurent, 'Gwerz an Aotrou Kergwezeg', *Planedenn*, 6 (1980–1), 13–43.
67   Constantine and Porter, *Fragments and Meaning*, pp. 167–83.
68   For discussions about the origins and authors of the *gwerziou*, see Guillorel, *La Complainte et la Plainte*, pp. 100–7.
69   See for example François-Nicolas Pascal de Kerenveyer, *Ar farvel göapaër. Le bouffon moqueur*. Texte traduit et présenté par Ronan Calvez (Brest: Centre de recherche bretonne et celtique, 2005).
70   See Charles Chassé, 'Les charivaris d'Hennebont', *Le Fureteur breton*, 55 (1919), 12–14.

texts themselves, which can lead to quite incompatible conclusions; in separate studies of the same *gwerz* about a murderous rift between two noblemen in 1707, Daniel Giraudon argues that the author must have been a clergyman, while Ronan Calvez sees it rather as the work of a member of the nobility.[71]

As with most song traditions, the Breton *gwerziou* show interaction between oral and written or printed sources, and between languages. There are some clear cases where French printed sources (ballads, news stories, trial proceedings) have served as raw material for the Breton tradition, as in the *gwerz* based on a printed account of the trial following the murder of the Marquise Dégangé in south-west France in 1667, which reached Brittany through the networks of *colporteurs* (itinerant peddlars selling ballads and broadsheets).[72]

Though such material does not seem to be a major source of inspiration for the *gwerziou*, it is perhaps worth, nonetheless, trying to distinguish the orally transmitted narrative songs from the large body of printed broadside ballads or *feuilles volantes* (which also sometimes call themselves *gwerziou*). These latter songs belong to the Europe-wide tradition of 'news' ballads, sold in markets and fairs and relaying sensational current events. They begin to appear in significant numbers in Breton from the very end of the 18th century (there is little secular literature of any kind in Breton before then, although hymns and religious pieces circulate much earlier in broadsheet form). They have a different aesthetic from the oral ballads, borrowing more heavily from French and being more sentimental and/or moralistic in tone.[73] Though more work needs to be done in this area, the printed ballads appear not to have borrowed from or contributed much to the oral *gwerziou* – a situation that contrasts with English-language ballads, where the interaction between oral and printed traditions can be traced much further back in time, and where broadsides played an important part in diffusing song types.[74] At the risk of perpetuating preconceptions and prejudices about a 'classical' oral tradition corresponding to F. J. Child's English and Scottish 'popular ballads' and a more ephemeral market-based broadside tradition, it does seem that Breton narrative song, for most of the 19th and part of the 20th century, ran in two fairly distinct channels. There are exceptions, of course. The *gwerziou* recounting the murder of a servant girl in Lannion (no. 28) and the fire in Quimper cathedral (no. 21) both have a complex relation to accounts in the printed tradition.[75]

71   Giraudon, 'Drame sanglant au pardon de Saint-Gildas à Tonquédec en 1707: Gwerz ar c'homt a Goat-Louri hag an otro Porz-Lann', *Annales de Bretagne et des Pays de l'Ouest*, 114 (1/2007), 75–77; Ronan Calvez, 'Du breton mondain', *Annales de Bretagne et des Pays de l'Ouest*, 115 (3/2008), 139.

72   Anatole Le Braz, 'L'origine d'une gwerz bretonne', in Joseph Loth (ed.), *Mélanges en l'honneur d'Arbois de Jubainville* (Paris: Fontemoing, 1906), pp. 111–28.

73   Giraudon, *Chansons populaires de Basse-Bretagne sur feuilles volantes*; http://www.kan.bzh.

74   Adam Fox, *Oral and Literate Culture in England, 1500–1700* (Oxford: Oxford University Press, 2000); David Atkinson and Steve Roud (eds), *Street Ballads in Nineteenth-Century Britain, Ireland, and North America: The Interface between Print and Oral Traditions* (Aldershot: Ashgate, 2014).

75   For other cases where a broadside has clearly influenced oral versions see Daniel Giraudon, 'Une chanson de conscrits en langue bretonne: Chanson Paotred Plouillio', *Mémoires de la Société d'Émulation des Côtes-du-Nord*, 116 (1987), 39–63; Daniel Giraudon, 'Gwerz sant Juluan. De la feuille volante à la tradition orale', in Blanchard, *Jean-Marie de Penguern*, pp. 139–67.

The *gwerziou* have no very obvious parallels with song traditions in the other Celtic languages – neither in Gaelic (Ireland, Scotland, the Isle of Man) nor in the linguistically closer but culturally quite different Welsh tradition. The most likely Celtic-speaking culture with a similar sociolinguistic background could well have been Cornwall, but so little has survived in Cornish that we can only guess at its lost oral heritage.[76] Welsh has a rich tradition of printed ballads for the 18th and 19th centuries, often produced by named authors and responding to local events (shipwrecks, court cases, news of the American war, the invasion scare of 1797) and also adapting freely from English broadsides.[77] These are the productions of a literate and profoundly Protestant society, well versed in the Bible, and with a moral, sometimes decidedly judgemental outlook. The Welsh oral song tradition, though considerably less rich (or dramatically less well recorded) than in other Celtic-speaking countries, is livelier, funnier, more playful – but rarely given to extended narrative. Nothing in Welsh song tradition really corresponds to the world of the *gwerziou* in terms of form, content and style.

Irish and Scots Gaelic have extremely rich and varied song traditions, with songs adapted to different occasions – songs for weddings and funerals, work songs, lullabies, love songs, and some political and prophetic songs that use the very old narrative technique of the dream vision (*aisling*).[78] Many of these domestic songs could be interestingly paralleled in the Breton *soniou*, but when directly compared to the *gwerziou*, the Gaelic tradition as a whole has a far more lyrical feel. The rich tradition of Ossianic songs, legends and ballads known as *Fianaigheacht* (material dating well back into the Middle Ages, parts of which were used by James Macpherson for his literary *Ossian* in the 1760s) shares with the Breton ballads an insistent quality of localisation, with named landscape features, hills, lochs and streams linked to episodes in the adventures of the legendary band of warriors associated with Fionn Mac Cumhaill.[79] The overriding concern of the *gwerziou* with 'true' local incidents, however, is far less in evidence. Although some songs can be linked to historical events, such as the lament on the death of Gregor MacGregor in 1570 in the context of a feud with the Campbell clan,[80] these tend to be rare cases.

There are, however, just one or two tantalising threads that appear to stretch directly from the Breton song tradition back to the early literatures of other Celtic-speaking countries. One is the long, strange and unique, rhymed text about 'Merlin' collected by La Villemarqué in the 1820s, which formed the inspiration for the some of the Merlin poems in the *Barzaz-Breiz*. It is hard to know quite how such a piece might have been performed in the 19th century, but it clearly

76   See Oliver Padel, 'Evidence for Oral Tales in Medieval Cornwall', *Studia Celtica*, XL (2006), 127–53.
77   Ffion Mair Jones, 'Welsh Balladry and Literacy', in Atkinson and Roud, *Street Ballads*, pp. 105–26. Mary-Ann Constantine (ed.), *Ballads in Wales-Baledi yng Nghymru* (London: FLS Books, 1999).
78   A good introduction to the variety of this material can be found via the Carmichael Watson project at http://www.carmichael-watson.lib.ed.ac.uk/cwatson/.
79   Anja Gunderloch, 'The Heroic Ballads of Gaelic Scotland', in Sarah Dunnigan and Suzanne Gilbert (eds), *The Edinburgh Companion to Scottish Traditional Literatures* (Edinburgh: Edinburgh University Press, 2013), pp. 74–84.
80   Martin MacGregor, '"Surely one of the greatest poems ever made in Britain": The Lament for Griogair Ruadh MacGregor of Glen Strae and its Historical Background', in Edward J. Cowan and Douglas Gifford (eds), *The Polar Twins* (Edinburgh: John Donald, 1999), pp. 114–53.

draws on an earlier body of material that might be called 'Arthurian'.[81] Another tantalising web of connections can be traced in the motif of the woman with the golden breast found in the ballad of 'Enori' (no. 2): the story is clearly derived from a Latin life of St Budoc, with analogues in French Arthurian literature, medieval Welsh triads, a Scots ballad and a Scottish-Gaelic folktale, discussed in the commentary to the ballad. As so often with the complex interactions of surviving Arthurian texts, these moments of international connection offer glimpses into a world of lost stories circulating among the medieval cultures of Europe's western seaboard.

Most teasing of all is the link between the ballad of the penitential figure Iannik Skolvan/ Skolan (no. 3) and an enigmatic little poem about a similarly guilt-ridden 'Ysgolan' in the Welsh *Black Book of Carmarthen*.[82] The Welsh poem, preserved in a 13th-century manuscript but potentially older, is in the form of an *englyn*: a stanzaic, highly elliptical form of art poetry, which frequently alludes to narratives that are now either lost or partially known from other sources; as Oliver Padel has observed, the *englyn* sequences often voice expressions of loss, regret and guilt.[83] The connections between the two pieces, clearly related but so far apart in time, are explored further in the case study accompanying the text.

III: One song, many stories: ways of 'reading' *gwerziou*

The richness of the *gwerz* repertoire encourages a wide range of critical approaches. In this anthology we have tried to offer, within the relatively restricted confines of individual short commentaries, a variety of different responses to the songs themselves. It is perhaps worth, however, setting out some of these approaches in more detail. They range from a focus on style, narrative technique and musicality to a concern with historicity, and the importance of a broader contextualisation which locates the song text within a wider nexus of performers and listeners.

Language, form and music

The texts themselves are valuable records for anyone interested in language and poetic form. *Gwerziou* almost all conform to a specific metre, with end-rhymed couplets of eight or thirteen stresses. Depending on the tune, these can be also performed as triplets or quatrains; the form when sung is naturally flexible enough to accommodate all manner of 'irregularities', and lines do vary considerably in length. Very occasionally, it is possible to detect traces of a more complex internal rhyme system, which is attested in other literary texts in Breton between 1350 and 1650,

81 Laurent, *Aux sources du Barzaz-Breiz*, 289–96; Constantine, 'Neither flesh nor fowl'.
82 Donatien Laurent, 'La gwerz de Skolan et la légende de Merlin', *Ethnologie française*, 1 (1971), 19–54.
83 Oliver Padel, 'Legendary poetry in *englyn* metre', unpublished article (pers comm). We are grateful to the author for sharing his ideas on this subject.

and which corresponds to the use of *cynghanedd* in Welsh poetry.[84] The language of the *gwerziou* is distinctive, it has its own poetic formality and is often rich in archaisms; though many ballads do preserve the dialect forms of their communities, they do not really reflect either the spoken day-to-day Breton of the singers or the *brezoneg beleg* – a form of Breton used by the church in catechisms, hymns and educational material such as printed texts, including songs. Singing may also alter the pronunciation of certain words, shifting the usual spoken stress patterns to fit the shape of the tune.[85]

Gwerziou share some of the well-known narrative techniques of other European ballad traditions – the dramatic 'leaping and lingering', sometimes concise to the point of ellipsis, and other times offering detailed, almost ritualised, descriptions. And, again as in other song traditions, *gwerziou* are composed of familiar phrasal building blocks (ballad commonplaces) which have both a mnemonic and a structuring role. These may be opening verses, readily adaptable to new names and new stories:

> [Iannik Kokard] *a lavare*
> D'he vamm, d'he zad, un deiz a oe
>
> [Character's name] said
> To his mother and father one day

Or (as in nos 12, 21, 23 and 24) they may invoke the listener's sympathy at a critical moment in the narrative:

> Kriz vije'r galoun na welje
> [En iliz Kemper] neb a vije
>
> Cruel the heart that would not have wept
> To be [in the church at Quimper]

They may also be smaller units, like the frequently repeated *seiz* (seven), or the *triwec'h* ('eighteen') which crops up with baffling regularity (eighteen lovers, eighteen dead soldiers, eighteen blows with a stick) until one realises that its role in ballad coinage is to express 'a large number'.[86] The function of these commonplaces in the preservation and renewal of song traditions has been the subject of a vast amount of critical attention, from the Parry–Lord theory of oral-formulaic composition derived from Homeric and South Slavic epic poetry, to more recent print-focused

---

84   Gwennolé Le Menn, 'La prosodie des chants en moyen-breton (1350–1650)', in Jean Quéniart (ed.), *Le chant, acteur de l'histoire* (Rennes: Presses universitaires de Rennes, 1999), pp. 13–21.

85   Francis Favereau, 'Phonologie des rimes et des vers dans la poésie chantée à Poullaouen', *Klask*, 3 (1996), 35–41.

86   Matthieu Boyd, 'The Female Jailer: Commonplaces in the gwerzioù', in Joseph Harris and Barbara Hillers (eds), *Child's Children: Ballad Study and Its Legacies* (Trier: WVT Wissenschaftlicher Verglag, 2012), pp. 186–204; see also Le Rol, *La langue des 'gwerzioù'*, pp. 108–60.

discussions of the Child ballads.[87] Traditionally understood as markers of an essentially oral tradition (a view which has been persuasively challenged by David Atkinson),[88] ballad commonplaces have been perceived both as proof that songs are continually recomposed with each performance,[89] with every singer reconfiguring the elements to create the ballad anew, and also, apparently to the contrary, as evidence of a mnemonic technique which keeps texts verbally stable generation after generation. Both, in a partial sense, may be true. Perhaps the least contentious way of understanding commonplaces in the *gwerz* context is to think of them as a language within a language, a store of phrases available to singers who, from deep familiarity with the 'grammar' of other songs, can extend or adapt certain aspects of the narrative (see, for example, the multiple endings of ballads associated with *gwerz* no. 26, 'Sea-changes'). Yet they clearly also function mnemonically and help to keep texts stable by structuring the story.

Set-piece endings – a miraculous rescue or, more likely, a good death – allow versions to develop in strikingly different narrative directions, sometimes quite brusquely. The cluster of different versions around a shipwreck ballad relating to St Mathurin Moncontour (no. 26) demonstrates this particularly effectively.[90] Dialogue occupies a large part of many ballads, and again certain classic dialogues of confrontation or denunciation may drift between versions with interesting narrative results. Above all the *gwerziou* are rich in idioms and expressions that derive from the culture and the language itself. Count Guillou warns his wife that, if she lies to him, she will be '*konfontet evel amann rouzet*' ('melted like burnt butter'). The terrified bride of a man bitten by a mad dog cries out: '*Ma é zeulegad én é ben/Avel guin ru en ur huéren*' ('The eyes in his head/ are like red wine in a glass'). At another level again is the constant irruption of the miraculous, the surreal – a star speaks, a girl shrivels to a 'little piece of heart', three thin-faced women in yellow silk ride past – in a language of symbolism heavily marked by, yet often weirdly subversive of, the Catholic church. Indeed, if one were to single out a stylistic characteristic of the *gwerziou* it might be a gift for *materialising* the miraculous. The bracken standing tall along the north coast is transformed into soldiers (no. 35). A simple gesture of physical contact allows a sceptical ship's captain to hear impossibly distant bells (no. 33):

> – O, 'me'añ, me na gredan ket se
> Klevfes kleier Kawan alese

87   For a stimulating review and discussion of the subject, with particular focus on the Child ballads, see David Atkinson, *The Anglo-Scottish Ballad and its Imaginary Contexts* (Cambridge: Open Book Publishers, 2014). See especially Chapter 3, which discusses 'sources of variance'.

88   'Accordingly – seductively – oral tradition comes to be equated with the very engine of ballad variation, that complex of processes involving remembering and forgetting, addition, subtraction and rearrangement, substitution, borrowing and consolidation (to name just a few) that scholars have codified to account for textual and melodic stability and change', Atkinson, *The Anglo-Scottish Ballad*, p. 49.

89   The theory of oral improvisation was advanced most comprehensively by David Buchan, *The Ballad and the Folk* (London: Routledge & Kegan Paul, 1972), and most strenuously refuted by Albert B. Friedman, 'The Oral-Formulaic Theory of Balladry – A Re-rebuttal', in James Porter (ed.), *The Ballad Image: Essays Presented to Bertrand Harris Bronson* (Los Angeles: Center for the Study of Comparative Folklore & Mythology, University of California, Los Angeles, 1983), pp. 215–40.

90   Constantine and Porter, *Fragments and Meaning*, pp. 101–11.

Klevfes kleier Kawan alese
Te ve'añ pemp kant lev dioute.

– Lakaet ho troad dehou war ma hini
Ha c'hwi klevo ma mestr kenkoulz ha me.

– Ah, he said, that I do not believe.
That you can hear the bells of Cavan from here

That you can hear the bells of Cavan from here
When you are five hundred leagues away from them.

– Put your right foot on mine
And you will hear, master, as well as I do.[91]

A musicologist would approach these pieces with further questions about the relationship between lyrics and tune; occasionally their findings might surprise. Thomas Price's comments about the primacy of words over tunes are not inappropriate here, in that melodies do tend to be subordinate, and are fairly readily interchangeable (it is difficult to think of any *gwerz* that is consistently sung to one single tune). Certain tunes hold sway over large swathes of the tradition at any given time; the best-known example being the air known as *Ker-Is*, which became very popular during the 19th century (included here with *gwerz* no. 21 and CD track 3).[92] Age and memory can also alter or reduce singers' melodic range. When a *gwerz* is put to a different use, however, the primacy of the narrative can be seriously destabilised. It regularly happens that ballad texts are used for dances – mainly group dances in the round – and here the rhythm of the piece is paramount, even when, disconcertingly, the story is a tragic one of rape or murder, such as the case of Marivonnik abducted by the English (no. 25 and CD track 15) or Perinaig Ar Mignon, the servant girl from Lannion (no. 28 and CD track 16).

History and memory: renewing the past

Historians are becoming increasingly interested in the nature of historical memory within popular and traditional genres. The Breton *gwerziou* offer many opportunities for such research, provided that the historian understands the internal 'rules' of the genre. Over the last century or so, some 40 separate studies have allowed us to identify specific historical events from the 16th to the

91   *Garan Ar Briz*, recorded by Claudine Mazéas from Jeanne-Yvonne Garlan, Minihy-Tréguier, *c.*1960–1. Dastum, NUM-2832.
92   Bernard Lasbleiz, 'Le timbre de Kêr Is: Un air populaire qui traverse les siècles', *Musique Bretonne*, 188 (2005), 34–8; Bernard Lasbleiz, 'War don… Les timbres des chansons et cantiques populaires en langue bretonne (17ᵉ–20ᵉ siècle)', unpublished doctoral thesis (Brest: Université de Bretagne Occidentale, 2012).

18th centuries which inspired *gwerziou* not collected until considerably later.[93] Wherever possible, multiple ballad versions are compared with information from more familiar written sources. Certain periods are especially well represented; there are several ballads covering the wars of religion in the last decade of the 16th century, often focusing on the troubles caused by the unruly followers of characters such as René de La Tremblaye, Marguerite Charlès or Guy Éder de La Fontenelle (nos 15, 16, 17), or referring to specific military actions, such as the siege of the town of Guingamp (no. 12).

Also well represented in the *gwerz* repertoire are ballads reflecting conflicts within the Breton nobility at the beginning of the 17th century, particularly encounters ending in duels (nos 23 and 24). Others focus on historical figures who left their mark on the popular imagination, such as the Marquis de Guerrand, the subject of several songs based on his turbulent youth and his penitent old age (no. 22), the Marquis de Pontcallec executed for treason (no. 30) and the Chouan leader Jean Jan (no. 34). Others preserve the memory of local events, such as the shipwreck at Penmarc'h (no. 11) and the murder of a group of merchants by Lord Villaudrain (no. 14).

The individual case studies are fascinating and often require considerable detective work. But the *gwerziou* as a body also permit a broader analysis through a cultural historical lens, offering a window onto Breton society under the *ancien régime*.[94] Any analysis needs to take account of the fact that songs are not preserved in aspic – that they change and adapt in the course of transmission. But the structure of the song, its form and its rhymes, quite apart from the status accorded the *gwerz* as a repository of 'truth', makes it inherently conservative. And comparison between the songs and the written evidence of the archives reveals that the historical *gwerziou* almost always offer closer reflections of the period of their composition (generally between the 16th and 18th centuries), than of the period during which they were collected (usually the 19th and 20th centuries).

They are detailed enough, for example, to allow the exploration of aspects of material culture, whether in terms of the built environment – the importance of the local manor house and its planted avenues of trees (no. 23) – or the furnishing of interiors, as with the use of coffers or chests (nos 19, 20 and 27). Styles and types of clothing are signalled in brief, significant details which permit the listener to identify the socioeconomic status of the protagonists: the rich with their ribbons, lace and high-status materials (nos 20 and 22); heiresses sporting beautifully ornate *coiffes* (no. 13); and nobles trying to escape justice dressed as peasants in garments of coarse linen (no. 30).

The *gwerziou* allow plenty of scope, too, for examining the relations between the world of the nobility and the labouring rural classes, as well as considering perceptions of the destitute and the socially excluded. The nobility they portray is far from uniform, from the rich ladies organising balls and dinners in their manor houses, or seeking to marry off their *pennhêrez* (heiress) (nos 13 and 24), to the impoverished aristocrats struggling to keep up appearances in front of an up-and-coming *paysan* class seeking to make advantageous marriages (no. 22). Nobles have the right to wear a sword or to retain a family pew at church (no. 24) – privileges which continue

---

93   For a list of dated *gwerziou* with accompanying case studies see Guillorel, *La Complainte et la Plainte*, pp. 122–4.
94   For a more detailed exploration of this point see Guillorel, *La Complainte et la Plainte*, pp. 290–490.

to distinguish them from the wealthy farming classes. For the latter, status is linked to material wealth – the size of their herds or the number of farms (no.18). Amid this broader network of social relations, certain themes appear specific to Breton-speaking Brittany. Among them we find the ostracism of 'kakous', a group believed to be descendants of lepers and excluded from taking part in normal society long after the disease itself was eradicated. Earning their living as ropemakers (the only craft permitted to them), they live apart, marry among themselves and are forbidden from mixing with the wider community, even at mass (no. 18).[95] Other ballads offer striking representations of diseases such as the plague (no. 8) and rabies (no. 9).

Gwerziou can also contribute a great deal to our understanding of popular religious belief and practice, reflecting as they do the characteristically intense religiosity of Breton-speaking Brittany well into the modern period.[96] They include accounts of local, often unofficial, saints (no. 6) and unusual representations of the afterlife (nos 1 and 3). Often richly detailed, they describe attitudes to death, prayers, processions, funerals and particular acts of charity towards the poor (nos 10 and 13). There are vivid vignettes of pilgrims circling churches on their bare and bloodied knees, heading for the numerous *pardons* – pilgrimages to favoured shrines at Sainte-Anne-d'Auray, Le Folgoët, Saint-Jean-du-Doigt and Le Yaudet. Once at church, they may offer votive gifts of long waxed cords ('ceintures de cire') in exchange for divine protection (nos 4 and 26). A recurrent protagonist in the ballads is the figure of the 'kloarek' ('cleric'), usually the son of a relatively wealthy farming family, pursuing religious studies, a situation which often sets up a painful conflict between the demands of a sweetheart at home and the desire of the kloarek's parents who wish to have a priest in the family (no. 22).

Strikingly, too, Breton ballads vocalise and form part of a world of constant movement – so many of the *gwerziou* begin with characters setting off for fairs, or the *aire neuve* (threshing floor, where dances are held), leaving for a pilgrimage or to try and make a living at sea. Also widespread are stories of soldiers heading off to war, or returning after many years unrecognised by their families or sweethearts (no. 32), often with tragic consequences. Descriptions of young men called up to the military by the drawing of lots (no. 33) correspond to known historical procedures from the 17th and 18th centuries.

And in a genre full of violent deaths it is not surprising to find references to various aspects of the judicial system of the *ancien régime*: arrests, trials, sentences and executions, with punishment often gradated by class – hanging for the lower classes, decapitation for the nobles and burning at the stake for women accused of witchcraft (nos 17, 20, 30). Several ballads use the motif of royal letters of remission or pardon for a criminal (no. 22). Others offer us glimpses of oral-based legal activities that leave little trace on the written record, such as unofficial negotiations resolving issues that would damage the reputation of families. In some cases, they shed new light on events known from other sources; the case of the murder of Loeiz Er Ravalleg, studied in detail by Donatien Laurent, is perhaps the best example of this. Where the contemporary written record

---

95   Constantine, *Breton Ballads*, pp. 83–128.
96   Croix, *La Bretagne aux 16ᵉ et 17ᵉ siècles*.

appears to have been deliberately muted in order to protect certain influential people, the *gwerz* and the handed-down knowledge that accompanies it have preserved a fuller and more damning account of events (no. 31).[97] The *gwerziou* thus permit us to read *ancien régime* history from unusual angles.[98]

While the stability and relative conservatism of the *gwerz* tradition lend it historical credibility, this does not of course preclude the songs being renewed in altered historical contexts. Several ballads relating to events from the 16th to the 18th centuries gain a new emphasis and new meanings during the 1789 French Revolution and its attendant counter-revolutionary rebellions. During this period of civil war, a period which scarred Brittany deeply, those who held revo-lutionary ideals confronted those who sought to uphold the authority of the monarch and the church (a group often, if rather too simplistically, labelled 'Chouans'). Some versions of the ballads on the murder of Perinaig Ar Mignon in 1695 (no. 28) or the death of the Marquis de Pontcallec in 1720 (no. 30) have clearly been 'updated' to reflect a counter-revolutionary perspective; this is especially the case in the Vannetais, where *chouannerie* was most active.

These kinds of meaningful alterations, only possible to detect where multiple versions of a single *gwerz* can be compared, offer further insights into the development of Breton society, and show the continued importance of certain key cultural or historical moments into the period when most of the songs were collected in the 19th and 20th centuries.

Performance and meaning: communities and individuals

Switching analytical focus, performance-oriented criticism steps outside the individual song text to ask questions about the meaning of a given song for its singers and their audiences. Song repertoires are intensely personal. Certain songs may have been learned from family members and carry with them a vivid penumbra of childhood associations; some may have been acquired during specific periods of close personal contact with other bearers of the tradition – for example, during apprenticeships or group work sessions. Personal taste – a penchant for a particular kind of ballad story – must also count for a lot. One might note the harsh religiosity of much of Marc'harit Fulup's repertoire, with its emphasis on bloody penitential acts, its investment in the notion of redemption bought through pain. Songs that play out dramas of violence against women or the loss of a son to the army may directly reflect and articulate lived experiences. It may not be pure chance that the repertoires of both Mari-Job Cado and Mari-Job Kerival, both of whom sang for Luzel, contain five different *gwerziou* about infanticide.[99] From what we know of the tradition, songs on such topics are virtually never sung by men. Under-represented in the written archive, acts of violence specifically relating to women, such as rape and infanticide (nos 25 and 27), are much in evidence in the *gwerziou*; they offer insights into a female discourse

---

97   Laurent, 'La gwerz de Louis Le Ravallec'.
98   Guillorel, *La Complainte et la Plainte*, pp. 173–288.
99   Guillorel, *La Complainte et la Plainte*, pp. 206–7.

which is rarely accessible through other sources. Elements of a ballad story may have a deeply hidden, indirect connection to the psychology of singers or listeners. Any information about the emotional importance of a particular song for an individual is precious (and largely missing, of course, for 19th-century versions), but one can also legitimately ask how society as a whole, or the parts of society that participated in the song culture, 'used' songs like these to deal with difficult, even taboo, subjects.[100]

More generally, one might ask how 'meaning' works for modern singers of ballads which date all the way back to the 16th century, but for whom that original historical context is lost. What keeps songs alive beyond the first context of their production? Aesthetic sensibilities must play their part, but narrative is fundamental. One of the most widely collected songs dating from the wars of the Ligue has a plotline eminently capable of being transposed in time (no. 16): should the young woman abducted by a captain kill herself to preserve her virginity? Female honour, an essential component of *ancien régime* society, retained its importance in successive generations; and the song remains a powerful one even in contemporary society, where the interpretation has shifted away from the subject of honour and virginity to focus on the trauma of rape.

In contrast, it is not hard to find examples of ballads that were hugely popular in the 19th century, yet fail to appear in later collections. The complex question of why some songs survive and others vanish is ultimately unanswerable, but once again, in at least some cases, the nature of the narrative must play a part. The ballad on the death of the Marquis de Guerrand – which took place in 1669 at Plouégat-Guerrand (Trégor) – is an astonishing rhymed tour de force setting out his bequest to some 30 or so religious establishments. Known in a dozen versions from 19th-century sources, it has never since been recorded. More than two centuries after the marquis' death, this endless litany, with minimal narrative impact, seems not to have carried much meaning for singers or audience, and thus fell out of the ballad tradition altogether.[101]

Performance context is equally important when trying to grasp the possibilities of meaning in songs. Most collectors will testify to the subtle invisible 'rules' that make certain songs singable in certain contexts and not others. We have already seen that class, gender and/or politics might constrain a singer's desire to share her repertoire with a collector, but even within communities certain songs may be held back in the presence of a singer with a better claim to it, or in favour of a different version – and perhaps, too, out of respect for the families. Where a song evokes real and tragic local events (no. 31), a singer might hesitate to sing it 'car la famille existe encore' (because the family still exists).[102] More practical circumstances also shape a repertoire; different pieces will be sung to accompany everyday chores, collective work outside or at a wedding party.

100   See, for the French song tradition, David Hopkin, *Voices of the People in Nineteenth-Century France* (Cambridge: Cambridge University Press, 2012); for anglophone tradition, David Atkinson, *The English Traditional Ballad. Theory, Method, and Practice* (Aldershot: Ashgate, 2002), pp. 1–38.
101   Guillorel, *La Complainte et la Plainte*, pp. 423–32.
102   See Patrick Malrieu, 'La chanson populaire de tradition orale en langue bretonne. Contribution à l'établissement d'un catalogue', unpublished doctoral thesis, 5 vols (Rennes: 1998), vol. 1, p. 132.

Conditions have changed dramatically, of course, over the last hundred years, with a shift from singing as a normal workplace activity in the fields or the domestic sphere, or as part of the long *veillées* combining work (such as spinning) and sociability, to the modern contexts of performance. The *veillées* continue, in pubs and village halls, as do the popular *festou-noz* where singing and dancing come together; but *gwerziou* may also now be heard in concert halls, on the radio or television, or on a CD played at home. Such audiences are wider but infinitely more disparate, and the meanings of these pieces for their singers and listeners are perhaps even more unknowable and unpredictable. What is certain, however, is that the meanings of songs can and will be renewed in quite different contexts, including in the privacy and silence of the printed page, and even refracted through another language. It is to be hoped that, in ways we cannot foresee, this anthology will help to give the Breton *gwerziou* a new lease of life.

Editorial Policy: Texts and Translations

Texts

The ballad texts in Breton reproduce the spelling of individual collectors, and are thus markedly different from each other, since Breton orthography varies across time and across the dialect regions, and collectors had their own ways of noting down songs. The internal division of songs into couplets or verses, on the other hand, has in a very few cases been altered for ease of reading. We have opted for a minimalist approach to punctuation – these words were sung, not written, after all – and we have, for the same reasons, reduced the sometimes dense punctuation of many of the Breton texts. It should be noted here, too, that the songs on the accompanying CD are not always the same versions as the printed text, but variant versions of the same ballad, often collected considerably later. Each ballad text is accompanied by an analysis which provides further context for the song – and, where known, information about the circumstances of its collection. A short bibliography notes any further studies of the piece in order of relevance.

Translations

Naming is a political act. In countries with two (or more) languages, where one language is officially dominant, simply choosing one form over another can have ideological implications. Should we be writing about Breiz-Izel or Basse-Bretagne? Montroulez or Morlaix? Should Luzel's most productive ballad singer be known as Marguerite Philippe, or Marc'harit Fulup (and for that matter, should Luzel himself be An Uhel?). Translating Breton songs and evoking Breton landscapes for an English-speaking audience adds another level of complexity to the problem. On one level it could be used as a way of bypassing 'French' culture altogether, since we could, in effect, access (or create) a thoroughly, if artificially, Bretonicised world. But how many English-speaking readers would be comfortable negotiating their way from Gwengamp to Kemper? And how many would recognise Kervarker as La Villemarqué? There is a tension between the desire for ideological correctness (and a desire to compensate for the erasure of a minority language by using its name forms) and the need to write naturally for an educated audience using the name forms that would normally appear in an English-language text about Brittany. That tension, as far as our editorial policy goes, has not been altogether resolved, but our discussions have been interesting. Both authors are used to working in bilingual cultures (French/Breton and English/Welsh), but, doubtless because of the different linguistic histories of the two countries, have different senses of what 'feels' natural or acceptable in print.

Our broad policy has been to use the better-known 'French' forms for places when writing in English (the Breton texts themselves, of course, retain the Breton forms), but to keep Breton forms for personal names (usually the singers, and characters within the ballads). Exceptions to this are well-known collectors (La Villemarqué, Luzel, Le Braz), most of whom, unlike their 19th-century informants, lived and worked through the French language, and who only occasionally used the Bretonicised forms of their names in the context of literary revival. An index of place names at the back of this book offers both forms so that readers may explore further; it is worth pointing out here that, as far as place names are concerned, 'French' forms, generally recorded earlier, can often preserve Breton etymologies more distinctly than their later oral Breton counterparts.

More generally, the translations have stuck close to the Breton text; occasional intractable words or phrases have been explained more fully in footnotes. In a small number of recurrent cases we have either opted to retain the Breton word or chosen an English word which closes down certain possibilities of meaning. They include *pardon*, an annual pilgrimage often focused on a local saint and involving the carrying of banners, the singing of hymns and, often, circuits of the church or precinct; many *pardons* attracted huge crowds and had a holiday aspect to them as well, with stalls selling food and religious icons, and couples enjoying a day out. The *leur-nevez*, or threshing floor, offered another space for sociability (and also, in the *gwerziou*, confrontation), where people would meet to dance. Like the *filajou* (*veillées*, evenings of song and storytelling), elements of rural labour (such as spinning) would often coexist with sociable gatherings and entertainment. The figure of the *kloareg*, translated as 'cleric' (pl. *kloer*), is a distinctive character in the ballads. Often, but not always, a trainee priest, the *kloareg* is a young man pursuing a course of religious studies, and his behaviour, especially in matters of love, is usually more that of the student than the man of the cloth. The *kloer* are often portrayed as poets, makers of songs (frequently love songs), and can become disruptive elements in the world of the *gwerziou*.

At a closer lexical level, other choices have to be made. The term of endearment *paour* (literally 'poor') is used frequently by characters (*ma mamm baour*, my poor mother) but sounds odd in English, possibly because 'poor' in Breton, and even French, retains some sense of 'blessed' which is missing in English. The various ways of translating title and rank have also caused problems, since an English 'Lord' does not always correspond to a Breton *Aotrou* or a French *Seigneur*, and the roles of vicars, priests and curates shift confusingly in space and time. In some cases, a 'best fit' policy has been adopted, which may not always be literally accurate; or titles have been kept (usually in French – 'the Marquis de Pontcallec').

The English versions of the *gwerziou*, then, may occasionally feel somewhat stilted or unnatural (and the absence of rhyme and metre is a huge loss), but this has to be preferable to the more mellifluous, medievalising style of earlier attempts, such as Tom Taylor's *Ballads and Songs of Brittany* (1865) based on the already much-smoothed texts of the *Barzaz-Breiz*. It is to be hoped that the rather more literal translations contained in this anthology will take curious readers, and Breton learners, back to the original texts.

A Note on the Versions on the CD

Thanks to over a century's worth of sound recordings we can now not only read, but listen to the *gwerziou*. A few of the songs in this edition are only known from 19th-century collections, and in their written form, but most have been collected and recorded many times since. Some of these continue to be regularly sung today, during social gatherings at *veillées* or *festou-noz*. All the versions on the CD were collected from traditional singers who learned their repertoires from family or neighbours, and virtually all were recorded in the field by amateur collectors.

As often as not, each *gwerz* presented a choice of recordings. Our final selection was guided by a desire to be as representative as possible, displaying a variety of singers and singing styles, as well as different dialects and different contexts for the performances – ranging from singers noted for their fine voices and their rich repertoires, to more intimate recordings. The geographical spread of the different versions (see Map 2) reflects the inequalities in collecting patterns across the different regions of Lower Brittany.

The creation of the CD was made possible through the support of Dastum. Set up in 1972, and initially run by volunteers, Dastum (which is Breton for 'collect') is a not-for-profit association dedicated to the collection, the preservation and the wider diffusion of Brittany's rich oral heritage. Based at Rennes, but with a network of associated groups across the whole of Brittany, Dastum works in collaboration with a number of different partners, including the Région Bretagne and the Bibliothèque nationale de France, and publishes or supports the publication of books and CDs, as well as editing the three-monthly review *Musique Bretonne*. The association also manages an impressive sound archive containing over 90,000 items recorded from some 5,000 different informants; a manuscript archive with over 250 song collections; and libraries holding some 30,000 song texts, printed ballads and stories, around 4,600 records and other sound media, and a picture archive with approximately 27,000 photos and postcards relating to Brittany's oral heritage. Dastum's sound archives can be accessed through the database 'Archives du patrimoine oral', from which the versions on the CD were selected.

In order to present as many different songs as possible on the CD, most of the versions selected have had to be cut short (some of the longer *gwerziou* last over 15 minutes). But the full versions, with transcriptions, can be freely accessed through the Dastum website: http://www.dastumedia. bzh (search for 'Miracles & Murders').

dastum

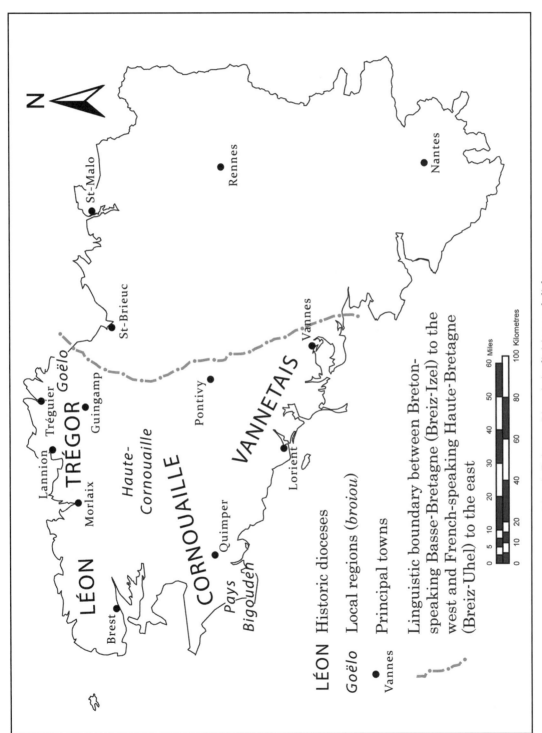

N

LÉON

TRÉGOR

Haute-
Cornouaille

CORNOUAILLE

Pays
Bigouden

VANNETAIS

Goëlo

Brest

Morlaix

Lannion

Tréguier

Guingamp

Quimper

Pontivy

Lorient

Vannes

St-Brieuc

St-Malo

Rennes

Nantes

LÉON Historic dioceses

Goëlo Local regions (broiou)

● Principal towns

Vannes

Linguistic boundary between Breton-
speaking Basse-Bretagne (Breiz-Izel) to the
west and French-speaking Haute-Bretagne
(Breiz-Uhel) to the east

0   5 10   20   30   40   50   60 Miles
0 10 20   40   60   80   100 Kilometres

Map 1 Brittany: Linguistic division and dialect areas.

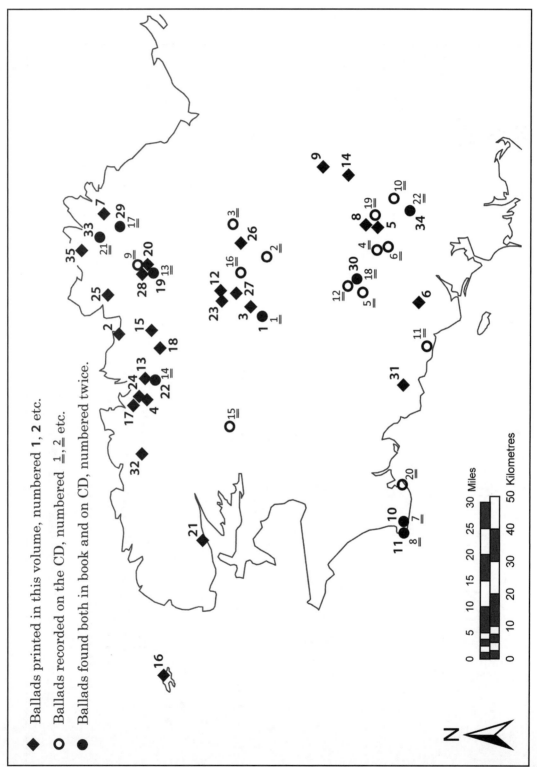

Ballads printed in this volume, numbered **1**, **2** etc.

Ballads recorded on the CD, numbered $\underline{\underline{1}}$, $\underline{\underline{2}}$ etc.

Ballads found both in book and on CD, numbered twice.

Map 2 Provenance of songs in the book and on the CD.

The Ballads

1. Lord Count and the fairy

An ô - trou   kont hag   e   bri - ed   oa a - bre - dig   mad   o   daou   di -

met,   oa a - bre - dig   mad   o   daou   di - met.

An ôtrou kont hag e bried	Lord Count and his bride
Oa abredig mad o daou dimet	Were married very young
Oa abredig mad o daou dimet	Were married very young
Un daouzeg vla, 'n heiñ all trizeg	One was twelve; the other thirteen
Eur mab bihan a zo ganet.	A little boy was born to them.
– Petra 'po bremañ 'vid ho koan	– What would you most like for dinner
P'e peus ganet eur mab bihan?	Now that you have given me a little boy?
– O kig keveleg pe kig gad	– Woodcock meat, or the meat of the hare
Pa ne ve d'ho poan da vond d'ar c'hoad.	if you don't mind going into the woods.
E toull ar c'hoad p'oa erruet	When he arrived, deep in the woods
Eur gornandonez 'neus gwelet.	He saw a fairy woman.
– Dibonjour dac'h, ôtrou ar c'hont	– Greetings to you, Lord Count
Me 'oa pell 'zo kas ho rankontr	I have been a long time waiting to meet you
Daoust a ve dac'h pe dimê d'in	Would you prefer to marry me
Pe chom seiz vla da langissi	Or spend seven years languishing
Kar soufr ar maro a zo kri?	For the pangs of death they are strong?
– Gwell e ve d'in mervel prontamant	– I would much rather die immediately
Evid chom seiz vla da langissañ	Than wait seven years languishing
Kar ma fried 'zo c'hoaz yaouank.	For my bride is still very young.
– Petra 'zo nê er maner-mañ	– What is new in this manor house
Pe ouel ar vitizien ar moz-mañ?	That the servant girls are weeping so?

– O kanna koue ez int bet
Ar c'haera niñsel 'neint kollet.

– O laret d'hê dihan da ouelo
Me am eus arc'hant hag a bêvo.

Petra 'zo nê er maner-mañ
Pe ouel ar vevelien ar moz-mañ?

– O toura 'r c'hezeg ez eint bet
Ar gwella jô a zo beuvet.

– O laret d'hê dihan da ouelo
Me am eus arc'hant hag a bêvo.

Petra 'zo nê er maner-mañ
Pe gan ar veleien ar moz-mañ?

– Eur paouar koz a oa lojet
Evid an noz eo desedet.

– O laret d'hê kano kano
Me am eus arc'hant hag a bêvo.

Petra 'zo nê er maner-mañ
O pe zon ar c'hleier ar moz-mañ?

– Ar paouar koz 'oa desedet
Hirio an de 'vo interet.

– O laret d'hê zono, zono
Me am eus arc'hant hag a bêvo.

Ma mamm, setu erru an tri mis
Poent bras eo din mond d'an ilis

Tapet d'in ma habit satin gwenn
'Vid ma hin da vinnigo ma fenn.

– Ma merc'h, brema 'ma 'r giz d'ar vro
Da vond d'an iliz en kañviou.

– They have been out washing the linen
And have lost the finest sheet.

– O tell them not to weep like that
I have money, and I will pay.

What is new in this manor house
That the servant lads are weeping so?

– They took the horses out for a run
And the finest horse of all was drowned.

– O tell them not to weep
I have money and I will pay.

What is new in this manor house
That the priests are all singing like that?

– A poor man who was lodged here
Passed away in the night.

– O tell them to sing, and sing again
I have money and I will pay.

What is new in this manor house
That the bells should be ringing like that?

– That poor old man who passed away
Will be buried here today.

– O tell them to ring, and ring again
I have money and I will pay.

Mother, now three months have gone
It is high time for me to be churched.

Pass me my dress of white satin
That I may go and receive my blessing.

– Daughter, it is the fashion in these parts now
To go to church in mourning dress.

En eur dremen dre ar vered	As she entered the church precinct
Be' e fried 'neus remerket.	She noticed the grave of her husband.
– Delet, ma mamm, ma alc'houeiou	– Mother, take my keys
Ha grêt ar vad gant ma madou	Put my possessions to good use
Ha kerhet d'ar ger gant ma mab	Go home to my little boy
Kar me 'chom amañ gant e dad.	I am staying here with his father.

Provenance:
Collected by Donatien Laurent from Maryvonne, Anastasie and Eugénie Goadec, Treffrin (Haute-Cornouaille), 1968. Published in *Tradition chantée de Bretagne. Les sources du Barzaz Breiz aujourd'hui*, CD track 1.

CD:
Track 1. Same version.

This classically beautiful ballad is one of the few Breton *gwerziou* that can unambiguously be assigned to an international ballad-type, being clearly related to the Scandinavian *Elveskud*, the Scots ballad *Clerk Colvill* (Child 42), and a host of other versions stretching from the Faroes to Italy. Much scholarly ink has been spilled trying to decide the source of the ballad and the nature of its dissemination across Europe. The story of the hunt and the encounter with a female otherworld presence are themes found in French and English versions of the elusive 'Breton lay', and some have made a case for Breton origins on the strength of this. With such a vast network of related songs in dozens of different languages, however, it is difficult to see how one could ever be sure.

La Villemarqué placed this ballad second in his 1839 *Barzaz-Breiz*, and Luzel used it as the opening piece in his *Gwerziou,* giving no fewer than three different versions. Dozens of other versions survive in 19th-century manuscript collections, and it was recorded orally many times in the following century. This version is from the repertoire of the famous Goadec sisters, who became widely known during the Breton cultural revival of the 1970s, partly thanks to their participation in concerts performed by Alan Stivell, the most high-profile singer of the period. The three sisters came from Haute-Cornouaille, a region which has maintained a strong tradition of Breton-language song to the present day, in part because of the popularity of *kan ha diskan* (a repertoire for dancing in the round), a form for which they were especially well known. The youngest, Eugénie, who died at the age of 93 in 2003, continued to sing to the end of her life, and to pass on her repertoire to her daughter Louise Ebrel, who remains an active singer. Various other 20th-century collections testify to the long transmission of this song; in 1980, for example, Yann-Fañch Kemener collected a version running to 34 couplets from Guillaume Bertrand in Saint-Nicolas-du-Pélem.

The Goadec sisters' version is textually very close to texts collected in the first half of the 19th century; and the tune is an old one, in three musical phrases with repetition of the second line of text. On the whole this is a stable *gwerz* with relatively few variables; though it is often known by the *Barzaz-Breiz* title 'Lord Nann and the Fairy', most versions have a 'Lord Count' or a 'Count Tudor' as their protagonist. They usually include the appearance of the young count's nemesis, who may be a fairy (*eur gornandez*) or a 'white lady' or 'old woman' (*groac'h*) and who initially asks the count to marry her before condemning him to death (in the Scandinavian versions she is often a jealous fairy lover). Most, too, linger over the various noises in the house heard by the young wife (still in her bed after childbirth) and deliberately misinterpreted for her by the mother. The Goadec sisters' version does not dramatise the moment of the young man's return, in which he asks his mother to hide the news of his imminent death from his wife. It is developed more fully in other versions, such as this one sung by Guillaume Bertrand, which recalls the insistent 'Mother, make my bed soon' of the well-known Child ballad 'Lord Randal' (Child 12):

Er gêr pa 'n 'eus bet erruet	When he arrived at the house
Digant e vamm 'n 'eus goulennet	He asked his mother
Digant e vamm 'n 'eus goulennet	He asked his mother
Gwele e gabined ma oa grêt.	If the bed in his closet was made.
– Ma n'e' ket grêt, grit-hañ ês	– If it is not made, make it so that I may rest
Birviken ken na deuin er-mêz	Never again will I leave it.
Nemet ur wech da liano	Except once to be wrapped in a shroud
Hag ur wech all da intero	And once more to be buried
N'anzavit ket deus ma fried	Do not tell my wife
Ken 'vin maro hag interet.	Until I am dead and buried.[1]

The version sung by the Goadec sisters is also relatively restrained in its development of the doubly tragic ending. In the *Barzaz-Breiz,* La Villemarqué makes the fairy rather more seductive, and causes intertwining trees, complete with turtledoves, to sprout from the young couple's grave.

Studies:
Donatien Laurent, 'Tradition and Innovation in Breton Oral Literature'.
Francis James Child (ed.), *The English and Scottish Popular Ballads*, I, pp. 371–87.
George Doncieux, *Le romancéro populaire de la France,* 'Le roi Renaud', pp. 84–124.
Yvon Le Rol, *La langue des 'gwerzioù' à travers l'étude des manuscrits inédits de Mme de Saint-Prix*, II, pp. 370–81.

1   Yann-Fañch Kemener, *Carnets de route*, pp. 136–7.

2. Saint Henori and the King of Brest

Ar roue a Vrest a so klanvet	The King of Brest is suffering
Gant eur c'hlenvet disesper meurbet	From a most desperate illness
Ma lavar dezhan ar brophetet	The prophets tell him
Mar deen eur vron merc'h a vo iac'het.	That a maiden's breast will cure him.
– Ez han breman da di ma merc'h henan	– I shall go to my eldest daughter's house
Hounnes am boa maget da gentan	She was the one I brought up first
Mar digwez d'ezhi ma refusi	If she should happen to refuse me
Me a bunisso anezhi	I will punish her
Me bunisso hi c'horf hag hi mado	I'll punish her body and her goods
Hag ho funisso war eur dro.	Punish them on the spot.
– Debonjour d'ac'h ma merc'h henan	– Good day to you my eldest daughter
Ha c'hui ma ziskourfe eun dra?	Will you do something for me?
Me so klanvet gant eur c'hlenved	I am afflicted with a disease
Ha so disesper meurbet	Desperate sickness indeed
Ha ma lavar d'in ar brofetet	And the prophets tell me
M'am be eur vron werc'h ven iac'haet.	That a maiden's breast would cure me.
– Euz an dra se n'ho sikourin ket	– From that I will not save you
Euz eun dra all na laran ket	Though from anything else I might
Merc'het all oc'h euz ho sikouro	You have other daughters to help you
N'e ket me, ma zad, a raïo.	My father, I will not.
– Me ia breman da di ma merc'h entrehenan	– I shall go now to my middle daughter's house
Hounnes a garan ar muian	She is the one I love the most
Mar digwez d'ezhi ma refusi	If she should happen to refuse me
Me a bunisso anezhi	I will punish her
Me bunisso hi c'horf hi mado	I'll punish her body and her goods
Hag ho funisso war eun dro.	Punish them on the spot.
– Debonjour d'ac'h ma merc'h entrehenan	– Good day to you my middle daughter
Ha c'hui ma ziskourfe eun dra?	Will you do something for me?
Me so klanvet gant eur c'hlenvet	I am afflicted with a disease
Hag a so disesper meurbet	Desperate sickness indeed

Ha ma lavar d'in ar brofetet
M'am be eur vron werc'h ven iac'haet.

– Euz an dra se n'ho sikourin ket
Euz eun dra all na laran ket
Merc'het all oc'h euz ho sikouro
N'e ket me, ma zad, a raïo.

– Na petra a rin me breman
P'on refuset gant an diou-man?
Ar re-ma 'm boa maget da genta
Hag a garien ar muia.

Breman ian da di ma merc'h Henori
Biskoaz vad n'am boa karet d'ezhi
Med hi chasseal euz hi bro
Hi friva kren euz hi mado.

– Dibonjour d'eoc'h ma merc'h Henori
Peseurt tiegez eo oc'h hini?
– Leal, ma zad, gwelet a ret
An douar ienn meuz da gousket
Hag eur men kalet da bluek.

– Me so klanvet gant eur c'hlenvet
Hag a so disesper meurbet
Ma lavar din ar brofetet
M'am be eur vron werc'h ven iac'haet.

– Komeret skabel hag azeet
Ho sikour ma zad a so gleet
Neuze ia Henori d'an daoulin
Da zispaka d'hi zad hi feutrin

Pa oa ar peutrin kaer dispaket
Eur serpant gant-han so lammet
Ha bron Henori neuz troc'het

Neuze tisken eun éel
'N he zorn gant-han eur vron sklezr
A servij da c'holou, da ganteler.

And the prophets tell me
A maiden's breast would cure me.

– From that I will not save you
Though from anything else I might
You have other daughters to help you
My father, I will not.

– Oh, what shall I do now
That those two have refused me?
The ones I brought up first
The ones I loved most.

I shall go now to my daughter Henori's house
I never loved her very much
But sent her from her country
And deprived her of her belongings.

– Good day to you, my daughter Henori
What kind of house do you keep?
– In faith, my father, you can see
I have the cold earth to sleep on
And a hard rock for a pillow.

– I am afflicted with a disease
Desperate sickness indeed
And the prophets tell me
A maiden's breast would cure me.

– Take a stool and sit down
It is my duty to help my father.
Henori goes down on her knees
To undo her breast for her father

When the beautiful breast was undone
A serpent leapt onto it
Henori's breast is cut off

And then an angel descends
With a shining breast in his hands
Which shines like a light, a chandelier.

Ar Roue a Vrest a lavare
D'he verc'h Henori eno neuse
– Breman emezhan ma merc'h Henori

Me a gomzo ho timezin
Da vraoa denjentil a gavin
Da vraoa denjentil vo er vro
Mar na ve Roue prins a vo.

Neuse oe komzet da Henori
D'ar Prins Efflam da zimesi
Daou vloavez antier ez int bet
Euz ho flijadur war ar bed

Ken a oa bolonté Doué
D'ezhi da gaout bugale
Med gant hi mam gaër ar Rouanez
Honnès a rè d'ezhi gwall vuhez.

Ar Rouanez koz a lavare
D'he mab er gêr pa'z arrue
– Eleal, emezhi, ma mab
C'hui c'heuz eureujet eur vreg vad

C'hui c'heuz eureujet eur vreg vad
Hag ema bed e bars ar c'hoad
Ema d'ezhi dre ar c'hoajou
O studia hi gwal-euriou.

– Tawet, ma mam, pec'hi a ret
Eur wreg a feson e ma friet.
– Me meuz hi gwelet er zolier
Gant paotr an aotro ar valeter.

– Ma ouifen ve gwir kement-se
M'hi c'hasfe d'hi zad Roue da Vrest
Hennes rofe d'ezhi eur maro prest

Hennes hi varno d'ar fouet pe d'an tân
Pe d'ar grouk so 'r maro buhan.

The King of Brest said
To his daughter Henori then
– Now, he said, my daughter Henori,

I shall see about marrying you
To the finest gentleman I can find
To the finest gentleman in the land
If he's not a king he'll be a prince.

It was arranged then that Henori
Should marry Prince Efflam
Two whole years they lived
In joy together on this earth

Until it was God's will
That she should have children
But then her mother-in-law the queen
Made her life a misery.

The old queen said
To her son when he came home
– Truly, my son, she said
You have married a fine woman

You have married a fine woman
Who goes into the woods
Who goes through the woods
Up to no good.

– Be quiet, mother, you sin
My wife is a respectable lady.
– I have seen her in the attic
With the chief valet's servant.

– If I knew that was true
I'd send her to her father, King of Brest
He would condemn her immediately to death

He will condemn her to the lash or the fire
Or to hanging, the swiftest death.

Ar Prins Efflam a vonjoure
'N ti he dad Roue pa'z arrue
– Debonjour a joa, ma zad Roue.
– Ha d'eoc'h ivé, ma mab Doue.

– Petore barn a vezo gret
D'eur wreg dizaboës d'hi friet
D'eur wreg so meurbet dirollet?

– Mar eo disaboës d'hi friet
Me ro d'ezhi eur varn galet
M'hi barno dar fouet pe d'an tân
Pe d'ar grouk 'so marw buhan.

– P'oc'h euz hi barnet, barnet é
Ma'z eo ho merc'h Henori ê.
– Ed d'an traon ha lavaret d'ezhi
Donet d'an nec'h da gomz ouz-in.

Ar Prins Efflam a lavare
Na d'he briet eno neuse
– Ma friet Henori mar am c'haret
D'an nec'h da gaout ho tad roue eet.

– Ia, ma fried, monet a rin
Senti ouzoc'h so dleet d'in.
Santez Henori vonjoure
D'ann nec'h hi zad roue pa zalude

– Debonjour d'eoc'h, ma zad roue.
– Ha d'eoc'h ive joa, ma merc'h Doue.
– Petore tolfet am euz gret
Ma roët d'in eur varn galet

Mar am barnet d'ar foet pe d'an tân
Pe d'ar grouk so eur marv buhan
Ha me ho tilamet euz a boan?

– Mar am euz ho barnet Henori
Me 'meuz ho barnet heb goud d'in
Med na vo ket vel se veso gret
Eur varn newez a veso gret

Prince Efflam made his greetings
As he arrived at the king his father's house
– Good day and joy, my father king.
– And to you the same, my son in God.

– What sort of punishment would you give
To a wife unfaithful to her spouse
To a woman utterly gone to the bad?

– If she is faithless to her spouse
I would give her a harsh sentence
I'd condemn her to the lash or the fire
Or to hanging, the swiftest death.

– Since you have judged her, judged is she
For it is your daughter Henori.
– Go back and tell her
To come up here to speak to me.

Prince Efflam said
To his wife then
– My wife Henori, if you love me
Go up to see your father the king.

– Yes, my husband, I will go
I must obey you.
Saint Henori greeted
Her father the king as she met him

– Good day to you, my father the king.
– And joy to you too, daughter given by God.
– What crime have I committed
To be given this harsh punishment

To be condemned to the lash or the fire
Or to hanging, the swiftest death
I who rescued you from pain?

– If I have judged you, Henori
I have judged you unwittingly
But it will not happen in that way
There will be a new judgement

Me lakaï ober eun donel skao glaz
Hag ho lakaïo seiz vloaz war ar mor braz
Ha pa vo ar seiz vloas achuet
Mar bec'h beo teufet d'am gwelet.

I'll have them make a barrel of green elder
And put it seven years on the wide sea
When the seven years are up
If you're still alive, come and see me.

Ha pa oa an donel achuet
Henori enn hi oa laket
Oa laket enn–hi Henori
Hag hi prest da wilioudi.

When the barrel was finished
Henori was put in it
Into it Henori was placed
Although she was about to give birth.

Pa oe ar seiz vloas achuet
Ar Prins Efflam d'hi c'hlask a so et.
Ar Prins Efflam a c'houlenné
Euz ar voardedi pa dremene

When the seven years were done
Prince Efflam went to look for her.
Prince Efflam questioned
The sailors as they passed

– Moardedi, d'in-me lavaret
C'hui n'oc'h euz gwelet tonel a-bed?
– Na ouzomb doare da hini
Med d'hini santez Henori
Avocadez d'ar Verdedi

– Sailors, tell me
Have you seen a barrel?
– We don't know anything about that
Unless you mean saint Henori's
She is the patron of all sailors

Ter fourdelisen exellant
So war galon hi inosant
Mar na ve roue 'veso sant.

Three beautiful fleur-de-lis
Over the heart of her innocent baby
If he's not a king, he'll be a saint.

– Debonjour d'eoc'h, ma friet Henori
C'hui so en grac Doue, me na on mui
Diwar ma zreid ez hon dizec'het
Ar bleo diwar ma fenn 'zo et
Ha ma mamm 'zo et gant an drouk speret.

– Good day to you, my wife Henori
You are in God's grace; I no longer am
The shoes are gone from my feet
The hair has gone from my head
And my mother has been taken away by devils.

Setu aman gwerz Santez Henori
M'ho ped holl d'hi c'honsideri
An neb hi c'hlevo a galon
Hen euz daou ugent a bardon

This is the *gwerz* of Saint Henori
I pray you all to consider it
Whoever listens to it with all their heart
Will have forty days of pardon

Hag an hi gan hen euz ouspenn
Hen euz hi gracz, hi gourc'hemenn
Ar Barados mar hen goulenn.

And, moreover, whoever can sing it
Will have grace and salutations
Even Paradise, if they ask.

Provenance:
Collected by François-Marie Luzel from Barba Lucas, Locquirec (Trégor), 1867. Bibliothèque municipale de Rennes, ms. 1023, 'Chansons populaires de la Basse-Bretagne recueillies par Luzel', fols 25 r–v. Published as 'Enori et le roi de Brest' in Donatien Laurent, *Études sur la Bretagne et les pays celtiques. Mélanges offerts à Yves Le Gallo*, pp. 220–2.

The ballad of Saint Henori – also spelt Enori – and the mysterious King of Brest has some fascinating analogues in the literatures, oral and written, of the other Celtic-speaking countries, and has been the subject of various in-depth studies. Though its opening scenario (an ailing, angry king and three daughters) is strikingly reminiscent of *King Lear*, the story it goes on to relate is most closely paralleled by the Latin *Life of St Budoc* (known from two 15th-century copies). Here the king's youngest daughter Azénor sacrifices a breast to save her father from a deadly serpent, receives a golden one in its place, and is subsequently calumniated and cast out to sea, where she gives birth to Saint Budoc. A different constellation of the same narrative elements appears in the story of Caradoc of Vannes, interpolated into the first *Continuation* of Chrétien de Troyes' *Conte del Graal*. References to Caradoc in medieval Welsh texts, particularly in the body of traditional lore preserved in the *Trioedd* (Triads), suggest the existence of a similar, but now lost, legend linking him to a faithful wife who sacrifices a breast (*Tegau Eurvron*, 'Tegau Goldenbreast'). The Scots ballad 'The Queen of Scotland' (Child 301) involves snakes, jealousy and the loss of a breast; two versions of a Scots-Gaelic folk tale likewise describe a young woman rescuing her future husband from a deadly snake by losing her breast, receiving a golden one and having subsequently to prove her fidelity. The tenacity (and mythic pull) of that core of story elements across the range of languages and genres does suggest a deep-rooted narrative, and it is striking that its geographical spread is mirrored by other Arthurian material.

Saints' lives are naturally a rich source for folkloric/legendary material, and they often provide the *matière* for subsequent oral forms. The ballad of Henori, though close to the written *Vita*, does not simply condense its plot, and the relationship between the two is not one of straightforward borrowing. In his study of this piece Donatien Laurent notes that *gwerziou* on religious themes may often be 'supported', directly or indirectly, over a long period of time by a parallel written tradition. The saintly protagonist and the theme of extreme penance (here an unmerited punishment) may account for this being one of several ballads (see also no. 3) graced with the promise of spiritual benefits for the singer.

Luzel collected this ballad in 1867 from Barba Lucas, a beggarwoman in her sixties from the coastal commune of Locquirec, in the westerly area known as 'Little Trégor'. Along with artisans, beggars were among Luzel's preferred informants, being notably visible in public spaces. Typically, she is also female: some 85 per cent of his *gwerziou* were collected from women, whom he favoured as the more reliable bearers of oral and customary tradition. Barba Lucas's long, detailed version (162 lines) is one of five texts for this *gwerz* collected by Luzel in Trégor. His thoroughness as a collector of songs is matched by his keen interest in collecting all manner of related material, from sayings and traditions to folk tales and popular religious drama.

Other versions of this *gwerz* collected by Luzel offer a more detailed account of one of the key motifs of the story: the new golden breast brought by an angel. One version collected at Plouaret makes the angel arrive at precisely the moment when the girl responds, rather bitterly, to her father's promise of a fine marriage as a reward for her sacrifice:

– Petra dal komz ma zimisi	– How can you speak of my marriage
Pa n'am euz ar iec'het em peutrin?	When my breast is far from healed?
N'oa ket hi ger peurlavaret	Scarcely had she said the words
Eunn el an Ef so diskennet	When an angel came down from heaven
Da zigas da Henori eur vrôn sklezr	To bring Henori a bright breast
'Veler golo deuz-hi er c'hartier	Which would light up all around her
Da zigass Henori eur vrôn aour	To bring Henori a golden breast
Biken goudé na vije paour.[1]	Never again would she be poor.

Another version, collected at Louannec, describes a golden breast:

Da servijoud d'ezhi da c'holou sclezr	Which would be a source of light for her
En noz da laret he fater.	At night, to say her *pater* by.[2]

Studies:

Donatien Laurent, 'Enori et le roi de Brest'. Republished in Donatien Laurent, *Parcours d'un ethnologue en Bretagne*, pp. 227–61.

Gwennolé Le Menn, *La femme au sein d'or*.

1   Donatien Laurent, 'Enori et le roi de Brest', p. 220.
2   Laurent, p. 222.

3. Skolvan, a penitent soul

Buhe Skolvan zo deut d'ar vro	The Life of Skolvan has come to these parts
D'an oll dud yowank d'he gano	For all the young people to sing
Ha d'ar re goz neb he gouio	And for the old, anyone who knows it
Neb he gouio, he gano bemdé	Anyone who knows it and sings it each day
'No daou hant de pard'n gand Doué	Will have two hundred days' pardon from God
E no daou hant devez pardon	He shall have two hundred days' pardon
Ha gand Doue e benediksion.	And from God his benediction.
– Piou 'zo aman poent-ma d'an noz	– Who is there at this time of night
'Skoi var ma dorejed jerr't kloz?	Knocking on doors that are safely locked?
– Me mamm baouer, ne spontet ket	– Mother dear, don't be frightened
Hoh mab Skolvan 'deuet d'ho kueled.	Your son Skolvan has come to see you.
– Ma e m' mab Skolvan deued aman	– If my son Skolvan has come here
Me malloz a leskan gantan	I put my curse upon him
Malloz e vreuded, e hoarezed	The curse of his brothers, of his sisters
Malloz an oll inosanted	The curse of all the innocents
Malloz ar stered hag al loar	The curse of the stars and the moon
Malloz ar gliz 'goue d'an douar	The curse of the dew falling on the ground
Malloz ar stered hag an heol	The curse of the stars and the sun
Malloz an oll inosanted.	The curse of all the innocents.
Na pe oa gand an hent honed	As he was going along the road
E dad peren 'na rankontret.	He met his godfather.
– Du e da varh ha du out-te	– Black is your horse, you are black yourself
Peleh oh bet ha da bleh het?	Where have you been, and where are you going?
– Deuz ar purgator dond a ran	I have come from purgatory
Ha d'an ivern mond a ran	And I am going to hell
Gand malloz ma mamm pe meus 'nan.	With my mother's curse upon me.

– O, ma fillor, deut war ho kiz
Me 'ha da houl vidoh eskuz.

– O my god-child retrace your steps
I am going to ask forgiveness for you.

– O petra 'ta, komer ingrat
Hui na bardonet ket hoh mab?

– O how is it, ungrateful woman
You cannot forgive your son?

O petra 'ta, a mamm dinatur
Pe na bardonet ket ho krouadur?

O how is it, unfeeling mother
You cannot forgive your child?

– N'e ket posib din e bardonin
N'eus groet med gwasan ma halle din

– I cannot possibly forgive him
He could not have done more to hurt me

Violet 'neus seiz deus e hoarezed
Ha lazet o inosanted
N'e ket ze e vrasan pehed

He raped seven of his sisters
And killed their innocent children
That was not his greatest sin

Mond en iliz ha torri gwer
Laz' ar beleg deuz an ôter
N'e ket ze e vrasan pehed

He went into church, smashed windows
Killed the priest at the altar
That was not his greatest sin

Poahet 'neus din triveh anel korn
Or hraou, or harrdi, on ti-vorn
N'e ket ze e vrasan pehed

He set fire to eighteen cattle
A stable, a cart-house and a bake-house
That was not his greatest sin

Laket an tan din bar me ed
Kaset hanon da glask ma boued
N'e ket ze e vrasan pehed

He set the fire among my wheat
Sent me begging for my bread
That is not his greatest sin

Me lewer bihan 'neus kollet
Oa skrivet gand gwad hom Zalver
O hez e e vrasan pehed.

He lost my little book
Which was written with the blood of our
    Saviour
That is his greatest sin.

– Ho lewer bi'n n'eo ket kollet
'Ma bar mor don triveh goured
E beg or pesk bi'n a vired

– Your little book is not lost
It is under the sea, eighteen fathoms deep
In the mouth of a fish, who guards it.

Neuz barz med teir feuill'n dianket
Eunan gand dour hag eun gand gwad
Eun gand dero ma daoulagad.

Only three pages are ruined
One with water, and one with blood
One with the tears from my eyes.

– Ma mamm baouer, ma bardonet
Me meus gret pinijenn galed

Me meus tremenet nozajo
'Tre treid ho kerzeg er parko

Didan an glao, an erh pe 're
Didan ar skorn pe rielle.

– Ma veh pardonet gand Doue
Ma mabig paour, me 'ra ive.

O pe oa gand an hent honed
E vamm bêren 'neus rankontret.

– Gwenn e da varh ha gwenn out-te
Peleh oh et ha da bleh het?

– Deuz purkator dond a ran
Ha d'ar baradoz mond a ran
Gand bennoz ma mamm pe meus 'nan

Bennoz m' breuded, me hoarezed
Bennoz an oll inosanted

Bennoz ar stered hag al loar
Bennoz ar gliz 'goue d'an douar

Bennoz ar stered hag an heol
Bennoz an daouzeg abostol.

Pa gan ar hog da hanternoz
'Gan an eled er baradoz

Pa gan ar hog da houlou de
Ha 'n Anaon paour dirag Doue
Me mamm baouer, me hei ive.

– My dear mother, forgive me
I have done hard penance:

I have spent entire nights
In the fields, between your horses' feet

Under the rain and falling snow
Under the ice when it froze.

– Since God has pardoned you
My poor son, I do too.

As he was going along the road
He met his godmother.

– White your horse, you are white yourself
Where have you been, where are you going?

– I come from purgatory
And I am going to heaven
With my mother's blessing upon me

The blessing of my brothers, my sisters
The blessing of all the innocents

The blessing of the stars and the moon
The blessing of the dew falling on the ground

The blessing of the stars and the sun
The blessing of the twelve apostles.

When the cock sings at midnight
The angels sing in paradise

When the cock sings at daybreak
And the poor souls go before God
My mother dear, I shall go too.

Provenance:

Collected by Donatien Laurent from Jean-Louis Rolland, Trébrivan (Haute-Cornouaille), 1967. Published in Donatien Laurent, 'La gwerz de Skolan et la légende de Merlin', pp. 51–2.

CD:

Track 2. Collected by Claudine Mazéas from Marie-Josèphe Bertrand (née Martail), Plounévez-Quintin (Haute-Cornouaille), 1959. Published in *Tradition chantée de Bretagne. Les sources du Barzaz Breiz aujourd'hui*, CD track 7; and in *Marie-Josèphe Bertrand chanteuse du Centre Bretagne*, CD track 2.

This must be one of the most beautiful, most mysterious and most moving of all the Breton *gwerziou*. The story of a penitential son returning, as a dead soul, to ask forgiveness from his mother for his horrendous crimes, it has the spacious quality of ballad narrative at its best. This version, collected by Donatien Laurent in 1967, is unusually finely structured, with its balancing imagery of darkness and light, cursing and blessing, black and white, coalescing around an intriguing central dialogue. It evokes the unseen but keenly sensed world of the *anaon* (souls), explored by Anatole Le Braz in his collection of popular stories, anecdotes and beliefs about the afterlife published as *La légende de la mort* in successive expanded editions from 1892.

The appeal of this *gwerz* may also have something to do with historical depth. It seems to be an old song, its many recorded versions and different branches suggesting deep roots in the tradition. It has attracted critical attention because of tantalising correspondences of plot, language and detail between certain versions (mostly, like this one, from Cornouaille) and an early medieval Welsh poem found only in one manuscript, the 13th-century *Llyfr Du Caerfyrddin* (Black Book of Carmarthen). It seems likely that the 'Skolvan' (or more often 'Skolan') of the Breton ballads is a later version of a shadowy character from Welsh tradition called 'Ysgolan', who is remembered as a destroyer of books. The elements shared between the *gwerz* and the Welsh poem are striking, and include the close verbal echo of the lines about a black figure on a black horse ('Du e da varh ha du out-te'), the destruction of a church, the slaughter of cattle, the all-important 'drowning' of a book and, above all, a shared atmosphere of pain endured as strange penance. The poem, in the *englyn* form (compact three-line stanzas, which often appear in sequences) is even more enigmatic than the *gwerz*, and short enough to quote in full:

Dv dy uarch du dy capan	Black is your horse, black your cape
du dy pen du du hunan.	Black your head, you are yourself black
i adu ae ti yscolan.	[So then] are you Ysgolan?
Mi iscolan yscolheic	I am Ysgolan the cleric
yscawin y puill iscodic.	Light in the head, flitting
guae ny baut a gaut guledic.	Woe that he drowns not who offends the Lord

O losci ecluis. a llat buch iscol.	For burning a church and killing a school cow
a llyvir rod y voti.	And drowning a given book
vy penhid. ys trum kynhi.	My penance is heavy suffering.
Creaudir y creadurev. perthidev muyhaw.	Creator of creation, greatest in marvels
kyrraw de imi vy gev.	Forgive me my wrong
ath vradas te am tuyllas ynnev.	He who betrayed you cheated me too.
Bluytin llaun im rydoded.	A full year I was placed
ym bangor ar paul cored.	In wattle on the pole in the weir
Edrich de poen imy gan mor pryued.	Look how the sea things hurt me.
Bei ys cuypun ar vn. mor amluc guint.	If I had known what I know – how keen the wind
y vlaen bric guit fallum.	In the tips of the [bare] trees
ar a vvneuthum e bith nys gunaun.	I would never have done what I did.[1]

Though the relationship between the Breton song and the Welsh poem, recorded hundreds of years apart, is clear, the significance of the connection is much harder to grasp. The two pieces undoubtedly illuminate each other, yet they do not fully 'explain' each other's narrative world. There is no reason to think, for example, that the unnamed interlocutor in the Welsh poem must correspond to the godfather on the road in the *gwerz*. Nor – though the emotional atmosphere is remarkably similar – need the guilt noted by Oliver Padel as a persistent feature of the elusive and elliptical *englynion* sequences in middle Welsh derive from the same sources as that of the Catholic penitential world of the *gwerziou*. Nevertheless, as Donatien Laurent has shown, the elements of guilt, of exile in wild places and the drowning of the book can also be found in the Irish legend of *Buile Shuibhne*, and evidently form some kind of broader narrative cluster across the Celtic-speaking cultures. And the much tighter correspondence between the Welsh and Breton versions of the Skolan/Ysgolan story does raise interesting questions about transmission across the southern Brittonic-speaking world (Brittany, Cornwall, Wales) in the Middle Ages. Once again, one would give a great deal to know more about the stories, songs and legends that must have circulated in the Cornish language before its demise.

As with 'Saint Henori' (no. 2), the *gwerz* has a strong Christian dimension, and promises its singers and listeners spiritual grace; in some versions Skolvan is described as the 'bishop of Léon' doing penance for his crimes in a forest. The importance of the written word as sacred object is emphasised in the crime that forms the culmination of a long and dramatic list, the loss of a 'little book' written with the blood of Christ. But the purgatorial world of this song, in which Skolvan spends his nights shivering in the fields between the horses' hooves, is a long way from orthodoxy.

---

1   Welsh text of 'Ysgolan' from A. O. H. Jarman (ed.), *Llyfr Du Caerfyrddin*, p. 55. Our translation.

The most distinctive versions of this ballad come from central Brittany, such as the 1959 recording by the singer Marie-Josèphe Bertrand, a 73-year-old clog-maker from Plounévez-Quintin (CD track 2). In her version the wanderings of Skolvan in search of absolution are described as a quest that has already lasted several years:

Ya, seizh vle zo 'c'h on war 'n henchoù	Yes, I have been on the roads for seven years
E treso ma gwall basajoù.	In reparation for my misdeeds.

Besides their poetic words, the Haute-Cornouaille versions are also notable for their tunes, which have a tercet structure and display characteristics of an older musical tradition. Marie-Josèphe Bertrand's version alternates lines of two and three syllables:

Her style is remarkable, and her interpretation of 'Skolvan' has gained an almost mythic status among subsequent generations of singers of *gwerziou*.

Studies:

Donatien Laurent, 'La gwerz de Skolan et la légende de Merlin'. Republished in Donatien Laurent, *Parcours d'un ethnologue en Bretagne*, pp. 111–88.

Mary-Ann Constantine, *Breton Ballads*, pp. 66–70.

A. O. H. Jarman, 'Cerdd Ysgolan'.

Oliver Padel, 'Legendary poetry in *englyn* metre'.

4. Maharit Lorançe saved from the gallows

Maharit Lorançe zo bed tri de deus ar grouk	Maharit Lorançe was three days on the gallows
Dre grass Santez anna nen deus ket bed a drouk.	Through the grace of Saint Anna she was not harmed at all.
Eun devez eur c'hloarek o tremen ar potenç	One day a cleric came past the hanging tree
– Benos Doue var da c'hene maharidig Lorançe.	– The blessing of God upon your soul, Maharidig Lorançe.
– Neket red dit kloaregik pedi gant va hene	– O cleric, you don't need to pray for my soul
Me zo ken dispos aman vel ma zout te aze	I'm as comfortable up here as you are down there.
Kers al lesse kloaregik, kers al lesse dan noblançe	Go, cleric, go, and tell them at the big house
Na da lakat va distaga na dimeus ar potenç	To come and get me down from the gallows.
Pa kano eur c'habon rostet tre ar plad hag ar ber	– When the roasted fowl sings between the plate and the skewer
Neuse te vezo kredet kloaregik ar gueïer	Then, dear cleric, all your lies will be believed.
Pa gano ar c'habon rostet en kreïs entre an daou Plad	When the roasted cockerel crows between the two plates
Neuze te vezo kredet kloaregig a gaouiat.	Then you will be believed, you lying cleric.
Na ne voam ni ket hoas peurechu a leïna	We had scarcely finished our meal
Hag ar c'habon rostet a kommençe da kana.	When the roasted cockerel began to crow.
Kemen se a signifi, e lar d'he pot merchossi	As soon as it had spoken, he said to his stable-boy
– Dib dime va inkane ma zin peteck heni.	– Fetch me my horse so I may go to see her.
Deud geni me maharid deud ganeme dam zi	Come with me my Maharit, come with me to my house
Me lakeï va cheghiner da ficha ho dijuni.	I will order my cook to make your dinner.
– Me ne meus defot da zebri ken neubeut da c'heva	– I have no desire to eat, nor to drink
Ken a vin bed dar folgoët a da Santez Anna.	Until I have been to Le Folgoët, and to Sainte-Anne-d'Auray.

– Deud ganeme Maharit var geïn ma inkane
A me ho kasso d'ar Folgoët a da Santez Anne.

– Come with me Maharit on the back of my
    horse
And I will take you to Le Folgoët, and to
    Sainte-Anne-d'Auray.

– Na din var geïn inkane ken neubeud na zin var
    droad
Var beno va zaoulin noas mar gel va c'halon pad.

– I will not go on horseback, nor even by foot
But on my bare knees, if my heart can take it.

Kris a vije ar galon a kris ma na welche
He gweret Santez Anna an hini a vijé

Cruel the heart that would not weep
In the graveyard at Sainte-Anne-d'Auray

Welet ar c'hoad ag ar min bez ho rucha
Gant daoulin Maharit Loranç o voada

To see the wood and the gravestones flowing
With blood from the knees of Maharit Loranç

Neb rus e ve ar fumelen e iafe di ie goude.

And happy the woman who might follow her.

Kris a vije ar galon a kris ma na voelche
Bars er goëret ar Folgoat an hini a vije

Cruel the heart, and cruel he who would not
    weep
In the graveyard at Le Folgoët

Goelet ar greanigou nag ive o ruïal
Gant Daoulin maharit a voa ho voada.

To see the gravel rolling
Under the bleeding knees of Maharit.

Na pa voa ie arruet e kichen an or vras
– Echu e va finigen ma vijen bed he gras.

And when she arrived by the great door:
– My penance is done, may I now find grace.

Ar c'hleïer komanç bralla ne voa den var ho zro
An orojou digeri eb den nag alc'houecho.

The bells all started ringing of their own accord
The doors opened wide, with no-one there, and
    no keys.

Provenance:
'Maharid Loranç', collected by Jean-Marie de Penguern from Louisa Herviou, Taulé (Léon), 1851. Bibliothèque nationale de France, Fonds des manuscrits basques et celtiques, ms. 89, 'Chants populaires de Léon (Bretagne) recueillis par M. de Penguern', fols 132–3. Published in *Dastumad Pennwern*, 'Gwerin 5', pp. 113–14.

This *gwerz* combines two striking motifs. The first, which can be traced back in the European literary tradition as far as the 6th century in the writings of Gregory of Tours, describes a falsely accused and innocent person hanging unharmed from the gallows.[1] The second motif, the cock-erel which crows after being roasted, appears in association with the story of Judas in a Greek manuscript of the apocryphal gospel of Nicodemus; it was subsequently widespread across Europe during the Middle Ages.[2] The latter miracle also appears, rather appealingly, in an early English carol known as 'King Herod and the Cock' or 'St Stephen and Herod' (Child 22):

If this be the truth King Herod said
That thou hast told to me
The roasted cock that lies in the dish
Shall crow full senses three

O the cock soon thrustened and feathered well
By the work of God's own hand
And he did crow full senses three
In the dish where he did stand.[3]

The theme of the hanged innocent is widespread across Europe; in the French tradition, both written and oral, the condemned protagonist is often a pilgrim en route to Compostela who is falsely accused of stealing. The Breton *gwerziou* dramatise instead the fate of a young woman accused of infanticide. This aspect is elided in the version given here, collected by Jean-Marie de Penguern from Louisa Herviou, a favourite informant from his home village of Taulé near Morlaix. Instead, the emphasis is almost solely on the miracle itself, and on the subsequent pilgrimage which Maharit undertakes in gratitude for her rescue. A version collected by Luzel offers more detail on the nature of the miracle, which is attributed to the girl's intensely localised devotion to the Virgin:

Ma a oa en em westlet d'ann itron ar Folgoat	I dedicated myself to Our Lady of Folgoët
Hag a deuz laket d'in-me skabel endann ma zroad	And she placed a stool beneath my feet
Me a oa en em westlet d'ann itronn a C'houlvenn	I dedicated myself to Our Lady of Goulven
Hag a defoa preservet ma c'houk euz ar gordenn.[4]	And she saved my neck from the rope.

1   Grégoire de Tours, *De Gloria Confessorum*. Latin and French translation cited in Gaël Milin, 'De Saint-Jacques-de-Compostelle à Notre-Dame-du-Folgoët: les voies de l'acculturation', pp. 23–4; English translation available in Raymond Van Dam (ed.), *Glory of the Confessors*. See also Pierre Saintyves, *En marge de la légende dorée: Songes, miracles et survivances. Essai sur la formation de quelques thèmes hagiographiques*.
2   For a study of the motif in its European context see Francis James Child (ed.), *The English and Scottish Popular Ballads*, I, pp. 233–42.
3   Cecil Sharp, *English Folk Carols*, p. 2.
4   François-Marie Luzel, *Gwerziou Breiz-Izel: Chants et chansons populaires de la Basse-Bretagne. Gwerziou I*, pp. 214–16, sung by 'Ar c'hemener bihan' (the little tailor), Plouaret, 1863.

The second half of the song focuses on Maharit's journey of pilgrimage – made on her bare knees, and bleeding copiously – to shrines at the two most important religious centres in Lower Brittany, Le Folgoët and Sainte-Anne-d'Auray (see also no. 18). The image of the bloodied knees appears in a number of similar *gwerziou*; the miraculous survivor of a shipwreck thanks Saint Maturin of Moncontour in a similar fashion:

Ter dro d'ann iliz a deuz gret	Three times she made the tour of the church
Hag euz ar goad 'vije c'heuillet	One could have followed her by the traces of her blood
Euz hi daoulin 'koeze ar goad	Blood flowed from her knees
Ann daelou euz hi daoulagad.[5]	And tears flowed from her eyes.

Those bloodied knees are not simply a poetic image. Various written sources testify to this practice at several shrines in Brittany under the *ancien régime* (including accounts for the upkeep and repair of paths around churches, worn out by constant use). The song thus reflects certain culturally specific religious attitudes, distinguished from other regions in France by their exceptional intensity.

Studies:

Gaël Milin, 'De Saint-Jacques-de-Compostelle à Notre-Dame-du-Folgoët: les voies de l'acculturation'.

Éva Guillorel, *La Complainte et la Plainte: Chanson, justice, cultures en Bretagne*, pp. 408–16.

---

5   Luzel, *Gwerziou Breiz-Izel: Chants et chansons populaires de la Basse-Bretagne. Gwerziou I*, p. 128, sung by Fanch Ar Roue, Plouaret, 1847.

5. Dom Jean Derrian's journey to Santiago de Compostela

Dom Jean Der - rian dré ur hui - ren, Dom Jean Der - rian dré ur hui -

ren E re-mer - kas ur sti - re - den, E re-mer - kas ur sti - re - den.

Dom Jean Derrian dré ur huiren	Dom Jean Derrian, through glass
E remerkas ur stireden	Noticed a star
Hanval mat e oé d'oh ur voéz	And it was like a woman
E vehé bet é creis er gloéz.	Suffering great pain.
Dom Jean Derrian aben e yas	Dom Jean Derrian swiftly went
De gonz dehi, hag e laras	To talk with her, and said
– Stireden, d'ein é larehet	– Star, tell me now
Petra é représantehet?	What is it that you represent?
– Me mabig peur, ne ouiet ket?	– My darling boy, do you not know?
Mé-é en hani dès hou kañnet.	I am the one who gave birth to you.
– M'ar d'oh en hani dès me gañnet	– If you are the one who gave birth to me
A b'ban é tet, ha men é het?	Where do you come from, and where are you going?
– E han de San Jacque é Galice	– I'm going to Santiago in Galicia
Léh me has Doué en é justis	Where God in his justice has sent me.
D'oh ein, me mab, hou péet truhé	My son, pity me – I only progress
Ne rhan meit hèd me hleur bamdé.	The length of my coffin every day.
– Me mammig peur, d'ein larehet	– O mother dear, please tell me
Eit oh m'ar don mad de vonnet.	If I may go on your behalf.

– Ya, mès, me mab, me larou d'oh
Ol hou ç'amzér e riñkehoh

Hag eit hou tispãgn piar hant scouët
E vehé hoah ret d'oh cavet.

– Me mammig peur, n' det ket pelloh
Me hrei er voyaj aveit oh.

– M'ar groet eit on er voyaj-sé
Kousket de noz, kerrhet d'en dé

Pé ur loñnig vil hou kavou
Ha kent pêl, hi hou tispennou.

– Me mamig peur, sur ne vankein
D'hobér er peh e laret d'ein.

– Kerrhet enta, ha d'hou preder,
Laret: M'ès hur voyaj d'hobér.

Kent pêl, d'hé verdér dastumet
Dom Jean Derrian en doé laret

– D'hobér ur voyaj pêl é han
Mès piar, pemb kant scouët e rinkan.

Hañni dehou ne reskondas
Mès é hoér Mari e laras

– Berman m'en d'oh hui beléguet
Guelet bro aben é klasket.

– Dé ket de redek bro é han
Monnet de Sant Jacque é houlennan

Monn't de Sant Jacque, me hoèr Mari
Aveit me mam hag hou ç'hani

Laret enou en overen
E ma guerço d'oh é goulen.

– Yes, my son, but I say to you now
It will take you all the time you have

And, in addition, four hundred *écus*
Which you will also have to find.

– Mother dear, go no further
I will make the journey on your behalf.

– If you make this journey for my sake
Sleep at night, walk during the day

Or else a wicked beast will find you
And tear you to pieces on the spot.

– My dear mother, I will not fail
To do everything just as you have said.

– Go then, and say to your brothers
'I have a voyage to make.'

Soon after, his brothers gathered round,
Dom Jean Derrian said

– I have to go on a long journey
But I will need four or five hundred *écus*.

No-one replied to this
But his sister Mari, who said

– Now that you are a priest
You want to travel the world.

– I am not travelling the world
I want to go to Santiago

To Santiago, my sister Mari
For my mother and yours

And there I will say the mass
That she has long been asking for.

N'oé ket achiùet hoah é lar
P'oé lan é zeulegad a zar.

– Kerrhet, mem brér, oh ya, kerrhet
Groeit er voyaj e huès grateit.

– Me mamig peur, m'hou télivrou
Hag en néan d'oh me zigourou.

Mem berder, d'oh hui kenavo
Pedet Doué eit ma t'ein én dro

Ben seih vlé m'ar n'arrihuant ket
Groeit m'interr'mant ha me eihved.

Nezé Dom Jean Derrian e yas
D'hobér er voyaj get joé bras

Liés é oé guélet é laret
Pedenneu er ré trémenet.

Ar vord er mor p'oé arriùet
En hum gavas skontet meurbet

Hur hogic ru hum brezantas
Ha dehou aben e laras

– Men é het-hui, filajour noz
Deit d'em jeînein é me repoz?

Troeit hou rodeu, kerrhet en dro
Pé é kreis er mor m'hou taulo.

– Tré Doué, nehoah, emb sekouret
É Sant Jacque é karehen bet.

Scarcely had he finished speaking
When his eyes filled with tears.

– Go, brother mine, oh yes go
Make that journey you have promised.

– Mother dearest, I will redeem you
Heaven's gate will open for you.

Brothers, I bid you farewell
Pray God that I will return

If I do not return within seven years
Hold my funeral mass, and my *huitaine*.[1]

And so Dom Jean Derrian set about
His voyage with great joy

Often he was seen reciting
The prayer for the departed.

But when he arrived at the coast
He had a terrible fright

A little red cock appeared
And said to him at once

– Where are you going, night-traveller
Disturbing me in my sleep?

Retrace your steps, return whence you came
Or I will fling you into the sea.

– Oh Lord, give me your aid
I wish I were at Santiago.

---

1   The 'messe de huitaine' is a commemorative mass celebrated on behalf of the deceased person, in theory after eight days although often later.

N'oé ket hoah é gonz reih laret	Scarcely had he spoken these words
Pe oé ar drézen Sant Jacque rantet.	When he found himself at the entrance to Santiago.
– Eutru Person, m'hou ped, reit d'ein	– Monsieur priest, give me, I beg
Permission d'overennein	Permission to hold a mass
De laret amen m'overen	To say my mass here
E ma m' mam peur d'oh é goulen.	As my poor mother asked.
Eit é vam get dévotion	With great devotion for his mother's sake
Ean bayas de Zoué é ranson.	He paid God his ransom.
Dom Jean Derrian é tonn't d'er gér	As Dom Jean Derrian made his way home
Hum gavas groñnet a sklerdér	He found himself wrapped in a brightness
Ligernus bras a drest é ben	Shining in brilliance above his head
Ean e huélas ur stireden	He saw a star
Hanval mad d'oh ur voés e oé	And it was like a woman
E vehé bet é kreis er joé.	Who might be in the very midst of joy.

Provenance:
Collected by Augustin Guillevic in Melrand (Vannetais), 1883. Published in Augustin Guillevic and Jean-Mathurin Cadic, *Chants et airs traditionnels du pays vannetais*, pp. 10–13.

CD:
Track 3. Collected by René Richard from Élisa Le Moigne, Kerpert (Haute-Cornouaille), 1979. Dastum NUM-23242. Published in Éva Guillorel, *La Complainte et la Plainte: Chanson, justice, cultures en Bretagne*, CD track 17.

Among the many *gwerziou* dealing with pilgrimages, this ballad relates to one of the oldest stories on that theme. Known in scores of versions (usually under the name 'Dom Yann Derrien'), it evokes a journey to the shrine of Saint James of Compostela, also known – as in this version collected by the priest Augustin Guillevic – as Saint James of Galicia, and also as 'Sant Jakez an Turki' (Saint James of Turkey). The song opens with the return of the penitent soul (Breton *anaon*) of the hero's mother. She asks her son, a priest, to carry out on her behalf a pilgrimage she had promised to make when alive; without having accomplished it she cannot gain entry into heaven. This motif recalls numerous legends and traditions about the *anaon* collected by folklorists such as Luzel and Le Braz, who were particularly inspired by the wealth of Breton material concerned with death and the afterlife. Other versions note that the dead mother had failed to repay a debt of two *sous*, and that this paltry sum is preventing her from finding eternal peace.

The ballad then recounts a voyage of several months, if not several years, since in some versions Dom Jean Derrian repeats at various points 'Hir eo an hent ha pell mont di' (the way is long and it is far to go). It begins with nicely concrete details relating to the young priest's travel preparations: finding money for the journey, persuading family and friends to let him go, choosing the right attire. One version collected by Yann-Fañch Kemener in Haute-Cornouaille notes that he should learn 'seven kinds of languages' – a symbolic number which underlines the difficulty of the enterprise.[2] The obstacles, both natural and supernatural, which the protagonist must face are legion; he must first of all confront the attacks of the devil, who appears in the form of a red rooster (or sometimes a black dog). His ship is then attacked and he is taken prisoner by Turkish pirates (an episode that has fallen out of this typically condensed Vannetais version). It is only thanks to his prayers and to a sequence of miracles that he achieves his goal and returns safe and sound to Brittany.

The atmosphere of the miraculous which permeates the Guillevic version – beautifully conveyed by the opening and closing image of the star 'in pain' and 'in joy' – is enhanced in other versions by the edifying and holy death of the pilgrim, once his task has been accomplished. He returns from Compostela on the very day his family, thinking him dead after many long months away, are holding his funeral. In the version collected by Yann-Fañch Kemener, the priest's sister approaches him in order to wipe the sweat from his brow – a gesture which recollects that of Veronica wiping the face of Jesus as he climbs up to Golgotha. But the Breton priest replies:

Ma c'hoer Vari, 'ma zorchit ket   My sister Mari, do not wipe my face
Glizh ar maro a dorchihet.[3]   It is the dew of death you would wipe away.

Another text has the pilgrim return with a handkerchief which he gives to his sister, saying that she must never wash it for it contains the Saviour's blood. When the young woman, unbelieving, dips the cloth in the river where she is doing her washing, the water dries up miraculously.[4] The mother appearing as a star is particularly interesting given that, according to Daniel Giraudon, *Hent Sant Jakez* (the road to Saint Jacques) is a Breton name for the Milky Way, which was imagined as a kind of purgatory for 'souls in transit'; those who made the journey in their lifetimes were spared the slow celestial progress after their death.[5]

Besides being part of a rich and Europe-wide literary tradition connected to Santiago de Compostela, the *gwerz* is witness to the historical practice of pilgrimage in Brittany as attested in

2   Yann-Fañch Kemener, *Carnets de route,* p. 95, version sung by Françoise Méhat, Laniscat, 1982.
3   Kemener, *Carnets de route,* p. 95.
4   Collected by Jean-Marie de Penguern, BnF, ms. 91, fols 154r–155v. Published in *Dastumad Penwern. Chants populaires bretons de la collection de Penguern*, pp. 327–30.
5   Daniel Giraudon, *Traditions populaires de Bretagne: Du soleil aux étoiles*, pp. 93–7.

written sources. A Breton nobleman is mentioned as having undertaken the journey as early as the 11th century, and the golden age for this pilgrimage from Brittany was during the 12th and 13th centuries, before a withdrawal to geographically closer shrines. From Brittany, the journey was usually undertaken by sea, and once again the archives attest to the misadventures of Breton pilgrims who fell victim to pirates from the north coast of Africa or from Britain. The difficulties of Dom Jean Derrian's journey are a vivid reminder of the genuine perils of travel.

This ballad is sung to a number of tunes. The version by Élise Le Moigne from Kerpert (CD track 3) is sung to the popular air 'Ker-Is', which is also that used for 'The fire in the lead tower' (no. 21).

Studies:
Éva Guillorel, *La Complainte et la Plainte: Chanson, justice, cultures en Bretagne*, pp. 368–76.
Jean Gauter, *Mémoire contée et chantée du chemin de saint Jacques en Bretagne*, pp. 39–88.
Patrick Malrieu, 'Les pèlerinages… dans la chanson de tradition orale en breton'.

6. Saint Iañn Bubri, murderer and rapist

Chi - la-wet ol ha chi-la - wet ur huer-zen a ne - ùé za - wet.

[Chilawet ol ha chilawet
Ur huerzen a neùé zawet][1]

[Listen, all, to a song
A song newly composed]

Zawet ziar on stereden lostek
Seitek vlé so n'é ket guélet

Made about a comet
No-one had seen for seventeen years

Seitek vlé so n'é ket guélet
Kent er blé-men noz Nédeleg

No-one had seen for seventeen years
Until this year, on Christmas Eve

Kent er blé-men noz Nédeleg
Sant Iañn Bubri 'n es hi guélet.

Until this year, on Christmas Eve
When Sant Iañn Bubri saw it.

Sant Iañn Bubri 'n es hi guélet
Ba' i è Bubri, ba' i er véred

Sant Iañn Bubri saw it
In Bubry, in the graveyard

Ba' i è Bubri, ba' i er véred
Ha geti é oè pet spontet.

In Bubry, in the graveyard,
And he was frightened by it.

San Iañn Bubri en es ion groeit
Peh n'es chet greit biskoah dén erbet

Sant Iañn Bubri has done
What no man alive ever did

Peh n'es chet greit biskoah dén erbet
É dad, é vam en ès lahet

What no man alive ever did
He killed his father and his mother

É dad, é vam en ès lahet
Hag é dér hoér en ès violet

He killed his father and his mother
And raped his three sisters

Nag é dér hoér en ès violet
Beb a vab bihan ou doè pet

He raped his three sisters
Each had a little child

---

1   This traditional opening has been added to make sense of the following couplet (Eds).

Beb a vab bihan ou doè pet
Hag ou sri é mant pet lahet

Each had a little child
And all three of them were killed

Nag ou sri é mant pet lahet
Ou sri é mant pet intèrêt

All three of them were killed
And all three were buried

Ou sri é mant pet intèrêt
Didan d'hornèg sen en oèled

All three of them were buried
Under this corner of the hearth.

Ne iélè dein lonjein é gampr
Ged er hri e oè en tri inosant

No-one could sleep in that room
For the crying of the three innocents

Ged er hri e oè en tri inosant
'Houlenné oleù er vadiant

For the crying of the three innocents
Asking for baptismal oil

'Houlen oleù er vadiant
Ou mameg por er zakremant.

Asking for baptismal oil
And the sacrament for their poor mothers.

Sant Iann Bubri hag e larè
D'i hoér Mari, on noz e oè

Sant Iañn Bubri said then
To his sister Mari one night

– Zau ahanese d'alum goulow
Ma hréemb-ni hor pakadow

– Get up from there and fetch a light
So we may pack up our belongings

Ma hréemb-ni hor pakadow
Eit mont de vala dré er vrow

So we may pack up our belongings
To go and journey through the land

Eit mont de vala dré er vrow
De glah belek d'hon euredo.

To go and journey through the land
And find a priest who will marry us.

– Ne chet beleg é Breih-Izél
Euredehè er breur hag en hoér.

– There is no priest in Lower Brittany
Who would marry brother and sister.

Zan Iañn hag e larè
Treah Porh Louis on dé i e oè

Sant Iañn said one day
On the beach at Port-Louis

– Pe chet guélet aùit en dé
Tér famelen pasein anzé

– Have you not seen today
Three women passing this way

Tér famelen bizajow moen
Ha iè guisket ér sei mélein

Three women with thin faces
All dressed in yellow silk

Ha iè guisket ér sei mélein	They are dressed in yellow silk
Getè beb a varh-du poulain?	Each on a black foal?
Zan Iañn hag e larè	Sant Iañn said one day
'Treah Porh-Louis on dé i e oé	On the beach at Port-Louis
– Er mor e ru doh men guélet	– The sea turns bloody at the sight of me
Hag en doar bras me andur ket	And the earth does not endure me
Nag en doar bras mé andur ket	The earth does not endure me
Er vein didan d'ein zo faoutet.	The rocks split beneath me.
Me gemérei résolusion	I make a resolution
Monet bamdé d'en ovèren	To go to mass every day
Monet bamdé d'en overen	To go to mass every day
Beb en eil dé d'en absolven.	And every other day to absolution.

Provenance:
Collected by Yves Le Diberder possibly from Perrine Daniel, Pont-Scorff (Vannetais), 1910. Collection Le Diberder, Archives départementales du Morbihan, 2Mi113. Published in Yves Le Diberder, *Chansons traditionnelles du pays vannetais*, II, pp. 840–1.

When François-Marie Luzel asked the bishop of Saint-Brieuc for advice on publishing *gwerziou* which put the clergy in a bad light, he was urged, vehemently, to desist. And it seems, by and large, that Luzel quietly censored the second volume of his *Gwerziou Breiz-Izel* to avoid any further disturbance; certain songs in the first volume had apparently been controversial enough. One wonders what the reading public of the 19th century would have made of a ballad such as this. In *Sant Iañn Bubri*, sanctity and transgression seem collapsed together – and the protagonist, no wild student *kloareg*, no merely corrupt priest, is a 'saint', no less, guilty of horrible crimes and driven by his guilt on a penitential journey. The sins, and the urge to penance, link this character perhaps to the world of *Skolvan* (who is sometimes referred to as the 'Bishop' of Léon, see no. 3), but this strange little piece is different from that classic *gwerz* in many respects.

It was collected in 1910 in the Morbihan by Yves Le Diberder, who responded to its enigmatic brevity by insisting that it must be a 'fragment' of a longer, lost narrative. Loss, erosion, occlusion are all terms that feature significantly in commentaries on texts from the Vannetais area, which was not properly explored by the first wave of earlier song collectors. Le Diberder was one of the most prolific collectors for the region, and it is really only recently that his work, including a particularly rich collection of folk tales, is beginning to receive much attention. It is true that many Vannetais versions of the long, circumstantial and richly detailed ballads from the Trégor and Léon often seem thinner and more elliptical than their northern counterpoints – a feature which can be explained by their relocation away from the historical *mise-en-scène*, and perhaps, too, by the proximity of the French song tradition, much lighter and more lyrical in style (see also nos 15 and 29).

Vanishing narratives have a particular force, however, in a cluster of Vannetais songs that deal with local saints. Here, the brevity and mystery of songs like this one come to seem emblematic of a more comprehensive loss of knowledge about highly localised (and deeply unorthodox) saints such as Sant Iañn himself. Another intriguing and evocative song, collected the same year by the abbé François Cadic, tells of three unnamed saints arriving from Rome to Melrand 'in a box':

En ur stanken é tevalan	They arrived in a marsh
Itré Lan Georj ha Koët-Buman	Between Landes-Georges and Buman wood
Deit-ind èn ur stanken tihouél	They came to a dark marsh
Mén ne skoa ket na éaul na luér	Where no sun or moon ever shine
Meit ur stirén de holeu-dé	Though the morning star
Splan asset é en dachén-sé	Is bright enough in that place
Ag er gurun bras e gorné	The thunder roared loud
En aüel kri e hargeissé.	And a strong wind howled.[2]

Cadic is still able to supply names for the three saints – Rivalain, Bieuzy and Gildas – because they are associated with features in the landscape (tiny secluded chapels, a cave by the river). But he writes, too, that this knowledge is fragile and highly circumscribed – the cult of Rivalain, he says, is barely known outside Melrand.

Le Diberder's brief notes to *Sant Iañn Bubri* propose another kind of 'vanishing', familiar to those who work on highly local saints' cults. The church at Bubry, in the Morbihan, is actually dedicated to St Yves, ostensibly the Trégor cleric Yves Hélori, who became one of Brittany's most successful saints, acquiring a kind of 'national' status. But the local Breton form of his name, *Sant Iwann*, is very close to the Iañn of the ballad; the occlusion of tiny cults by more popular ones is a common occurrence in Brittany as elsewhere, and Le Diberder suggests that the song preserves the memory of a now-lost earlier saint. Songs like these have perhaps a slightly tangential relation to the more 'classical' body of *gwerziou*, and shade into the more distinctly religious world of the *cantique* or hymn. They are nevertheless clearly conceived of as stories in the *gwerz* style, full of journeys and tribulations, and lit up by moments – those thin-faced women dressed in yellow silk – of startling poetic imagery.

---

2   *Paroisse bretonne de Paris*, juin 1910. Published in François Cadic, *Chansons populaires de Bretagne publiées dans la Paroisse bretonne de Paris*, p. 301.

Studies:

Mary-Ann Constantine and Gerald Porter, *Fragments and Meaning in Traditional Song*, pp. 177–9.

Mary-Ann Constantine, 'Saints Behaving Badly: Sanctity and Transgression in Breton Popular Culture'.

7. Bertet, midwife to the Virgin Mary

Piou ê ar plac'hic 'c'h a gant ar ru	Who is that girl who goes along the road
Gant he mantel c'hlaz, he brozic ru	With her red dress and her cloak of blue
Hac hi kerzed ken diread	And who walks so beautifully
He c'hof ganthi beteg he lagad?	Her belly up to her eyes?
Mari Jouassin rer anezhi	They call her Mary Joachim
Ha Zant Joseb a zo ganthi	And with her is Saint Joseph
Ha Zant Joseb a zo ganthi	And Saint Joseph is with her
Conductor d'ar Werc'hes Mari.	Guide to the Virgin Mary.
'N ti ann den cruel p'int arruet	When they arrived at the cruel man's house
Goulenn da lojan hi ho deus grêt.	They asked for lodgings.
– Leun ê ma c'hambrjo he leun ma zi	– My rooms are full and my house is full
Bemdez, deuz a dremeneri	Every day, with passers-by
Bemdez, deuz a dremeneri	Every day, with passers-by
Ha na vefet ket lojet, Mari.	You cannot be lodged here, Mary.
Beza 'n efoa eur mab cloarec	He had a son who was a cleric
Na d'he dad hen eveus laret	Who said to his father
– Allas! ma zad, c'hui 'zo manket	– Alas! Father, you have not done well
Na pa n'ho peus Mari lojet.	To refuse Mary a lodging.
– Na ma na teus truez outhi	– Well if you feel that sorry for her
Kerz war he lerc'h ha distro hi	Go after her and bring her back
Kerz war he lerc'h ha distro hi	Go after her and bring her back
Hac hi laka er marchossi.	And put her in the stable.
Er marchossi p'int arriet	When they arrived in the stable
Mari da Joseb deus laret	Mary said to Joseph
– Joseb, Joseb, hastet buan	– Joseph, Joseph, hurry quickly
Deuz ar merc'hed clasket unan	And fetch one of the girls

Clasket unan deuz ar merc'hed	Fetch one of the girls
Rac ma foaniou a zo cresket.	My pains are getting worse.
En toul ann nor p'ê arriet	When he got to the door of the house
Na Joseb hen eveus laret	Joseph said
– Laret deus Mari d'in donet	– Mary asked me to come
Da glasc unan deuz ho merc'hed.	And fetch one of your daughters.
– Ma merc'hed 'zo êt da gousked	– My girls have all gone to bed
Ken a vo dez na zavfont ket	They won't get up before it is day
Met Berta 'zo war ann oalet	But Berta is at the hearth
Honnes a peo, mar keret.	You can have her if you like.
N'oa ket ar gir peurachuet	Scarcely had he finished speaking
Nac ar Werc'hes 'zo arriet.	When the Virgin arrived.
– Bertet, Bertet, goure ma mab	– Bertet, Bertet, deliver my son
Me roïo dit eur gopred mad	I will reward you well
Zantes er Baradoz a vi	You shall be a saint in Paradise
Da oel a vo 'roc d'am hini.	Your feast-day will be before my own.
– Penoz 'c'h alfenn ho sicouri	– How can I come and help you
Ha me n'am eus ma izili	I who have no arms
Ha me n'am eus na brec'h na dorn	I who have no arms nor hands
N'am eus met bete ma as-dorn?	Nothing but stumps?
N'oa ket he gir peurachuet	Scarcely had she said the words
Brec'h ha daouarn defoa Bertet	When Bertet had arms and hands
Brec'h ha daouarn defoa Bertet	Bertet had arms and hands
Coulz ha hini he c'hoarezed.	As good as those of her sisters.
Na 'bars er c'hraou p'oant arriet	When they got to the stall
Bertet neuze deveus laret	Bertet said
– Ma ve bolonte ann nôtrô	– If it is the will of Our Lord
Am emp eur pennadic golo.	Let us have a little stub of candlelight.

N'oa ket he gir peurachuet	She had hardly finished speaking
C'huec'h pilad coar 'zo allumet	When six wax candles all lit up
Ha war lerc'h c'huec'h ez oa daouzec	After six, there were twelve
Rac beza oa loar ha stered	For there were stars and a moon
Rac beza oa loar ha stered	There were stars and a moon
Da c'henel Redemptor ar bed.	For the Redeemer's birth to this world.
Creiz tre 'n ijen hac eun azen	Between an ox and an ass
Mesq eun dornad bihan a foënn	In a handful of hay
Mesq eun dornadic a foënn glaz	In a handful of fresh hay
Ez eo ganet ar Messias.	The Messiah was born.

Provenance:
Collected by François-Marie Luzel from Jobenn Daniel, Pleudaniel (Trégor), 1888. Published in François-Marie Luzel, *Soniou Breiz-Izel: Chants et chansons populaires de la Basse-Bretagne. Soniou II*, pp. 308–11.

Tune collected by Maurice Duhamel from Maryvonne Nicol, Plouguiel (Goëlo). Published in Maurice Duhamel, *Gwerziou ha soniou Breiz-Izel: Musiques bretonnes: Airs et variantes mélodiques des 'chants et chansons populaires de la Basse-Bretagne' publiés par F. M. Luzel et A. Le Braz*, p. 218.

CD:
Track 4. Collected by Jean-Yves Monnat from Élise Nignol, Bubry (Vannetais), 1976–7. Dastum NUM-65214.

This song, with its strikingly physical opening describing the heavily pregnant Virgin 'with her belly up to her eyes', was often used as a Christmastide *chant de quête*. It combines elements from medieval French and from Irish folk tradition; the story derives from an apocryphal account of the Nativity in which a handicapped young woman (Bertha, Berc'hed, Brigit) miraculously grows hands in order to help the Virgin give birth. The narrative can be found in dozens of medieval French manuscripts dating from the 13th to the 15th centuries; folk songs on the same subject have been collected across a range of francophone traditions, from French-speaking Belgium via Poitou, Quercy and the Limousin. Links to various international folk tales appear in the Aarne-Thompson-Uther (ATU) classification, such as *The mother who did not bear me but nourished me* (ATU 713) and *The maiden without hands* (ATU 706).

But a number of elements link this song to a more specifically Celtic tradition associated with Saint Brigit, a figure of considerable importance in Ireland. Unlike this version, which follows French tradition in opting for 'Berta' and an intermediate 'Bertet', most Breton versions give their protagonist the name 'Berc'hed', and include couplets (not attested in the French tradition) which make the link with an Irish Brigit very clear; many of them, for example, contain a dialogue between Mary and Brigit, in which the Virgin promises that the young girl will have her feast-day before her own (Saint Brigit's day is the first of February; Candlemas, the purification of the Virgin, the second). Brigit is also a popular saint in Breton tradition, and other genres attest to a general interest in this story, from prose accounts revisiting the story of the young girl who helps deliver the infant Jesus to a hoard of agricultural proverbs and sayings linking the feast-days of Saint Brigit and Candlemas. Brigit was also a favourite in Breton tradition among women seeking to have children and those fearing a difficult pregnancy or with an inadequate supply of breast milk.

The song has been collected all over Lower Brittany, with certain areas of concentration, notably in the Vannetais where it appears in virtually all of the main collections. Le Diberder has some lovely versions. One of them, collected at Riantec in 1911, gives a vivid account of the reward offered to the handicapped young woman:

Berhet, deit te sekour Mari	Berhet, come and help Mary
Our goubre kaer hou pou geti	You will be well rewarded
Our goubre kaer hou pou geti	You will be well rewarded
Hi rei d'oh daulegad ha fri	She will give you eyes, a nose
Hi rei d'oh daulegad ha fri	She will give you eyes, a nose
Ha divréh de sekour Mari	And arms with which to help Mary
Hi rei d'oh fri ha daulegad	She will give you a nose, eyes
Ha divréh de sekour er Mab.	And arms to help the son of God.
Dé ket ir hampeu aleuret	Not within golden chambers
I ma pet gañnet Salùèr er bet	Was born the Saviour of the world
Ha ba 'n or marchosi hemb tuén	But in a stable without a roof
Iter oun oujon hag oun azen	Between an ox and an ass
Iter oun oujon hag oun azen	Between an ox and an ass
Ar un dornadik plouz ha foen	In a handful of straw and hay

Ha ba 'n or marchosi distou	In a stable without a roof
Dign ar en doar ne hazé inon	Where no-one would have sat
Ha ba 'n or marchosi distér	In a humble stable
Durheit t'er glaù ha d'en aùél.	Open to the wind and rain.[1]

The version presented here, collected by Luzel at Pleudaniel, has, as usual, no tune; but the musician Maurice Duhamel, who set out in the first decade of the 20th century to retrace the territory of Luzel's singers and discover their melodies, found an appropriate tune for this song some 10 kilometres from Pleudaniel:

The Brigit story also makes an appearance in a Christmas recitation (part sung, part spoken) known in the Vannetais region as a *tragélie*. The second section (there are five in all) dramatises the Virgin's lying-in and the help she receives from a young woman without arms. A fine version (CD track 4) was recorded from Élise Nignol, a farmer from Bubry born in 1907. She had learned the piece from her father Jean-Marie Le Nozach, who had learned it from his mother, and recited the *tragélie* to his children every Christmas Eve.

Studies:

Donatien Laurent, 'Brigitte, accoucheuse de la Vierge. Présentation d'un dossier'. Republished in Laurent, *Parcours d'un ethnologue en Bretagne*, pp. 217–26.

Donatien Laurent, 'Une chantefable en pays pourlet: la "tragélie"'. Republished in Laurent, *Parcours d'un ethnologue en Bretagne*, pp. 191–216.

---

1   Yves Le Diberder, *Chansons traditionnelles du pays vannetais*, II, p. 812.

8. The plague in Langonnet

É   Lan – gon – net é   hès gla-har,   É   Lan   –   gon – net é   hès gla-

har.   É   Lan – gon – net é   hès gla-har,   Mar   dès   é   kan-ton ar en   douar.

É Langonnet é hès glahar	There is misery in Langonnet
Mar dès é kanton ar en doar	If in any parish on this earth
Mard dès é kanton ar en doar	If in any parish on earth
Huélet ur verh é touch er hâr	To see a girl driving a cart
Huélet ur verh é touch er hâr	To see a girl driving a cart
Eit kas hé zad, hé mam d'en doar	To bury her father and mother in the ground
Eit kas hé zad, hé mam d'en doar	Her father, her mother, in the ground
Hé brér, hé hoer, hé nessan câr.	Her brother, her sister, all her close kin.
É Langonnet, gavér ket dén	At Langonnet there is no one left
Na bugul seud, bugul devend	No-one herds cattle, no-one guards sheep
Na bugul seud, bugul devend	Not one herder of cattle, not one shepherd
Querr marhùe ind rah get er vossen.	All have died of the plague.
Person Langonnet en dès groeit	At Langonnet the priest has made
Pèh biskoâh den n'en dès guélet	Something never seen before
Pèh biskoâh den n'en dès guélet	Something never seen before
Ur berchen a drihuèh trueitéd	A pole, eighteen feet long
Ur berchen a drihueh trueited	A pole, eighteen feet long
Eit rein Sacremant en Nuied.	To deliver the Sacrament, the Last Rites.
– Langonnèdis, saùet hou pen	– People of Langonnet, lift your heads
Ha me rei d'oh en absolven	And I will give you absolution

Me rei d'oh Sacrement a Nouien

I will give you the Sacrament, the Last Rites

Dré er fenestr get er berchen.

Through the window, with this pole.

É Langonnet, ar er murieu

At Langonnet, on the walls

É varùe er piged a goubeu

The magpies die in pairs

Hag er piged hag er brañni

And if the magpies die, if the crows

En dud, perac ne varùen gui?

How then should the people not die?

É Langonnet tachen varad

In Langonnet in the market square

É ma hir er guiaud de falhat

The grass is high enough for cutting

É ma hir er guiaud de falhat

Grass, high enough for cutting

En eur milén de rosellat.

Yellow gold for raking.

Provenance:

'Complainte de la peste à Langonnet', collected by Augustin Guillevic in Melrand (Vannetais), 1883. Published in Augustin Guillevic and Jean-Mathurin Cadic, *Chants et airs traditionnels du pays vannetais*, pp. 18–19.

CD:

Track 5. Collected by Donatien Laurent from Maryvonne Bacon (née Mao), Berné (Vannetais), 1965. Published in *Tradition chantée de Bretagne. Les sources du Barzaz Breiz aujourd'hui*, CD track 9.

This tragic ballad was the first song published by La Villemarqué in the journal *Écho de la Jeune France* in 1836, where the text noted by his mother Ursule Feydeau de Vaugien was arranged for harp and piano. Since then, the piece has been collected all over Lower Brittany, with a concentration of versions in the south. Generally the action is located at Elliant in Basse-Cornouaille, although Vannetais versions, such as the one given here, often mention Langonnet, and Léon versions usually have Plouescat or Guimiliau. (The opening couplet is a *gwerz* commonplace adaptable to other contexts (see, for example, no. 9)). A web of anecdotes and stories form a backdrop to the song, many collected from the region around Elliant, which is still known as 'pays melenig' (the yellow region). They explain how the plague arrived from Quimper in the form of a 'white lady' or a wicked woman who persuades someone to carry her unwittingly into the village. The following Sunday she stands in the porch of the local church at the start of mass, and all the people she touches with her white stick fall ill and die. According to some versions she sometimes spares the life of the man who carried her into the village, or that of his mother – but never, despite his entreaties, his wife or children. The spread and persistence of these various traditions testify to the importance of this traumatic event in local historical memory, as do the numerous chapels dedicated to saints Roch and Sébastien, the healing saints most associated with protection against the disease. Episodes of plague were a grimly regular feature of life in Europe between the 14th and 17th centuries, making it difficult to ascertain the date of this particular account.

The scenes of plague unfold in a kind of static horror. Guillevic's text opens with a young girl pulling a cart loaded with the corpses of her family. The priest administers last rites on a long pole; even the birds die in pairs on the walls of the village. A version noted by Alexandre Lédan opens with a mother burying her nine sons:

O zad adrén o c'houibanad   Their father brings up the rear whistling
Collet gantàn e sqiant vad.   He has lost his reason.[1]

This was the image which, in 1849, inspired the painter Louis Duveau ('La Peste d'Elliant', Musée des Beaux-Arts de Quimper); the Pre-Raphaelite painter John Everett Millais would take the same tableau for his illustration of Tom Taylor's translations from the *Barzaz-Breiz* in 1865. La Villemarqué's version gives a figure of some 7,100 dead, and evokes the relentless succession of carts, in groups of 18, taking the bodies to the burial ground. In this dystopic vision two people alone escape the utter desolation:

É bro Elliant, heb lãret gaou   At Elliant, I tell no lie
É ma diskennet ann Ankaou   Death descended
Maro ann holl dut német daou.   And all the people died, but two.[2]

Other versions state that the graveyards have overflowed, and that fields have had to be blessed in order to receive the surplus of corpses.

The tune noted by Augustin Guillevic is not well known; most recorded versions give the air used by Maryvonne Bacon, a singer from Meslan recorded by Donatien Laurent in 1965 at the age of 67, when she was working in a crêperie in the parish of Berné (CD track 5). In ten concise couplets her version captures the emotional impact of this powerful piece, foregrounding the devastation caused by the plague and the grief of the mother burying her seven children.

Studies:
Fañch Postic, 'La peste d'Elliant'.
Bernez Rouz, 'Ar Vosenn e Breizh-Izel. Studiadenn war Hengoun ar Bobl'.
Fañch Gourvil, *Théodore-Claude-Henri Hersart de La Villemarqué (1815–1895) et le 'Barzaz-Breiz'*
    (1839–1845–1867), pp. 417–21.

1   Collection Lédan, Archives municipales de Morlaix, ms. 2, pp. 212–15.
2   Théodore Hersart de La Villemarqué, *Barzas-Breiz. Chants populaires de la Bretagne*, p. 46.

9. The bridegroom and the mad dog

E par-rez Mur é hès gla-har E par-rez Mur é hès gla - har E par-rez

Mur é hès gla - har Mar dès é par - rèz ar en doar.

É parrez Mur é hès glahar	In the parish of Mûr there is grief
É parrez Mur é hès glahar	In the parish of Mûr there is grief
É parrez Mur é hès glahar	In the parish of Mûr there is grief
Mar dès é parrèz ar en doar.	If ever in any parish on earth.
Komans e hra 'n iliz gloèbein	The church began to drip
Get plah en éred é ouilein	With the tears of the bride-to-be
Na dén erbet n'hi honsolé	And no-one comforted her
Meit ur brer béleg hi doé.	But her brother the priest.
– Men brer béleg, mar me haret	– My brother priest, if you love me
De heneh n'em érédet ket.	Do not marry me to him.
– Chiket, me hoer, ne ouilet ket	– Quiet, sister, do not weep
Rak mat e hret, ha mat é het	You are doing what is right and proper
Rak mat e hret, ha mat é het	You are doing what is right and proper
Un dén adres hui hues bet.	You have a very suitable husband.
– Mem brérig peur ne houiet ket	– My dear brother you do not know
Ne hues chet dohton mat sellet	You haven't looked at him closely
Ma é zeulegad én é ben	The eyes in his head
Avel guin ru en ur huéren	Are like red wine in glass
El guin ru pen dé guérennet	Like red wine held in a glass
Ne hra ket joéiusted erbet.	He has no joy at all.

– Lakamb en dud iouank de gousket
Pe ne hrant joéiusted erbet

Pe ne hrant joéiusted erbet
Lakamb int én ur gambr cherret

Débramb hag ivamb ér chervad
É ma en dud iouank ér leh mat.

– N'hellan ket débrein nag ivet
Rak un taul kri em es kleuet

Rak em es kleuet un taul kri
Hanval mat te me hoér Mari.

Ketan dor en dehoé digoret
N'en dehoé kavet nitra bet.

En eil dor dehoé digoret
É hoér Mari dehoé kavet

Hé oé ino é hoér Mari
Tennet hé halon anehi.

– Mem brérig peur, mar me haret
Get hou koutel n'em lahet ket

Get hou koutel n'em lahet ket
Mouget mé étré diù holhed

Paset é er pearzek loérad
Pe oen dantet é lér me zad

Pe oen dantet é lér me zad
Ar men deuhlin é patérat

Ar men deuhlin é patéret
Get ur hiig du barbouilleg

– Let us put the young people to bed
Since they take no pleasure

Since they take no pleasure
Put them in a locked room

Let us eat and drink at the feast
The young people are in the right place.

– I cannot eat or drink
For I have heard a cry

For I have heard a cry
Like that of my sister Mari.

The first door he opened
He found nothing there at all.

The second door he opened
He found his sister Mari

She was there, his sister Mari
Her heart torn from her.

– Oh my brother,[1] if you love me
Do not kill me with your knife

Do not kill me with your knife
Smother me between two mattresses

Fourteen moons have come and gone
Since I was bitten in my father's yard

Since I was bitten in my father's yard
As I was praying on my knees

As I was praying on my knees
By a vicious black dog

---

1   The groom is speaking here, so 'brother' means 'brother-in-law'.

Ne més chet santet droug erbet	I felt nothing wrong at all
Betag hinoah, noz me éred	Until this evening, my wedding night
Get en trouz ag er soñnerion	When the noise of the musicians
En des me lakeit de vet klan.	Brought the illness on.

Provenance:

Sent by the abbé Cadoux, Croixanvec (Vannetais), to François Cadic. Published in *Paroisse bretonne de Paris* (1926), pp. 5–7. Republished in François Cadic, *Chansons populaires de Bretagne publiées dans la Paroisse bretonne de Paris*, pp. 545–47.

CD:

Track 6. Collected by Jean-Yves Monnat from Élise Nignol, Bubry (Vannetais), 1976–7. Dastum NUM-64931.

In his discussion of this disturbing *gwerz* from the Vannetais region, Cadic roots the story firmly in the landscape of its provenance, using the topic of rabies to pull in traditions about local saints, particularly Saint Bieuzy, deemed especially efficacious against the bite of mad dogs. The afflicted animals themselves were supposed to run and drink from a holy spring on the outskirts of the little village named after the saint, Bieuzy-des-Bois, near Pluvigner. A local saying was good for avoiding unpleasant encounters:

Ki klan arajet tro a me hent	Sick mad dog turn from my path
Doué ha mé e vieu en hent	This path belongs to God and to me
Sant Bihui a zou bet gannet	Sant Bihui was born
Erauk ma hoeh ki arajet.	Before you became a mad dog.[1]

Versions of the ballad exist in the other dialects; one from Locmaria-Quimper published by Luzel in the 1880s is more gruesomely detailed, but less effective as a result. When Émile Ernault came across a literary-sounding version in the Penguern manuscripts he doubted that the song had any truly popular origin, and, suspecting interference by Penguern's colleague Kerambrun, recollected having read a similar story in a newspaper 'qu'on dirait s'être passé en Autriche' ('where it was supposed to have happened in Austria'). The detail of the young couple being left alone on their wedding night while others feasted was, for him, proof of 'foreign' provenance. But the ballad also brings to mind an account from 1526, when a royal pardon was issued to a man from Trébrivan in Central Brittany who had killed one of his sons. He explained his actions by claiming that he

---

1   *Paroisse bretonne de Paris* (1926), p. 7.
2   Archives départementales de Loire-Atlantique, B 31.

'avoit esté longtemps auparavant mordu d'un chien enragé, alloccasion dequoy, par chacune lunée, il souffroit grosse doulleur et troublement de ses scens et entendements' (had a long time previously been bitten by a rabid dog, and that ever since, at every full moon, he suffered great pain and was disturbed in body and mind).[2]

Both Cadic and Le Braz collected a number of further beliefs about the causes and symptoms of rabies; the recognition of the onset of the disease after 'fourteen moons' refers to the sometimes lengthy period of its incubation. The version collected from Élise Nignol (sung to a brisk rhythmic tune of a type often used in the Vannetais and in Upper Brittany when walking), reflects this tradition in referring to the bite of a little black dog 'on the day after the thirteenth moon' (CD track 6).

The bride's terror, the groom's red eyes and the cruelly locked door are Gothic enough, but conveyed with ballad precision and economy; what is made clearer from the other versions is that the last few lines are spoken by the afflicted groom, who asks to be killed through suffocation. The version collected at Locmaria-Quimper shows the husband, having killed his wife '*ken kaer 'vel ar bleun per*' ('as lovely as pear-blossom'), begging his new brother-in-law not to kill him with his silver pistol, but rather to suffocate him so that no blood will flow (presumably to avoid contamination). His entire family, he says, has been afflicted with the disease:

Tri breur oamb bars ar memeuz ti	Three brothers we were in the same house
Hon zri clanv gant clenved ar c'hi.	All three infected by the dog's disease.[3]

The final lines also reveal the concealed slow burn of his illness over many weeks, and add the oddly poignant detail that the madness only erupted when the wedding musicians, the *sonnerion*, played their instruments.

Studies:
François Cadic, *Chansons populaires de Bretagne publiées dans la Paroisse bretonne de Paris*, pp. 545–7.

---

3   Version collected from Juliette Moënner, published in *Mélusine*, 3 (1886–7), 394.

10. Seven years at sea

Chi - la - ouet holl   ha   chi - i - la - ouet,   ha   chi - i - la - ouet,

Eu - eur son a - ne - ve 'zo - o sa - vet,   Eu - eur son a - ne - ve 'zo - o sa - vet.

Chilaouet holl ha chilaouet, ha chilaouet	Listen all, and listen, and listen again
Eur zon a–neve 'zo savet	To a new song, recently made
D'eur vandennad martoloded	About a band of sailors
Seiz vloa 'zo a zo n'eus ket douaret	Seven long years since they touched land.
Ar brovision ganten a voe faehiet	They ran out of provisions,
Graet a voe ganten ar gomidi	And they acted out a comedy
Da laz't ar moustig da zibiñ.	Pretending to kill the cabin boy, and eat him.
Ar moustig paour, sur a ouele	The poor little cabin boy wept bitterly
Pa na nevoe den d'e goñsole	And there was no-one to console him
Nem' ar c'habiten a levere	But the Captain, who said
– Moustig bihan, moustig bihan	– Little cabin boy, little lad
Te a zo lijer, te 'yal buan	You are light and you'll be quick
Lamm d'ar vern vihan d'ar vern vraz	Climb up the masts, the mizzen and the main,
Da vell' hag-eñ 'velli douar braz.	To see if you can see land ahead.
En eur vont el laeh eoñ a c'hoarze	As he climbed up high, he was laughing
En eur zont en traoñ eoñ a ouele.	When he came back down, he was weeping.
– Moustig bihan, petra t'eus gwellet	– Little cabin boy, what have you seen
Ha pa out te ken glac'haret?	And why are you so distressed?
– Netra netra 'm eus ket gwellet	– Nothing, nothing have I seen
Nemet seiz batimant Spagnolet	But seven big Spanish ships

O seiz emañ e liou ar gwad
Desin ar brezel pe ar gombad.

All seven of them the colour of blood
Sign of war and battle.

Int a lêre atao d'an eil d'eben
– Ar moustig bihan vo debet da goen.

All of them said, one to the other
– The little cabin boy will be eaten for dinner.

– N'eo ket an dra-se hag a vo gwraet
Ar blouzenn verr a vo tennet.

– It will not be decided like that
We shall have to draw lots.

Ar blouzenn verr pa voe tennet
Gant ar c'habiten 'voe degouezet.

And when the short straw was drawn
It was the Captain who had chosen it.

– Imposubl eo, ma martoloded
Imposubl eo a vehen debet.

– It is impossible, my sailors
It is impossible that I should be eaten.

Int 'lakê eur pod da virviñ
D'ober d'ar re all da zibiñ.

They set the pot to boil
To make a meal for the others.

– 'Mije ket ka't diaez e vervel
Paneve 'm eus eur bugel 'n e gavell

– I would not have found it hard to die
If I did not have a baby in the cradle

A vez atao é c'helver tad
Biskoaz n'eus gwell' ma daoulagad.

Who cries out for his father
He has never looked into my eyes.

Moustig bihan, moustig bihan
Te a zo lijer, te 'yal buan

Little cabin boy, little lad
You are light, and you'll be quick

Lamm d'ar vern vihan d'ar vern vraz
Da vell' hag-eñ 'velli douar braz.

Climb up the masts, the mizzen and the main,
To see if you can see land ahead.

En eur vont el laeh, eoñ a ouele
En eur zont en traoñ, eoñ a c'hoarze.

As he climbed up, he was weeping
When he came back down, he was laughing.

– Moustig bihan, petra t'eus gwellet
Ha pa out te ken joaiustet?

– Little cabin boy, what have you seen
To make you so happy?

– Netra netra 'm eus ket gwellet
Nemet tour Sant Jakez benniget
Hag ar brosesion en overn-bred

– Nothing, nothing have I seen
But the tower of the blessed Saint-Jacques
And the procession for high mass

Hag eur c'hornig deuz ar vered	And a little corner of the graveyard
E lec'h ma mamm 'zo interet.	Where my mother lies buried.
Person Sant Jakez pa 'n eus klevet	When the priest at Saint-Jacques heard the news
E overn-bred 'n eus achuet	He finished his high mass
Da vord an aod eoñ a zo eet	Down to the beach he went
Da glask sikour d'ar vartoloded.	To bring help to the sailors.
Lod a c'houle bar', lod a c'houle dour	Some asked for bread, some asked for water
Lod a c'houle Doue d'o sikour.	Some asked God for salvation.
– Fi a yal d'ar gêr me na yan ket	– You go home, I shall not go
Fi a ray ma c'heloù da ma gwreg	You will give the news to my wife
Fi a gaso dei ma roched liou ar gwad	You will take her my blood-red shirt
Evit gwello deuz ma c'hombat	So she may see I have been in combat
Fi a lavaro da ma c'hoerezed	And you will tell my sisters
O, kemer un' deuz labourioù douar	Oh, to choose a farming man,
Kar rankont ket monet var ar mor.	For they do not have to go to sea.

Provenance:
'Ar moustig bihan', collected by René Hénaff from Mari An Drev, Penmarc'h (Basse-Cornouaille), 1956. Dastum, NUM-30056. Published in Éva Guillorel, *La Complainte et la Plainte: Chanson, justice, cultures en Bretagne*, pp. 392–3 and CD track 19.

CD:
Track 7. Same version.

Several *gwerziou* are based on themes common to song traditions in other languages, and adapt them to a particular local context. This *gwerz* about a group of sailors adrift for seven years, who draw lots to decide which of them will be eaten first, is one of the best examples of this process. Frequently collected in French (and still highly popular today as the children's song *Il était un petit navire*) this ballad also appears in Scandinavia from at least the 17th century, and in the British Isles, the Hiberian peninsula, and in South and North America where it travelled with the immigrant Portugese, English and French communities.

In this version, collected from the little coastal village of Penmarc'h in the *pays bigouden* (the extreme south-west corner of Cornouaille), the structure of the story is much the same as in the

French versions; before sacrificing one of the crew members, the captain sends the little cabin boy up the main-mast to scan the horizon. The boy climbs up in tears and descends laughing, with news that land is in sight. Although Mari An Drev's version says that he can see the bell tower at Saint-Jacques, it is almost always the 'Tower of Babylon' – a name redolent of the exotic and the miraculous – which is noted in both languages.

But here the similarity ends. In many of the French songs, the little cabin boy describes a scene of bucolic content, entirely in keeping with the usual ballad tropes in this genre of songs. He sees the castle of his father the king, and the sheep grazing on the slopes tended by graceful shepherdesses, amongst whom he recognises his former sweetheart. The wandering life of the sailor thus ends in a series of joyful reunions. In the Breton versions, however, the narrative is considerably darker. Some songs speak of Spanish (or Turkish) ships with blood red sails, massing to attack. Then the cabin boy spies the priest of Babylon processing around the church and graveyard where his mother lies buried; he comes down to meet the sailors as they leave the ship in order to give them their last rites, prior to their burial in the same grave. Confronted by such extreme human distress, the priest himself sometimes dies too and, as a version collected by Luzel has it:

Êt int ho zregont 'n ur poullad	All thirty of them were put in the same hole
Doue da roï d'hô maro mad.	May God give them all a good death.[1]

Other texts show the dying Captain begging for someone to take his blood-spotted shirt to his wife.

A similarly grim atmosphere haunts many of the Scandinavian versions, some of which, like their French counterparts, actually portray the sacrificial act and subsequent cannibalism: the captain is served with the intestines of his first mate. Others add a penitential element reminiscent of Coleridge's *The Rime of the Ancient Mariner*, by showing the ship mysteriously becalmed in open sea because a blasphemer and rapist has come on board; the ship starts to move again only after the crew discover him and throw him into the sea. These tragic outcomes are not part of the corpus of versions in English and Portugese; and in Brazil where the song is still well known, the story of the sailors drawing lots has attached itself to the real wreck of the *Catrineta*, a ship attacked by privateers during a voyage between Portugal and Brazil in 1565. Different cultures, then, have taken up this internationally known story centred on a taboo subject and treated it in many different ways (and, as Gerald Porter has shown, its various afterlives in literary forms reflect society's willingness, or otherwise, to 'sing the unspeakable').[2] As far as the Breton versions go, the dominant features here can be found in many other *gwerziou*; this is a narrative genre of deep religiosity, thoroughly haunted by notions of death.

---

1 François-Marie Luzel, *Gwerziou Breiz-Izel: Chants et chansons populaires de la Basse-Bretagne. Gwerziou I*, pp. 186–7.
2 Mary-Ann Constantine and Gerald Porter, *Fragments and Meaning in Traditional Song*, pp. 59–62.

Studies:

George Doncieux, *Le romancéro populaire de la France*, 'La courte-paille', pp. 243–51.

Éva Guillorel, *La Complainte et la Plainte: Chanson, justice, cultures en Bretagne,* pp. 391–5.

Gerald Porter, '"Eaten with Merriment and Sport": Cannibalism and the Colonial Subject'.

Mary-Ann Constantine and Gerald Porter, *Fragments and Meaning in Traditional Song*, pp. 55–62.

11. Shipwreck at Penmarc'h

Bre - man bloa da foar San-tez Ka - tell Sor - ti - as ar flod deuz ster Bour-

del, Sor - ti - as ar flo - od deu - euz ster Bour - del.

Breman bloa da foer santez Katell	A year ago on St Catherine's day
'Sortias ar flod deuz ster Bourdel	The fleet left the river at Bordeaux
'Sortias ar flod deuz ster Bourdel	The fleet left the river at Bordeaux
Ha pa voe var ar rad mouilhet	And when they lifted anchor in the harbour
Na voe banne avel ebet	There was not the slightest breath of wind
Ha kaer a doe-e naviget	And for all their navigation
Avel avoalc'h ne gavent ket.	They could not get enough wind.
Pa voent erru var tal Penmarc'h	When they arrived close to Penmarc'h
Int a doe kavet avel avoalc'h	Then they found wind enough
Goulou var dreon, goulou var rôk	Lights behind, lights ahead
Int a zonje den be' kreiz ar flod.	They thought they were in the midst of the fleet.
– Kouraj, kouraj, bugaligou	– Courage, courage, my boys
Da vont 'benn d'an avel d'ar C'helou.	Head into the wind for the Étocs.
– Ma yim benn 'n avel d'ar C'helou	– If we go straight for the Étocs
Nin 'vo kaet e Penmarc'h en aochou.	They will find us on the beaches at Penmarc'h.
Petra c'hoarvez gant Penmarkiz	What has come over the people of Penmarc'h
O terhet goulou 'n noz 'n o iliz?	That they keep fires in their churches at night?
Krest a galon neb na ouélé	Cruel the heart that would not weep
Var dal Penmarc'h neb a vezé	To be near Penmarc'h

E vel' ar mour bras o virvi	And watch the great sea seething
Gant ar vartoloded e vuizi	With the sailors drowning
E vel' ar mour bras o ruian	And watch the great sea reddening
Gant gwed ar gristenien 'n ennañ.	With the blood of the Christians in it.
– Piou 'gaso kelou da Voaien	– Who shall take the news to Audierne
Eo kollet ar flod nemet unan?	That the fleet has perished but for one?
Piou fell doc'h nem' eur chas-mare	What would you have but a *chasse-marée*[1]
Nemed eur chas-mare na rafe	What but a *chasse-marée* would do it
Eur chas-mare e Porz Louizou	A *chasse-marée* from Port-Louizou
Hag a zonjfe touffi ar c'helou?	[Thinking to stifle the news]?[2]
Oe ket e gomz peurlavaret	Scarcely had he spoken
Gant eun taol mour a neus int beuzet.	When a huge wave drowned them.
Nin a vele merc'hed Goaien	We saw the women of Audierne
E tont en aod vras gant licheriou moan	Coming to the wide beach with fine sheets
Kant intanvez deuz bae Goaien	A hundred widows from Audierne bay
A gasas ganto kant licher venn.	Bearing a hundred white sheets.
Int a c'houlas an eil d'eben	They asked each other
– Na peus ket gwelet korf ma den?	– Have you not seen the body of my man?
– Penôs mi gwelet korf ho ten	– How should I have seen the body of your man
Pa man e tibi gant kranked melen?	Since the yellow crabs are eating it?
Krest a galon neb a oele	Cruel the heart that would not weep
E korn an Dorchen neb a veze	To be at the point of La Torche
Vel' ar c'horviou maro e tont	And see the bodies of the dead
Ive da Benhors he d'ar Gador	Arrive at Penhors and at La Chaise
E Plozeved er parkou 'maint	At Plozévet in the fields
Goueliou lian er flod o sec'hañ	The linen sails of the fleet are drying

1   *Chasse-marée* can refer to either the person or, by extension (and most probable here), the swift boat used to deliver fresh catches of fish to shore.
2   This line could be emended to make better sense as 'thinking to pass the Étocs', since *ar C'helou* is the Breton name for these rocks.

Red eo binnigi ar parkou
E-vit douari ar horviou.

They have to bless the fields
To bury the bodies.

Ha 'n oac'hig Dreo 'zo eun den mad
Neus sternet e gar d'o charreat

Old Dreo is a good man
He has saddled up his cart to carry them

Evit o gas da zaou da dri
Da vered Sant Per da interi.

To carry them, in twos and threes
To Saint-Pierre graveyard for burial.

– Malloz, malloz da Benmarkiz
Hag a zalc'h goulou noz 'n o iliz

– Cursed, cursed be the people of Penmarc'h
Who keep fires in their church at night

Da Benmarkiz, da Blozevet
Ivez da Benhorz ha d'an Dreded

The people of Penmarc'h, of Plozévet
Those of Penhors and La Trinité

A zalc'h goulou 'n o ilizou
'Vit ma yal d'an aod batimañchou

Who keep fires in their churches
So that ships go onto the coast

Tudou Penmarc'h zo tud daonet
Birviken mi gant Doue vefe pardonet.

The people of Penmarc'h are a people damned
Never again will God pardon them.

Provenance:
Collected by Donatien Laurent from Nicole Pochic, Penmarc'h (Basse-Cornouaille), 1992. Published in Donatien Laurent, 'Mémoire et poésie chantée en Pays Bigouden: La gwerz de Penmarc'h', pp. 185–7.

CD:
Track 8. Collected by Michel Colleu and Pierre-Yves Pétillon from Nicole Pochic, Penmarc'h (Basse-Cornouaille), 2011, during one of the *veillées* organised by Dastum Bro Gerne-Centre du patrimoine oral de Cornouaille.

In a ballad tradition rich in shipwrecks, *Gwerz Penmarc'h* is exceptional. And this, the most recently collected of a handful of versions, is an exceptional version. It is another very precisely located *gwerz*, charting the course of an ill-fated flotilla of Audierne ships returning from Bordeaux, and passing the dangerous rocks near the coast at Penmarc'h in the *pays bigouden* (these are the 'grisly rokkes blake' which cause so much concern in Chaucer's *Franklin's Tale*). The strength and direction of the wind, the named rocks, the location of the church at Penmarc'h, all these elements in the seascape are not details, nor 'colour', but utterly necessary to the unrolling of the story of the disaster. Much of the poignancy of the aftermath – the arrival of the women of Audierne, the sails drying in the fields at Plozévet, the named local man shifting the bodies in cartloads to the church at Saint-Pierre – also comes from that deep sense of place and community evoked in small details.

The quality and clarity of the ballad's language has attracted comment. Donatien Laurent has argued that, although the earliest recorded version is late 19th century, we are dealing here with a very old song recording an event that took place many centuries ago. No records of the disaster survive, but taking into account various factors including the presence of merchant ships in Bordeaux from both Audierne and Penmarc'h, the absence of the lighthouse at Saint-Pierre (constructed in the 16th century), the name of one of the ships and the practice of lighting fires in churches, he offers the 15th century as a possible historical context. This also accords with a period of great prosperity in Breton maritime commerce, owing to Brittany's key position between the Channel and the Atlantic. Other *gwerziou* preserve memories of the busy merchant trade with La Rochelle, Gascony and Spain – and later, Newfoundland and the Americas. Shipwreck ballads are, like their subjects, notoriously liable to narrative break-up, and it is of course impossible to say with absolute certainty that this *gwerz* does *not* contain layers of memory of different wrecks.

Most known versions of the *gwerz* of Penmarc'h were collected in the *pays bigouden*, although some come from other maritime communities, such as the island of Ouessant. Nicole Pochic, herself from Saint-Pierre-en-Penmarc'h, learned the version given here in the 1960s from her grandmother and her two great-aunts, who sang it as they mended fishing nets. The oral transmission of songs remained strong in the Penmarc'h area until very recently (see no. 10), partly because of the fish canneries, which kept up a tradition of collective singing while working.

One of the most distinctive aspects of this *gwerz* is the reference to wreckers lighting fires in church towers in order to lure ships onto the rocks and obtain their cargo. The passionate final stanzas cursing the inhabitants of Penmarc'h and neighbouring villages remind us that (as in Cornwall and Wales) wrecking is a sensitive and elusive subject, perceived differently by different groups and often hard to trace in the historical record. The first written mention of the practice in Brittany is in the work of the traveller Dubuisson-Aubenay in 1636.[3] Shipwrecks remain to this day a feature of Breton life, though since the 1960s they are now most often associated with the wrecks of tankers and the regular appearance of *marées noires* ('black tides', slicks of crude oil) which pollute the coasts in their wake. The shipwreck song, one of the oldest and most widespread song types in the Breton tradition, is also one of the most readily renewable, as the songs composed about the *marée noire* that followed the wreck of the *Erika* in 1999 testify.[4]

Studies:

Donatien Laurent, 'Mémoire et poésie chantée en Pays Bigouden: La gwerz de Penmarc'h'. Republished in Donatien Laurent, *Parcours d'un ethnologue en Bretagne*, pp. 309–21.

---

3   Alain Croix, *La Bretagne d'après l'itinéraire de monsieur Dubuisson-Aubenay* (Rennes: Presses universitaires de Rennes, Société d'Histoire et d'Archéologie de Bretagne, 2006), p. 356.
4   See for example Ifig Castel, *Amzer vat* (Kreizenn sevenadurel Lannuon, 2004), CD track 12. This song composed by the Trégor-based singer Ifig Castel won the 'prix de création' at the prestigious *Kan ar Bobl* competition in 2000.

12. The siege of Guingamp

Ebars ar blaves mil a pemp kant	In the year one thousand five hundred
E teuas ar sézic war Guingamp	The siege came to Guingamp
Ha brema ar bloaz mil pemp kant seiz	And now in the year one thousand five hundred and seven
Oa disquennet ar sézic war Breiz.	The siege has descended on Brittany.
War porz Miguel oa ar Saozon	The English were at St Michael's gate
An Allemantet war porz Roazon	The Germans were at the gate of Rennes
War porz ar Ploum ber oa ann Irlantet	At the Ploubezre gate were the Irish
Ac enn eur plaç all ar Flamantet.	And the Flemish were in another square.
Ar prince Dénoblin a goulenné	Prince Dénoblin called out
War porzou Roazon pa zarbaré	As he manoeuvred at the gate of Rennes
– Porzer! digoret ar percher-ma!	– Porter! Open up these gates!
Ar prinç Dénoblin a so ama	Prince Dénoblin is here
Ar prinç Dénoblin a so ama	Prince Dénoblin is here
Triwac'h mil cavalier so gant-han	Eighteen thousand cavalrymen at his side
Triwac'h mil cavalier paotret vaillant	Eighteen thousand brave men
Da lakaat ar sézic war Guingamp.	To lay siege to Guingamp.
Hac ar porzer kos pa a glevaz,	And the old porter when he heard that
D'ar prinç Dénoblin a respontaz	Replied to Prince Dénoblin
– Ar percher-ma ne vont ket digoret	– These gates will not be opened
Na d'eoc'h, na da prinç all a bed	Not for you, nor any other prince
Ken na mo goulennet digant an Dukes Anna	Until I have asked the Duchess Anna
Hounnes a so mestress war ar percher-ma.	She is the mistress of these gates.
Dukes, digoret e vezo ar percher-ma	Duchess, Should we open the gates
D'ar prinç Dénoblin so arruet ama?	For Prince Dénoblin, who has just arrived?
Triwac'h mil cavalier tud vaillant	Eighteen thousand cavalry, brave men
Da lakaat ar sézic war Guingamp.	Come to lay siege to Guingamp.
An Dukes Anna a respontas	The Duchess Anna replied
D'ar canonier kos pa glevas	To the old gunner when she heard that

– Va doriou a so moraillet	– My gates are well locked
Ha va mogueriou a so cimantet	My walls are reinforced
Ne rann ket kaz ho gwelet	I do not want to see them
Kear Guingamp ne vezo ket kemeret	The town of Guingamp will not be taken
Mar hoc'h heus ar canoun bras karget	If you have the big cannon loaded
Ar kear Guingamp a vezo diffenet	The town of Guingamp will be defended
Ha pa vijent tri mis anter azé	And if they were to spend three whole months there
Ne rann ket kaz eus a nicun arré.	I am not concerned with any of them.
Ar canonier koz a respontaz	The old gunner replied
D'ar Dukes Anna, pa lavaraz	To the Duchess Anna, when she spoke
– Brema e teuann d'har karga	– I have just this moment charged it
Tregont boulet rolet so ama	There are thirty round cannonballs here
Barr eun hanter poëzel a mitraill ploumb	And a half bushel of lead mitraille
Mui pe kémend all a poultr a canoun	More, or as much cannon powder
Ha mui pe kemend all a dragé braz	And more, or as many again, of silver bullets
Da rei d'ar prinç Dénoblin war he faç.	To give Prince Dénoblin to his face.
Na oa ket hé guer peur achuet	Scarcely had the words been said
Ar canonier kos a so lazet	When the old gunner was killed
Gant eun tenn poultr gwen demeus eur gambr	By a blast of white powder shot from a room
Gand eur cavalier hanvet Goasgarant.	Delivered by a cavalryman named Goasgarant.
An Dukes Anna a lavare	The Duchess Anna said
D'ar canonieres kos neuze	To the old gunner's widow then
– Aoutrou Doué, petra vezo grët?	– Lord above, what shall we do?
Ar canoun bras a so braket.	The great cannon has taken aim.
Ar canonieres a lavare	The gunner's widow said
D'ar Dukes Anna, pa glévé	To the Duchess Anna, when she heard
– Pa ar canoun bras so karget	– Since the big cannon is fully charged
M'em bezo rebech va priet.	I will take revenge for my husband.
Na oa ket ho guer peur achuet	Scarcely had she said those words
Ar vogueriou a so bet freuzet	When the walls were breached
An doriou a so bet torret	The gates were broken down
Karguet oa ar kear a soudardet.	And the town was filled with soldiers.

Ar prinç Dénoblin a lavaré
Ebars ar kear Guingamp, pa rentré
– D'heoc'h, va soudardet, ar merc'hed koant
Ha d'in an aour ac an arc'hant.

An Dukes Anna a lavaraz
D'ar prinç Dénoblin, pa zaludas
– Ma vije bet karget ar canoun bras
Mé mé gounet hirio va goaz.

Ar Dukes Anna en em strinkas
War an douar ien ha noaz
– Itron Maria a guir chicour
Pliget ganeoc'h hor sicour!

Ar canonieres a lavaré
D'ar bec ann tour plat pa arrué
– Me wel azé eur régiment o c'hoarzin
D'abord c'houi ho welo chagrin.

N'a oa ket he guer peur achuet
Ann tan d'ar canoun he deus laquët
Triwac'h kant ar-ré he deus lazet
Mui pe kemend all he deus blecet.

Ar prinç Dénoblin a goulenné
Gant eur furor bras, pa tremene
– Pelec'h-emâ merc'hed ar kear-ma
A laka ar canoun da strinka?

Kriz ê vijé ar c'haloun n'a gwelgé
Ebars ar kéar Guingamp, hini è vijé
Da welet ar merc'hed, ar gragé
O touguen an diliat ho gwélé

O lakaat diliat ha liennach
Evid en em cuzaat eus an arrach
Evit prenna prenestou ha camprou
En em zavetei eus ar canoniou.

Prince Dénoblin said
In the town of Guingamp, as he entered
– You, my soldiers, take the pretty girls
And I will have the gold and the silver.

The Duchess Anna said
To Prince Dénoblin, as he saluted her
– If the big cannon had been charged
I would have won my husband today.

The Duchess Anna threw herself
Upon the cold, bare ground
– Our Lady Maria of Salvation
May it please you to save us!

The gunner's widow said
As she arrived at the top of the tower
– I see there a regiment laughing
Soon you will see them disappointed.

Scarcely had the words been said
When she lit the fuse on the cannon
Eighteen hundred of them she killed
And injured the same, or more.

Prince Dénoblin demanded
In a great fury, as he passed by
– Where are the women of this town
Who fire off the cannon?

Cruel the heart that would not have wept
In the town of Guingamp
To see the girls, the women
Bringing the linen from their beds

Bringing out sheets and linen
To hide themselves from the fury
Closing up the windows and rooms
To save themselves from the cannon.

An Dukes Anna a redaz
Ebars an ilis bras en em strinkaz
– Itron Maria a guir chicour
Grit deomp tréc'hi war hon adversour!

Ha c'houi ve countant Guerc'hes Marie
Da lakaat hô ti da varchossi
Hô sicristiri da c'hav ar guin
Hag hoc'h auter bras d'ann daol guégin?

N'a oa ket hé féden peur achuet
Ar kléier da zonna so commancet
Eo commancet ar kléier da zoun
Hag ar spouranné enn oll c'haloun.

Ar prinç Dénoblin a commandé
D'hé pagic bihan, hac en galvé
– Pagic, pagic, va pagic bihan
Te a so diligant ha buhan

Kerz buhan d'ar bec ann tour plat
Da gouzout piou a so d'ho brancellat
Ha mar deus den unan d'ho zoun
Plant da glévé enn hé galoun

Ouz da gostes te euz sabrenou
Gant da zaouarn t'en em ziffennaut.
He a ia é crec'h ô cana
Hag a zisken enn traon ô guéla.

– Enn bec ann tour plat me a so bet
Ha, mad ann doué, me m'eus guelet
Nemet ar Verc'hes Marie hag he Vab
Ar ré so d'ho brancellat.

Ar prinç Dénoblin a lavaré
D'hé oll soudardet, pa ho glévé
– Profit, va soudardet, pep hini eur skoed
Hac ann dud noblanç a roio deck

The Duchess Anna ran
She flung herself into the great church
– Our Lady Maria of Salvation
Let us triumph over our enemy!

Would it please you, oh Virgin Mary
To see your house used as a stables
Your sacristy as a cellar for wine
And your high altar as a kitchen table?

She had scarcely finished her prayer
When the bells began to ring
The bells began to ring
And there was fear in every heart.

Prince Dénoblin called for
His little page and gave him orders
– Little page, my little page
You who are so diligent and quick

Climb quickly up to the tower
To find out who is making them ring
And if there is someone there pulling them
Plant your sword in his heart

You have sabres by your side
Defend yourself with your own hands.
He climbed up singing
And he came down again weeping.

– I have been up on the flat tower
And lord knows I saw nothing
Except the Virgin Mary and her Son
They are making the bells ring out.

Prince Dénoblin said
To all his soldiers, when he heard them
– Make an offering, my men, one *écu* each
And the noblemen will each give ten

Me va unan a brof daouzeck	Myself, I will give twelve
Da repari an domach me m'eus grët	To repair the damage I have done
Bridomp hon keseck, ha deomp enn hent	Saddle up the horses, and let's be on our way
Ha lezomp ho ziez gant ar sent.	Leave the saints to their houses.
Ar prinç Dénoblin a lavaré	Prince Dénoblin said
Eus a kear Guingamp pa partié	As he left the town of Guingamp
– O veza 'r kear Guingamp kemeret	– Though I took the town of Guingamp
Ouz penn c'houec'h kement me m'eus kollet	I lost more than six like it
Ma kollann va buez ô vont d'ar guer	If I lose my life returning home
Me em bezo kollet tout enn entier	I will have lost altogether
Kerzomp buhan kostes hon bro	Let us now go quickly to our own country
Evit ma kemerimp repo.	That we may take our rest.

Provenance:

'Sezic Guingamp', collected by Barbe-Émilie de Saint-Prix in the area of Callac (Haute-Cornouaille) in the 1820s or 1830s. Published in Chevalier de Fréminville, *Antiquités des Côtes-du-Nord*, pp. 375–86.

CD:

Track 9. Collected by François Vallée from Marc'harit Fulup, Pluzunet (Trégor), 1900. Dastum NUM-26140. Published in *Tradition chantée de Bretagne. Les sources du Barzaz-Breiz aujourd'hui*, CD track 4.

Songs about towns under siege are well known in French, appearing in prerevolutionary printed texts and collected later from oral tradition. The *gwerz* describing the siege of Guingamp is the only thing of this kind in Breton. This version from the manuscripts of Barbe-Émilie de Saint-Prix was the first ever collected, and was included among the small group of ballads studied by Fréminville in 1835, some four years before the publication of La Villemarqué's *Barzaz-Breiz*. Since then, it has been collected numerous times.

The dates of 1500 and 1507, given in the opening couplet, are not to be trusted; as is common in the *gwerziou*, the act of providing the date is more significant than any particular number, and serves to remind listeners that the song is true in the ballad sense. Nevertheless, the way in which the events are described, combined with the presence of certain named characters, allows us to locate a real historical context for this song. The account appears in fact to conflate memories of two sieges suffered by the Trégor town of Guingamp. The first took place in 1489 during the final major confrontation between the independent Duchy of Brittany and the kingdom of France; the second, over a century later, took place in 1591 in the midst of the period of religious unrest

known as the Wars of the League. The *gwerz* tells of a certain 'prince Dénoblin', who must be
an altered version of Dombes, the king's lieutenant general who laid siege to the town in 1591.
Other versions mention a 'Melkunan', who is identifiable as the Duke of Mercœur, governor
of Brittany and a man of considerable influence during the last decade of the 16th century;
the 'Goasgarant' who kills the gunner may well be the nobleman Coetgourhant, mentioned in
contemporary chronicles from the same period.

The main female character, however, is none other than the Duchess Anne herself – which sends
the action back to the last decade of the 15th century and the loss of Breton independence. Anne, last
Duchess of Brittany and Queen of France, remains to this day a profoundly significant character in
Breton popular imagination, and yet the ballad of the siege of Guingamp is the only *gwerz* in which
she plays an important part. Her role in the action is unexpected to say the least, since she appears
to be posted on the ramparts in the midst of the battle, directing operations; when the wife of the
gunner killed in action takes her husband's place at the cannon to fight alongside her, the ballad takes
on a distinctively proactive female tone, intriguingly at odds with its very masculine subject.

The siege and the battle are described in the exuberant poetic terms of the ballad cliché:
18,000 soldiers take the town by storm; 1,800 are killed in the cannon volleys of the gunner's
widow. And the song's ending develops the more miraculous aspects of its story – the shamefaced
withdrawal of the conquerors, awed by the supernatural ringing of the bells – by bringing in other
ballad clichés as narrative building blocks. The little page who is sent up the tower laughing and
who comes down weeping is structurally parallel to the little cabin boy who climbs the ship's
mast in many maritime ballads (see no. 10). Another popular *gwerz* motif – that of church bells
spontaneously ringing to protect a sacred precinct from assault (see nos 4 and 15) – can be found
in written sources as early as the medieval Chronicle of Alain Bouchart, printed in 1514 where it
is linked to the entry of the English into Rennes in 1357.

There are various tunes associated with this piece. In 1839 La Villemarqué set his version of
the song to the Welsh air *Rhyfelgyrch Cadben Morgan* (Captain Morgan's War March), but he had
spent several weeks in south Wales just prior to the book's publication, and the notion that this
tune was popular in Brittany before the *Barzaz-Breiz* seems improbable. Trégor singers furnished
a number of subsequent tunes; indeed, *The Siege of Guingamp* was among the first (strange, and
not terribly audible) sound recordings made on wax cylinders by François Vallée from the singing
of Marc'harit Fulup in 1900 (CD track 9). Polig Monjarret noted seven separate tunes in the
Guingamp area in the 1940s, and the most recent version of the song was collected by Ifig
Troadeg from the singer Yvonne Garlan in 1980.

Studies:
Yann-Ber Piriou, 'La gwerz du "Siège de Guingamp" et la duchesse Anne dans la tradition orale'.
Donatien Laurent, 'Le siège de Guingamp'. Republished in Donatien Laurent, *Parcours d'un ethno-
logue en Bretagne*, pp. 265–78.
Yvon Le Rol, *La langue des 'gwerzioù' à travers l'étude des manuscrits inédits de Mme de Saint-Prix*, II,
pp. 655–64.

13. The Heiress of Keroulas: a forced marriage

Ar Pen - he - rez a Ker - ou - las Nag he deuz eur Pli - ja - dur braz

Da zoug' eur zaë a sa - tin glas, Pa - ra gant Au - trou - nez dan - sâ!

Ar Penherez a Keroulas	The Heiress of Keroulas
Nag he deus eur Plijadur braz	Must be truly happy
Da zoug' eur zaë a satin glas	Wearing a dress of blue satin
Pa ra gant Autrounez dansâ.	To dance with these *messieurs*.
Evelse ê gomsed er zall	That is what they said in the ballroom
Pa zeue ar Penherez er ball	As the heiress entered to dance,
Rag Marquis Mezl voa erruet	For the Marquis de Mezl had arrived
Gan he vamm, ag eun heul bras meurbed.	With his mother, and a great crowd of followers.
– Me a garje bea Goulmic glas	– I wish I were a little blue pigeon
Var an Doen e Keroulas	Up on the roof of Keroulas
Evit clevet ar complidi	To hear the plotting
Entre he vam a va hini.	Between his mother and mine.
Me a gren gant ar pez a velân	I tremble at what I see
Neket heb eur sonj int deut amân	It is not without intention that they have come
Deuz a Gherne, pa so en ti	From Cornouaille, when there is in the house
Eur Penherez da simizi.	An heiress to be married.
Gant he madou ag he hano brudet	For all his wealth and his illustrious name
Ar Marquis ze d'in ne a plij ket	That Marquis does not please me
Mæz Kerthomas, deuz a bell so	But Kerthomas, for a long time now
A garan a garin atô.	I love, and will love forever.
Enkrezet voa ive Kerthomas	Kerthomas himself was much disturbed
Gant tud ze deut ê Keroulas	By the people come to Keroulas
Rag he a gared ar Penherez	For he loved the heiress
Ag voa clevet lavaret aliez	And could often be heard to say

– Me a garje bea Crag-houad
Var ar lenn e welc'her he dillat
Evit glebia va daou lagad
Gand an dour demeus he dillat.

Ar Penherez a lavare
D'he Mam-Itron, euz an de ze
– M' vel eru Marquis Mezl amâ
A lakas va c'haloun d'a ranna.

Va Mam, Itron, a me ho ped
D'ar Marquis Mezl n'em roït ket
Da va reï kent da Penanrün
Pe mar kirit da Salaün

Va roït kentoc'h da Kerthomas
Henez en deuz ar muïa graçz
En ti man he zeu aliez
Hên a lezec'h d'in ober al lez.

En Gastelgall me a zo bet
Mad, en Doue, n'emeuz gwellet
Nemet eur gôs sall voghedet
Ag ar prenechou hanter torret.

En Kerthomas me a so bet
Madou avoalc'h em meuz gwellet
An norojou zo arc'hant gwenn
Ar prenechou zo aour melen.

– Va Merc'h, ancounît an holl ze
Trakent ho mad n'a dal gan me
Roet ar gheriou: an dra so græt
D'ar Marquis Mezl vihot demezet.

– Eur goalen aour ag eur signet
Gant Kerthomas oent din roet
Hô comeris, en eur gana
Ag hô restaulin en eur woela.

– I wish I were a teal
On the lake where she washes her clothes
So I could bathe my eyes
In the water that falls from her clothes.

The heiress said
To her lady mother, one day
– I see the Marquis de Mezl arriving
My heart is torn to pieces.

My mother, Lady, I beg you
Do not give me to the Marquis de Mezl
Give me rather to Penanrun
Or even to Salaün

O give me instead to Kerthomas
For he is the kindest of all
He often comes into this house
And you allow him to court me.

I have been to Châteaugal
But, in God's name, all I saw
Was an old smoke-filled room
And the windows half-broken.

I have been to Kerthomas
I saw plenty of nice things
The doors are bright silver
The windows yellow gold.

– My daughter, forget all of this
Nothing matters to me but your advantage
The word has been given, the thing is done
You will be married to the Marquis de Mezl.

– A gold ring and a signet
Were given me by Kerthomas
When I took them, I was singing
When I give them back, I will be weeping.

Dalc'hit Kerthomas ho goalen aour	Take, Kerthomas, your golden ring
Hô signet gant carcaniou aour	Your signet with its chains of gold
Na ven ket leset ho kemeret	Since I am not allowed to accept you
Miret ho re ne zlean ket.	It is not right for me to keep them.
Crîz vije ar galoun n'a woelje	Cruel the heart that would not have wept
En Keroulas neb a vije	To be at Keroulas
E velet ar Penherez kez	And see the poor heiress
E poket d'an nor, pa ïe er mæs.	Kiss the door as she went through it.
– Adieu, ti bras a Keroulas	– Farewell, great house of Keroulas
Biken en oc'h ne a rin pass	Never again will you see me here
Adieu, va amezeïen kez	Farewell, my dear neighbours
Adieu, breman a da jamæs!	Farewell, now and forever more!
Peorien ar Barez a woelje	The poor of the parish wept
Ar Penherez hô gonsole	The heiress consoled them
– Tevit, Peorien, ne woelet ket	– Hush, poor people, do not cry
Da Gastelgall deuit d'am gwelet	Come and find me at Châteaugal
Me a roïo aluzen pep de	I will give you alms every day
Teïr gwech ar sizun eur charité	And three times a week I will give in charity
Triouec'h palevars a gwiniz	Eighteen quarters of wheat
Ag eï, a kerc'h ive roïz.	And barley and oats besides.
Ar Marquis Mezl a lavare	The Marquis de Mezl said
D'he grœg nevez, pa he gleve	To his new wife, when he heard her
– Evit pep de ne root ket	– You will not give every day
Rag va madou ne batfen ket.	For my possessions will not last long.
– Marquis Mezl, heb cahout ho re	– Marquis de Mezl, without touching your goods
Me raïo aluzen pep de	I will give alms every day
Evit destumi pedennou	That we may gather prayers
Goude omp maro, d'hon eneou.	After our deaths, for our souls.
Ar Penherez a goulene	The heiress asked
Er Castelgall pa errue	As she arrived at Châteaugal
A n' gaffe ket eur messager	If there was a messenger
Da gass d'he mamme eul lizer.	Who would take a letter to her mother.

Eur paj yaouank a respontas	A young page replied
D'ar Penherez, pa he glevas	To the heiress, when he heard her
– Scrivit lizerou pa gherfet	– Write all the letters you like
Messagerien a vo cavet.	Messengers will be found.
Coulscoude eul lizer a scrivas	Straight away she wrote a letter
A d'ar paj en berr hê roïas	And gave it quickly to the page
Gant gourc'hemenn evit hê cass	With the order to take it
Ragtall d'he mamm e Keroulas.	Immediately to her mother at Keroulas.
Pa erruet al lizer gant hi	When the letter arrived
Hi a voa er zall e ebatti	She was in the ballroom, entertaining
Gant lod a Noblanz euz ar vrô	A number of noblemen from the region
Kerthomas voa ive eno.	Kerthomas was there as well.
Pa 'n devoa he lizer lennet	As soon as she read her letter
Da Kerthomas hi a lavared	She said to Kerthomas
– Likit da zibra kezec affô	– Saddle the horses right away
Da Gastelgall a ann fenôs.	I leave this instant for Châteaugal.
Itron Keroulas a goulene	The Lady of Keroulas asked
Er Castelgall pa errue	As she arrived at Châteaugal
– Petra nevez so en ti man	– What has happened in this house
Ma ê steignet ar perc'hier er ghis mân?	That I see the doors covered like this?
– Ar Penherez a voa deut aman	– The heiress who came here
A zo decedet an nôs mân.	Died in the night.
– Mar dê maro ar Penherez	– If the heiress died
Ah, me a so, gwir, he lazerez	I am, indeed, her murderess
Meur vech endoa din lavaret	More than once she told me
Dar Marquis Mezl n'hen rofen ket	Not to give her to the Marquis de Mezl
He roï kentoc'h da Kerthomas	But rather to give her to Kerthomas
Pini en doa ar muïa graçz.	For he was the kindest of them all.
Kerthomas ag ar vam diseuruz	Kerthomas and the distraught mother
Scoet gant eun taul ker truezuz	Shaken by such a heart-breaking event
Hô daou gonsacras da Zoue	Both devoted themselves to God
Er Claustr, ar rest eus hô pue.	In a cloister, for the rest of their lives.

Provenance:
Collected by Aymar de Blois from women in the village of Troudousten near Morlaix (Trégor), 1823. Published in Donatien Laurent, 'Aymar I de Blois (1760–1852) et "L'héritière de Keroulas"', pp. 415–27.

This *gwerz* was the first ever oral ballad to be the subject of a critical edition in France, thanks to the work of Aymar de Blois de La Calande, who wrote his account of the piece in 1823 and published it five years later. In 1839 another version was included in the *Barzaz-Breiz*, and it has been an important point of reference in discussions of the tradition ever since, proving as it did to a literary public that historical narrative songs, comparable to ballads found across Europe, could also be found on French soil. Some ten or so texts are known from right across Lower Brittany, though with only two tunes: the one given by Aymar de Blois is quite distinct from the air made popular by the *Barzaz-Breiz*.

The *gwerz* – Aymar de Blois used the French term *romance* – had all the necessary elements to capture the imagination of a cultivated reading public eager for long, dramatic and historical ballads preserved by an idealised peasantry. The song tells the story of the unhappy Marie de Keroulas, married against her will to François du Chastel, lord of Mesle and Châteaugal. The marriage, attested in written documents, took place in the early 1570s. The dramatic power of the *gwerz* derives from the young woman's heart-breaking farewells to her family, her sweetheart and the manor house where she has spent her childhood. The procession of paupers all weeping over her departure increases the sense of despair, and Marie's own death, the night she arrives at her husband's manor, is the tragic and inevitable denouement. In actual fact, the heiress died four or five years after her marriage, leaving three children behind her.

One distinctive feature of this piece not found in other *gwerziou* is the motif of wishing to be a little bird – first, in this version, Marie herself anxiously wishing to overhear her mother's plans for her future; and then her sweetheart Kerthomas, longing to be near her. Other versions of the ballad play some lovely variations on the theme. Several appear in the notebooks of Jean-Marie Perrot, who early in the 20th century collected a rich repertoire of songs in Léon, not far from the Keroulas domain:

Me garje beza koumik c'hlaz	I wish I were a little blue dove
War ar maner a Geroulaz	In Keroulas manor
Evit gwelet ar bennherez	To watch the heiress
O vont dar gousperou d'ar Vrelez.	Going to vespers at Brélès.
Me garfe beza goulmik wenn	I wish I were a little white dove
En he jardin war ur rozen	In her garden, on a rose
Pa deui da zestum bokedou	When she comes to pick a bouquet
Ni a raïo diskour hon daou.	The pair of us would talk.[1]

1   'Barzaz Bro-Leon' (unpublished collection in private hands).

The *pennhêrez*, the heiress of a good family, though not necessarily of the nobility, is a recurrent character in the *gwerziou*. Sometimes (as in no. 22) she has as her sweetheart a *kloareg* (a young cleric pursuing his studies); the tension of the ballad often revolves, as here, around rivalry for her hand which sets in play various questions about class and wealth. The emotional strength of the *gwerz* of Marie de Keroulas has made her a kind of exemplar of the romantic heroine forced to sacrifice her own happiness in the interests of the family name.

Studies:

Gaston de Carné, 'L'héritière de Keroullas'.

Donatien Laurent, 'Aymar de Blois (1760–1852) et les premières collectes de chants populaires bretons'. Republished in Donatien Laurent, *Parcours d'un ethnologue en Bretagne*, pp. 13–21.

Donatien Laurent, 'Aymar I de Blois (1760–1852) et "L'héritière de Keroulas"'.

14. Lord Villaudrain and the merchants

E ha Eouannik Berjen d'er vin eur, *lira*	Eouannik Berjen is going to the goldmines, *lira*
'Ben ma téi indro ne vo ket peur.	When he returns, he will not be poor.
Hag er boufamik koh e oé in ti	In the house there was a little old woman
Karget é halon a velkoni.	Her heart was filled with anxiety.
Er goh boufamik e oé ir manér	The little old woman was in the manor
Hag e droé bamdé ar er vangoér	And paced the battlements every day.
Troein e ré 'r boufamik dré er manér	The little old woman paced through the house
– Pegours téi Eouan Berjen d'er ger?	– When will Eouan Berjen come home?
Hi oeit a kriet dé a boez é fen	One day she shouted at the top of her voice
– Mé huél trégont jau in er vanden	– I see thirty horses in a group
Me huél Eouannick Berjen é tonet	I see Eouannick Berjen coming
Ardro geton hes seih kar karget	And with him seven carts full to the brim:
E beg er marh ketan er brid argant.	In the mouth of the first horse, a silver bit
E goust mat dehon er skouid ha kant	Which easily cost him a hundred and one *écus*
Lost er har ketan er perroked glas	Behind the first cart a green parrot
E ra d'em halon plijadur vras.	Which brings great delight to my heart.
– Keh charterion, touchet dous ha plain	– Dear cart-drivers, drive gently and straight
É passein doh porh er Villaudrain.	As you pass by the gates of Villaudrain.
Doh dor er Villaudrain, él ma passé	As he passed by the door of Villaudrain
Aoutrou Villaudrain er saludé	Lord Villaudrain saluted him

– Eouannik Berjen, deit té in me zi
Ha te goénio ardro genemb ni.

– Aoutrou er Villaudrain, ma em haret
D'er gér me lauskehet de vonet

D'er ger me lauskehet de vonet
Seih vlé bremann ir ger ne don bet.

– Eouannik Berjen, é men ho bet té
Ha pe doh oeit érauk ker pel sé?

– Me zo mé bet gol bel in doar neùè
Aveit klah er perroet glas-zé.

E beg er marh ketan en dés kroget
Hag ir marchausi dés er staget.

– Reit hui kerh de me jau, er pé garo
Rak marsé me buhé éon sauvo.

Eouannik Berjen gomans de sonné
Get er flaouit argant en deoé

Ne oé ket a galon vat é sonné
Més 'veit hirat 'n tammig é vuhé.

– Aoutrou er Villaudrain, ma em haret
É plas hou ti ne me lahet ket

Hui me haso é kreiz er marchausi
Ma huélein hoah me marh Tourlbandi.

– Naren, te varh Tourlbandi, 'n huélet ket
Rak ré abil tes bet eàn disket.

– Aoutrou er Villaudrain, ma em haret
Ne lausket ket men goéd de ridek

Pehed vé ma chuilh men goèd ar en doar
Rak me zo ag er ligné roïal.

– Eouannik Berjen, come into my house
And you shall dine in our company.

– Lord Villaudrain, if you love me
You will allow me to return home

You will allow me to go home
It is seven years since I was there.

– Eouannik Berjen, where have you been
Since you have been gone for so long?

– I have been far away in an unknown land
Searching for this green parrot.

He grabbed hold of the mouth of the leading horse
And tied it up in his stable.

– Give my horse all the oats he can eat
For he may just save my life.

Eouannik Berjen began to play
A silver flute he had with him

He did not play for pure pleasure
But to extend his life a little longer.

– Lord Villaudrain, if you love me
Do not kill me inside your house

Take me out to the stable
That I may see my horse Tourlbandi once more.

– No, you will not see your horse Tourlbandi
You have taught him too cleverly.

– Lord Villaudrain, if you love me
Do not allow my blood to flow

It would be a sin to let my blood flow to the ground
For I am of royal descent.

– Me mes mé chas, Eouan, més levréri E lipo te hoéd, p'en taulehi.	– I have dogs, Eouan, I have greyhounds To lick up your blood when it flows.
Eouan Berjen grié a boéz é ben – Forh sekour, oh me marh Tourlbannen!	Eouan Berjen cried with might and main – Help me, oh my horse Tourlbannen!
Er marh Tourlbannen, ha pe dés kleuet Tér dor hoarn ir porh e dés torret	The horse Tourlbannen, when he heard this Smashed through three iron doors in the castle
Ha pe devé torret er baderved Buhet é vestr en devé sauvet.	If he had smashed the fourth He would have saved his master's life.
Jardrin er Villaudrain hés bet kavet Seih kalon in en darn bod salet	In Villaudrain's garden were found Seven salted hearts in a broken pot
Ia, seih kalon in en darn bod salet Ré er varhaderion hostinet.	Yes, seven salted hearts in a broken pot Those of the murdered merchants.

Provenance:
Collected by François Cadic around Noyal-Pontivy (Vannetais). Published in *Paroisse bretonne de Paris* (1905), pp. 8–10. Republished in François Cadic, *Chansons populaires de Bretagne publiées dans la Paroisse bretonne de Paris*, pp. 167–9.

CD:
Track 10. Collected by Jude Le Paboul and the Cercle celtique de Baud from Emmanuel Le Sergent, Guénin (Vannetais), 1960. Dastum NUM-63917. Published in Éva Guillorel, *La Complainte et la Plainte: Chanson, justice, cultures en Bretagne*, CD track 9.

There are some 30 written and sound recordings of this ballad from all over Brittany, a few of them relatively recent. They divide into two branches, split roughly north and south. In the northern Trégor versions the murdered merchant is called Erwanig Prigent; in the southern Vannetais region he is most usually Ivon Berjen or, as in Cadic's text here, the variant Eouannik. Various features of the Trégor versions are absent from the southern versions, including extensive comparisons between the wealth of the merchant and the poverty of the nobleman who kills him; a dialogue between Erwanig Prigent and a maidservant whom he takes for the lady of the house (and to whom he offers his parrot); and an account of the dice-game organised after supper and won by the merchant. The Vannetais versions make more of the Ivon Berjen's exotic travels, and the role of his horse, who attempts to save him from his horrible fate.

The name of the murderous aristocrat is more stable than that of his victim, with all versions identifying him as Lord Villaudrain – a name which makes it possible to link even this fairy-tale-style ballad to a datable and locatable historical event. In the middle of the 17th century, the monks of Lantenac Abbey launched an enquiry into the circumstances surrounding the destruction and pillage of their monastery; Hervé de Kerguézangor, lord of Villaudrain, was found to have been heavily involved. Six witnessses present at this enquiry (four of them merchants) also described how he had murdered a group of merchants around the year 1569, a crime which led to his arrest and execution by the Parlement de Bretagne. The archives held at the abbey are brief and clearly dated; the ballad is expansive and full of vivid details but not anchored in place or time.

Interestingly, the murder seems to have taken place at Cadélac, which is on the francophone side of the linguistic border in Central Brittany. It is in Breton, however, that the account of the event has been preserved; one or two fragments of verse and some local stories collected in the 19th century suggest that there may well have been a French ballad on the same subject, which has not survived. The preservation of such a story over some four centuries in Breton oral tradition is remarkable; besides the song, a whole web of stories and legends concerning the sinister goings-on of Kerguézangor (and, subsequently, of his ghost) were collected by folklorists during the 19th century.

This is a real action ballad, full of vivid and dramatic scenes. In fact, it feels closer to the world of the Breton folk tale than many of the other *gwerziou*, with its mnemonic patterning, stylised characters and colourful, rather bizarre details. An old woman – who in some versions turns out to be the wife of Villaudrain – watches for passing travellers from the battlements of the manor house; sometimes armed with a telescope (*ul longuevu*) she can see them coming from seven leagues away. The merchant explains that he has spent seven years in the New World, and has brought back a multicoloured, trilingual parrot (*a oar al latinn, al gallek/kerkoulz ma oar ar brezonek:* 'which knows Latin and French as well as it knows Breton').[1] And Ivon Berjen's horse, hearing its master in trouble, smashes down three doors to come (usually, alas, in vain) to his aid.

The very last stanzas of the song are, as so often in the *gwerziou*, the part most susceptible to change. Most versions end with the death of the hero and his merchant companions, occasionally followed by the arrest and execution of Villaudrain and his wife (in that, at least, they coincide with the historical narrative). Four Vannetais versions recorded in the second half of the 20th century have – in an upbeat Hollywood ending – Ivon Berjen rescued by his faithful horse. The text given here is the only one to offer the strange and troubling final image of the seven salted hearts preserved in a pot. It was collected from an unknown singer in the Vannetais area and published in 1905 in the *Paroisse bretonne de Paris*, a journal aimed at Breton *émigrés* to the French capital.

---

1   François-Marie Luzel, *Gwerziou Breiz-Izel: Chants et chansons populaires de la Basse-Bretagne. Gwerziou I*, p. 464.

The song on the CD (no. 10) is one of the 'happy ending' versions, and replaces the horse with a dog which saves its master. It was recorded in the course of a *filaj* ('veillée', or evening singing session) at Guénin. Here all the participants respond to the lines sung by Emmanuel Le Sergent, according to a practice only found in Breton in the Vannetais region, but which is common in the francophone singing traditions of Upper Brittany.

Studies:

François Cadic, 'Le Sire de Villaudrain'. Republished in François Cadic, *Chansons populaires de Bretagne publiées dans la Paroisse bretonne de Paris*, pp. 167–9.

Éva Guillorel, *La Complainte et la Plainte: Chanson, justice, cultures en Bretagne,* pp. 242–59.

15. Fontenelle and his bandits

Fontenelle an eus grët lé	Fontenelle swore an oath
Biquen en Léon ne entréje	That he would never enter Léon
A gouscoude en neus lavaret gaou.	And yet he lied.
Tremenet gantan Plonevez ar Faou	After passing Plonévez-du-Faou
Méné Aré, Plougouvez	The Monts d'Arrée, Plougouves
Ar chapel nevez	And La Chapelle-Neuve
Fontenelle a houlenne	Fontenelle asked
En Coadelan pa arrué	At Coadélan, when he arrived
— Bonjour a joa en ty-man	— Greetings and joy to this household
Ar bennerez pelec'h e-man?	Where is the heiress?
— Ar bennerez a so cousquet	— The heiress is asleep
Teulet evoës ne diffunet.	Take care you do not wake her.
— Rey-tu dime an alc'houéau	— Hand me the keys
Mar de cousquet me he diffunau.	If she sleeps, I will wake her.
Ar bennérès à lavare	The heiress said
Da Fontenelle pa diffune	To Fontenelle when she awoke
— Me ne gredan quet a vale	— I do not dare to take a walk
Gant aoun rac Fontenelle	For fear of Fontenelle
Clevet em eus lavaret	For I have heard it said
Et tébauche merc'het, ac spécial pennerézet.	That he ravishes young girls, especially heiresses.
— Mar de rac Fontenelle et spontet	— If it's Fontenelle you fear
Eh dioutan e parlantet.	Then you are talking to him now.
Ar bennerez a lavare	The heiress said
De mathés vian eno neuse	To her little servant girl then
— Mathés vian am sicouret	— Little servant girl, help me now
Evit courage ne vanquan quet.	When it comes to courage I am not lacking.

Eun hach pennec a voa ganti	She had a sharp pointed axe
Ac e prétande er sceï.	And made as if to strike him.
Fontenelle a lavare	Fontenelle said
D'ar bennérés eno neuse	To the heiress then
– Pennérés n'em scoët quet	– Heiress, do not strike me
Péotramant c'hui a vo n'ec'het	Or it will be the worse for you
Mar galvan ma soudardet	If I call my soldiers
Pennérés enno e cren-fet.	Heiress, you will tremble then.
Fontenelle a houlenne	Fontenelle asked
Eus ar bennérés enno neuse	The heiress at that moment
– Pennerez din er lavaret	– Heiress, tell me, will you come
A c'hui a deufe ganen da zouar galled	With me into the land of France
Da gabitenés voar deir armé	To be captain of three armies
A da briet da Fontenelle?	And the wife of Fontenelle?
– Goel ec'he ganen mont da zouar ar Folgoët	– I'd rather go to the country around Le Folgoët
A hanné e voélin douar ma sat	From there I would see my father's lands
A ray vat d'am daoulagat.	And that would bring pleasure to my eyes.
Fontenelle a lavare	Fontenelle said
De pach bian enno neuse	To his little page then
– Pach bian, quet da houlen digor digant Mari	– Little page, go and ask Mary to let us in
Ma ne houlen quet diéri, tory	And if she will not open, break the door down
Lac an illis vras da varchossy	Turn the church into a stable
Ar secrétéri d'ar sellier ar guin	And the sacristy into a wine cellar
An n'auter vras da dol guiguin.	Make the high altar a dining table.
Pa voa guella ganté ar cher vat	As they sat there enjoying their meal
E commanças ar cleyer da brancellat	The bells began to ring
Fontenelle a leusque huannad	Fontenelle gave a sigh
– Pachic, pachic bian	– Page, oh little page
Te a so diligent ha buan	You are quick and lively

| Quet buan ebars en tour | Go swiftly up to the tower |
| Da c'hout piou a so eus o son. | To find out who is ringing. |

| Ar pach bian a lavare | The little page said |
| Deus an tour pa disquenne | When he came down from the tower |

| – Huellan ma hellan hon bet | – I went up as high as I could |
| Den a bet na m'eus guelet | And I saw nobody there |

| Nemet ar Voerc'hes ac et map | But the Virgin and her Son |
| A so o daou eus o brancellat. | Both ringing the bells. |

| Fontenelle a lavare | Fontenelle said |
| De soudardet eno neuse | To his soldiers then |

– 1200 soudardet a so ganen	– I have 1200 soldiers here with me
Profomp aman pep a scoët nevez	Let each leave one new *écu*
Ar bennérés a me a profo daouzec	The heiress and I will give twelve

| Ha deom-ni breman gant hon n'hent | And now let us be on our way |
| Ha laisomp ho zies gant ar sent. | And leave the saints to their own houses. |

| Fontenelle a c'houlenne | Fontenelle asked |
| En Trévrian pa arruë | At Trébriand when he arrived |

– Ma merrer dign e lavaret	– Farmer, tell me
Pelec'h e-ma ho merc'het?	Where are your daughters?
Unan a renquan da gaët.	I need one now.

| – Autro, mais ma excuset | – *Seigneur*, you will excuse me |
| N'o c'heus quet eom ma merc'het | But you have no need of my daughters |

| E m'an gannec'h pennérés Coadelan | You have with you the heiress of Coadélan |
| Coanta plac'h a so er bet-man. | The loveliest girl in the land. |

| Deut so liser da Fontenelle | A letter has come to Fontenelle |
| Da vont da gaët ar Roué. | He must go and speak with the king. |

| Fontenelle a lavare | Fontenelle said |
| D'eus Trévrian pa sortie | As he left Trébriand |

– Quen a vo da bardon Trémel
Mar bean bëo e theuin d'ar guer
Ma marvan e theui liser.

Fontenelle a lavare
En palès ar Roué pa arrue

– Bonjour Roué a Rouannès
Deut on do coëlet do palès.

Ar Roué a respontas
Da Fontenelle pa en clèvas

– Pa oh deut mat e viet
Evidoc'h d'ar guer n'a héet quet.

Fontenelle a respontas
Dar Roué pa en clèvas

– Re yaouanc ec'h eo da varna
Da laquat ar c'hanon-me d'ar maro.

Ar Roué a respontas
Da Fontenelle gant maliç bras

– Mar don-me ré yaouanc da varner
Té a so ré gos da ravager.

Fontenelle a lavare
De pach bian, eno neuze

– Pach, pach bian
Té so diligent a buan

Quet breman da Coadelan
Da vit eur c'houplat linceil moan dam lienan.

Ar Roué a respontas
Da Fontenelle pa en cleivas

– Farewell to the *pardon* at Trémel
If I live, I will return home
If I die, a letter will be sent.

Fontenelle said
In the king's palace as he arrived

– Good day to you, King and Queen
I have come to see you in your palace.

The king replied
To Fontenelle when he heard this

– Since you have come, you are welcome
You will not be going home.

Fontenelle replied
To the king when he heard this

– He is too young to judge
That I should be condemned to death.

The king replied
To Fontenelle with great spite

– If I am too young to judge
You are too old to lay waste to the land.

Fontenelle said
To his little page then

– Page, my little page
You are quick and lively

Go now to Coadélan
And fetch a pair of fine sheets to be my shroud.

The king replied
To Fontenelle when he heard him

– Salocroas, Fontenelle ne vet quet
E quartiero dispennet

– In heaven's name Fontenelle, you will not
Be torn into quarters

Dispennet é quartiero
A laquet voar coz inchau.

Torn up into quarters
And scattered on the old road.

Fontenelle a lavare
Dé pach bian eno neuze

Fontenelle said
To his little page then

– Pach bian, pach bian
Quet breman da Coadelan

– Little page, my little page
Go now to Coadélan

Da vuit eur plat alaouret
Da laquat ma fen pa vo trohet.

And fetch a gold platter
To carry my head when it is cut off.

Ar Roué a respontas
Da Fontenelle pa en cleivas

The king replied
To Fontenelle when he heard him

– Ne vit quet voar ar pavé tolet
Da ober boul hillaut dar vugalet.

– You will not be thrown onto the cobbles
For the children to play skittles.

Fontenelle a lavare
De pach bian eno neuzé

Fontenelle said
To his little page then

– Dal eur guichennat eus ma bleo melen
Da stagan eus pors Trévrian

– Take a few strands of my yellow hair
And tie them to the church door at Trébriand

Evuit ma laro Trevriennis
– Bénédiction Doué voar iné ar marquis.

So that the people of Trébriand will say
– The blessing of God be on the soul of the
     marquis.

Provenance:
Collected by Jean-François de Kergariou, Trémel (Trégor). Published by Chevalier de Fréminville as 'La complainte de Fontenelle', *Antiquités des Côtes-du-Nord*, pp. 392–5.

CD:
Track 11. Collected by Donatien Laurent from Jeanne-Marie Guyomarc'h, Clohars-Carnoët (Cornouaille), 1956. Archives du Centre de Recherche Bretonne et Celtique, Université de Bretagne Occidentale, Brest. Dastum NUM-a75253.

This *gwerz* on the death of La Fontenelle is well attested, and is yet another song linked to the religious Wars of the League from the last decade of the 16th century (nos 12, 16 and 17). It recounts three episodes from the life of the bandit leader Guy Éder de La Fontenelle. In the first, he kidnaps an heiress whom he subsequently marries, an event well documented in written sources – the girl in question was Marie Le Chevoir, the heiress of Coatezlan. The subsequent account of the church sacrilegiously turned into a stable and dining room is less 'factual', but concentrates in a single stylised scene a whole range of known depredations carried out by La Fontenelle and his men during this period of civil war: the pillaging of monasteries, massacres of local populations and attacks on towns – notably the west-coast port of Penmarc'h in 1595. The *gwerz* here uses traditional ballad clichés found in other songs, such as the bells which ring miraculously to repel the intruders (no. 12) and the little page who climbs the tower to see what is going on (no. 10). Finally, La Fontenelle's death (its violence evoked in this version curiously indirectly) is a reminder of his execution in Paris in 1602 – he was in fact condemned to the wheel, though the ballad versions offer various other scenarios.

Fascinatingly, given the facts of his career, La Fontenelle is a character who appears in the *gwerziou* in a largely sympathetic light (one might compare the cluster of anglophone folk songs similarly sympathetic to Napoleon).[1] He is often introduced as '*braoa den-jentil 'wisk dillat*' ('the handsomest gentleman who ever wore clothes'); the kidnap of the heiress takes place without either violence or dishonour, and La Fontenelle is invariably shown as unjustly condemned to death. Yet this positive portrayal is not, it seems, the result of a divergent popular tradition at odds with the written record (which has nothing good to say about him at all); there is no shortage of legends, expressions and proverbs, all collected orally, which paint him in a far blacker light. As early as 1839, the English traveller Thomas Adolphus Trollope was surprised to hear a range of terrible stories about him, a phenomenon also noted a few years later by François-Marie Luzel.[2] Other writers report that his name was regularly used to frighten disobedient children, and the author Pierre-Jakez Hélias recalled that in Cornouaille at the beginning of the 20th century it was still extremely insulting to say that someone came from the 'race de La Fontenelle'.[3]

The idealised view of La Fontenelle is thus restricted to the *gwerziou* – and links the Breton ballad tradition with a far wider international body of similar songs about outlaws and bandits influentially explored by Eric Hobsbawm in his book *Bandits* (1969). In the case of La Fontenelle, that sympathy is focused intensely through a transformative final scene, in which the suffering of the bandit-chief effectively absolves him from his crimes and turns him into a hero. Different versions summon up striking images to convey this: a golden plate is brought to hold the decapitated head; local children play skittles with it; and La Fontenelle himself asks that a lock of his blond hair be taken to the parish of his birth. Various features of this execution scene also appear in the *gwerz* on the death of the rather less violent Marquis de Pontcallec (no. 30), leading to a kind of narrative collision and conflation common enough in ballad traditions, and no doubt

---

1   Oskar Cox Jensen, *Napoleon and British Song 1799–1822*.

2   Thomas Adolphus Trollope, *A Summer in Brittany*, pp. 378–80; François-Marie Luzel, *Journal de route et lettres de mission*, p. 97.

3   Pierre-Jakez Hélias, *Le cheval d'orgueil*, p. 277.

thereby helping La Fontenelle's cause. A version from Trégor collected in 1980 by Ifig Troadeg from Yvonne Détente takes this to its logical conclusion and has the bandit chief vindicated and rescued by his devoted wife, who (as in no. 24) travels to Paris and persuades or threatens the king to release him.[4]

Most versions – over 20 of them – were collected from Trégor, the scene of many of his depredations, and are long and richly detailed. But the *gwerz* has travelled south, appearing in the Vannetais region as the far more spare and lyrical *Mab er Brigand* ('the brigand's son'). Following a distinct Vannetais aesthetic for stripped-down narrative (see no. 29) it reduces the unnamed protagonist's crimes to the symbolic theft of '*ur goh goutel hag ur mouched / Nag ur verh iouank de drihuéh vlé*' (an old knife, a handkerchief and a young woman of 18), and elevates his death to something almost Christlike, as he looks down from the scaffold to see his mother approaching, bearing a gold platter for his soon-to-be-decapitated head. A version collected by Loeiz Herrieu from Joachim Er Baill at Lanester finishes thus:

Rak, allas! me horv peur nen dei ket	For alas, my body will not follow
É kosté ur hlé é vou taolet	It will be thrown beside the ditch
É kosté ur hlé é vou taolet	Beside the ditch it will be thrown
De zèbrein get brandi ha piked.	To be eaten by crows and magpies.[5]

A similar ending can be found in the fine version of the *gwerz* collected by Donatien Laurent from Jeanne-Marie Guyomarc'h of Clohars-Carnoët (CD track 11). Besides the crows and magpies, she sings, the brigand's corpse will also be picked over by wolves and the big dogs from Pontcallec manor.

Studies:
Louis Le Guennec, 'Un épilogue ignoré de l'histoire de La Fontenelle'.
Julien Trévédy, 'Le dernier exploit de La Fontenelle'.
Éva Guillorel, *La Complainte et la Plainte: Chanson, justice, cultures en Bretagne*, pp. 463–75.
Mary-Ann Constantine and Gerald Porter, *Fragments and Meaning in Traditional Song*, pp. 173–80.
Yvon Le Rol, *La langue des 'gwerzioù' à travers l'étude des manuscrits inédits de Mme de Saint-Prix*, II, pp. 496–505.
Bernard Lasbleiz, 'Fontanella, un héros de chanson populaire'. Republished in Bernard Lasbleiz, *Ma'm bije bet kreion: Chroniques musicologiques du Trégor et autres pays de Bretagne*, pp. 125–8.

4   Ifig Troadeg, *Carnets de route*, pp. 40–1.
5   Loeiz Herrieu, *Guerzenneu ha soñnenneu Bro-Guened: Chansons populaires du pays de Vannes*, pp. 50–1.

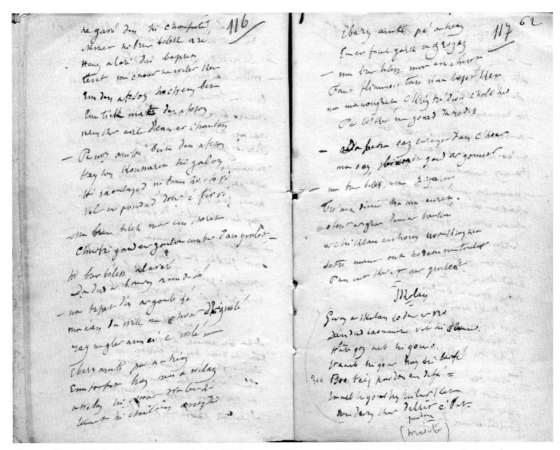

Pages from Théodore Hersart de La Villemarqué's second field notebook, containing the *gwerz* 'Skolvan', *c*.1841–2. (La Villemarqué family, private collection)

Plate 1

Plate 2

The singer Marc'harit Fulup (centre) with the collector Anatole Le Braz (fourth on right) and the daughter of singer and storyteller Barba Tassel (far right), in front of the birthplace of François-Marie Luzel at Plouaret during the inauguration of a commemorative plaque in his honour, 3 September 1906 (photo Joseph Ollivier, published in *Bretagne*, November–December 1930, p. 221. (CRBC-UBO-Brest))

Plate 3

The collector Donatien Laurent with the singer Maryvonne Goadec in her home
at Treffrin, Christmas 1967. (Photo Philippe-Étienne Raviart)

Plate 4

The *pardon* (saint's day pilgrimage) at Notre–Dame–de–la–Joie à Penmarc'h. Undated postcard (first half of the 20th century). Ed. Dantan. (Collection Dastum photo 7131)

Plate 5

The *grand pardon* at Notre-Dame-de-Folgoët. Undated postcard
(first half of 20th century). Ed. Hamonic. (Collection Dastum photo 13228)

Plate 6

The singer Yann Ar Rouz at home in Plounéour-Ménez, autumn 1974.
(Photo Roland Laigo)

Plate 7

The brothers Morvan singing at a *fest-noz* in August 1973. (Photo Daniel Le Couédic)

Plate 8

The singer Louise Le Bonniec on her doorstep at Pluzunet in 1981. (Photo Ifig Troadeg)

16. The kidnap and suicide of Jeannedic Ar Rous

Jeannedic ar Rous eo ar gaera
Zo crouet gant Doue er bed ma, allas.

Jeannedic Ar Rous is the fairest girl
Ever created by God in this world, alas.

– Va zad va mam c'hui ne doc'h quet fur
Laquad eured o merc'h da zul, allas

– Father, mother, you are not wise
To hold your daughter's wedding on a Sunday,
      alas

Me nac eb gouzout na clevet
Erru an Aotrou tremblet d'am guelet.

Before I knew or even heard about it
Lord Tremblet has come looking for me.

Ne voa quet e guer peur echuet
An Aotrou tremblet zo erruet.

Scarcely had the words been spoken
When Lord Tremblet arrived.

– Debonjour oll nac en ti-man
Ar plac'h neves peleac'h eman?

– Greetings to one and all in this house
Where is the newly married bride?

– Aman neus plac'h neves ebet
Nemet an dud en Oferen bred.

– There is no newly married bride here
Everybody is at high mass.

Neseu an Aotrou tremblet
D'an ilis a zo bet et.

And so Lord Tremblet
Went to the church.

– Digorit d'in me dor sacritiri
Pe me a gavo ar voyen de zerri.

– Open up the door of the sacristy
Or I will find a way to smash it down.

Dor sacritiri dezan zo digoret
Ar plac'h neves en deus cavet

The door of the sacristy was opened
And he found the newly married bride

A ioa ganthi eun habit seis melen
Evel gant merc'h eur c'habiten

Dressed in a gown of yellow silk
As befits the daughter of a captain

En e zreid eur botinezou satin guen
Eur c'hoef mountet var e fen.

On her feet, boots of white satin
A high *coiffe* upon her head.

Er plac'h neves en deus croguet
– A ganen me eo e teufet

He seized hold of the new bride
– You will come along with me.

– Va list da vont da guichen dor an ilis
Da lavaret adieu d'am broïs.

– Da guichen dor an ilis c'hui ne deot quet
Livirit alesse mar quirit Jeannette.

– Va list da vont da guichen dor ar porchet
Ma livirin adieu d'am fried allas.

– Da guichen d'or ar porched c'hui ne deot quet
Livirit allesse mar quirit Jeannette, allas.

– Adieu va mam adieu va zad
Adieu va fried evit mad, allas

Pa basein ti va mam a va zad
Mouchit d'in va daoulagad, allas

Mouchit din va daoulagad
Ma n'em bo quet quer bras calonad

Prestit din o poignard alaouret
Da drec'hi ceinturenic va eured

Da drec'hi ceinturenic va eured
A zo var va zro re stardet, allas.

Et boignard dezi en deus roet
Mes en e c'halon en deus en plantet.

– Ouman eo d'in me an drivac'hvet
Ag evit beza bet enlevet

Mes ouman eo an diveza
Pehini a laca va goad da yena.

Eun tantad tan zo bet gret
Ebars en e greis eo bet plantet, allas.

– Let me go at least to the church door
To say farewell to my family and neighbours.

– To the door of the church you will not go
Say your farewells here if you like, Jeannette.

– Let me go at least to the porch entrance
To say farewell to my husband, alas.

– You will not go to the porch entrance
Say your farewells here if you will, alas.

– Adieu my mother, adieu my father
Adieu my husband, for good, alas.

When I pass my mother and father's house
Cover my eyes for me, alas

Cover my eyes for me
So that I do not suffer so much.

Lend me your gilt dagger
That I may cut my wedding girdle

That I may cut my wedding girdle
It is too tight for me, alas.

He handed her his dagger
But she drove it into her heart.

– This is the eighteenth woman
I have abducted for myself

But this one is the last of all
She is the one who will make my blood go cold.

They have built a great pyre
And placed him at the centre, alas.

Provenance:
Song from the repertoire of Mme Noret, Ouessant (Léon). Sent by the singer to the song competition 'Barzaz Bro-Leon', 1906, collection Perrot. Published in Éva Guillorel, *Barzaz Bro-Leon: Une expérience inédite de collecte en Bretagne*, pp. 306–8.

CD:
Track 12. Collected in the 1970s by Jean-Yves Monnat from Jean Guégan, Kernascléden (Vannetais). Dastum NUM-65448.

This is the most widespread of the rich group of *gwerziou* dealing with events from the 16th-century Wars of the League. Over 30 versions are known from right across Brittany all the way to the west-coast island of Ouessant in Léon – a region which most 19th-century collectors wrongly believed to have little to offer in the way of oral traditions. In 1906, however, the young priest Jean-Marie Perrot organised a song-collecting competition under the title *Barzaz Bro-Leon*, with impressive results; the version given here was written down by the singer herself, Mme Noret, who contributed two school exercise-books filled with traditional songs. The ballad continued to be collected to the end of the 20th century; an example can be found in the version on the CD, collected in the 1970s from Jean Guégan in the Vannetais.

The ballad tells of René de La Tremblaye, a captain on the royalist side, who with his men carried out several highly destructive raids between 1590 and 1592 during the so-called Wars of the League. His actions are well documented in contemporary chronicles, none of which, however, mentions this episode of the kidnapping of Jeannedic Ar Rous. (The song, for its part, makes no mention of the crimes recorded in the written historical records.) Nevertheless, the clearly identified main protagonist, the backdrop of conflict between armed groups, and the reference in some versions to the Spanish soldiers who came to reinforce the *Ligueurs*, all point strongly to a historical context for the events related in the song.

This *gwerz*, however, is not at all interested in the broader aspects of the conflict, but dwells on the 'human interest' story of a young girl kidnapped on her wedding day who prefers to kill herself rather than lose her honour. Unlike the ballad of La Fontenelle (no. 15) the focus is firmly on the victim, her forebodings on her wedding morning, her forcible removal from the church where she has taken refuge, and her heartrending farewells to her loved ones. Other versions have Jeannedic hiding in a grave, while the priest pretends to be conducting a funeral in order to throw the men off track – the coloured ribbons of the congregation reveal the truth, and La Tremblaye takes her away. A version sung by Pierre Ollivier from Plussulien (Haute-Cornouaille) evokes this through a traditional sequence of questions and answers, often found in the *gwerziou*:

– Petra neve 'zo bet amañ	What is new here
P' emañ 'r merc'hed ker gwisket-mañ?	That the women are so finely dressed?
– Kapiten Tromble hon eskuset	– Captain Tromble, by your leave
Un interamant am eus bet.	I have just conducted a funeral.
– N'e' ket d'an interamañchoù	– It is not in order to go to funerals
'Douga 'r merc'hed kolinetoù	That women wear lace collars
Boukloù arc'hant war o boetoù	And silver buckles on their shoes
Ya d'un deme' pe d'un eured	But rather to an engagement party, a wedding
Pe d'un asamble gêr bennaket.	Or some other fine gathering.[1]

Jeannedic's suicide follows a familiar pattern, when she asks for a knife to cut the knot of her belt, or to loosen her dress, but then stabs herself in the heart. The trope of female honour and suicide occurs frequently in the *gwerz* repertoire (see no. 25), and reflects deep-rooted beliefs and expectations concerning the purity of women in a Catholic society. But it is the focus on personal tragedy that has, in all likelihood, kept this song alive over centuries, long after the original historical context, the lawlessness of the period of the League, has been forgotten. Many versions end with La Tremblaye regretting the deaths by suicide of all the young women he has kidnapped; Mme Noret's version, however, restores justice in a brusque, and conflagratory, final couplet.

Studies:
Éva Guillorel, *La Complainte et la Plainte: Chanson, justice, cultures en Bretagne*, pp. 453–8.
Laurence Berthou-Bécam and Didier Bécam, *L'enquête Fortoul (1852–1876): Chansons populaires de Haute et Basse-Bretagne*, II, pp. 564–7.

---

1   Yann-Fañch Kemener, *Carnets de route*, pp. 297–8.

17. Maharit Charlès and her bandits

C'houi a c'heus klevet e ze roud vad	Have you ever heard that any good
Klevet eur plac'h e c'houitellat?	Came of hearing a girl whistle?
Maharit Charles a c'huitelle	Maharit Charlès used to whistle
Hag a deus bet goall chanç a se.	And there was ill luck after that.
– Me zo groet din evel d'ar c'hi	– I am treated like a dog
A zo bet tollet e mes an ti	That is thrown out of the house
Zo bet tollet var ar pave	That is thrown onto the street,
Kris vije kallon merc'h na voëlche.	Cruel-hearted the girl that would not weep.
Hag hi o chonjal ober mad	And so, thinking to make the best of it
Mond da laeres d'ar c'hoad.	She became a bandit in the wood.
Er c'hoat pa zeo entreet	When she went into the wood
Pevarzek forban deus rankontret.	She met fourteen outlaws.
– Mar dan me da laeres d'ar c'hoat	– If I become a bandit in the wood
Me a ranko kaout eur gobri mad	I will have to have a fine reward
Eur siffl arc'hant da c'houitellat.	A silver whistle to whistle with.
Pevarzek forban a rankontras	She met fourteen outlaws
Da vont da laeres da ti he zad	Going to rob her father's house
Hag e mond a lavaret d'he	And she went and said to them
E vouie an douare gwel evit-he.	She knew the grounds better than they.
E ti he zad pa int arruet	When they arrived at her father's house
E voa ed an dud tout da kousket	Everybody had gone to bed
Nemet he breur hena na voa ket	Only her eldest brother had not
A voa or reï adkoan d'he ronset.	He was giving supper to his horses.
He breur hena e deus lazet	She killed her elder brother
A laket an tan var he ronset.	And set fire to his horses.

Ar Charles kos a lavare	Old Charlès said
De vugale eun deïs a voe	To his children one day
– Baleomp sioul dre ar c'hoat man	– Let us walk quietly through this wood
Va merc'h Maharit a zo enan.	My daughter Maharit lives in it.
Ne voa ket he hir peurachuet	Scarcely had he finished his words
E verc'h Vaharit an deus renkontret	When he met his daughter Maharit
E verc'h Vaharit ha rankontras	He met his daughter Maharit
Hag e lazas var ar plass.	And she killed him on the spot.
Maharit Charles na vouie ket	Maharit Charlès did not know
E voa he zad e devoa lazet	It was her father she had killed
Ken e voa goelet e vonnet	Till his hat was seen
Var ben eunan ar forbannet	On one of the outlaws' heads
Ken e voa goelet he gontel	Till his knife was seen
Var an dol en Koat an Drezen.	On the table in Drezen Wood.
Otrou Maner Koat an Drezen a lavare	The lord of Drezen Wood manor said
En Koat an Drezen pa errue	When he arrived in Drezen Wood
– Deud on do pedi, Maharit	– I have come to ask you, Maharit
Da zond da gomer dam priet.	To come as a godmother for my wife.
Maharit Charles a lavare	Maharit Charlès said to the lord
D'an otrou pa er c'hleve	When she heard this
– Parlantet sioula ma c'hellet	– Speak more softly if you can
Rag ar forbannet a zo kousket	Because the outlaws are asleep
A ma kleffent me ve gourdrouzet.	And if they heard I would be punished.
Otrou Maner Koat an Drezen a lavare	The lord of Drezen Wood Manor said
Da Vaharit Charles pa e c'hleve	To Maharit Charlès when he heard this
– Tollit ho droad var dailler va marc'h	– Put your foot on the stirrup of my horse
Neuze ni ielo sur avoalc'h.	Then we shall go, sure enough.

Otrou Maner Koat an Drezen a lavare
Er ger de dud pa errue

– Ma friedik, id en ho koële
Lavarit e zoc'h klan

Maharit Charles e zo deud aman

Pachik bien ke allesse
Lavar dan archerien dont ive.

An archer bras a c'houlenne
En Maner Koat an Drezen pa errue

– Petra zo a neves er maner-man
mar zon digemeret da zont aman?

An otrou sur a lavare
Dan archer bras pa er c'hleve

– Parlantet sioula ma c'helfet
rag Maharit Charles a zo tappet

Lamomp he c'hontellou digant-hi
He siffl arc'hant mar man ive.

– Maharit Charles deomp leveret
A ped paour kes o c'heus lazet?
Ag a ped dejentil o c'heus laeret?

– Seïz gontel zo em godellou
Ag an distera deus aneze
Nag a laze seiz den bemde.

– Maharit Charles, deomp leveret
A ped bugel ho c'heus bed?

– Seiz a meus bet deus va briet
A seiz all deus ar forbanet.

The lord of Drezen Wood Manor said
When he arrived home to his family

– My wife, go to your bed
And say you are ill

Maharit Charlès is here

Little page, go quickly now
And tell the soldiers to come here too.

The captain of the soldiers said
When he arrived in Drezen Wood Manor

– What is happening in this manor
That I am told to come here?

The lord said
To the captain when he heard this

– Speak more softly if you can
For Maharit Charlès is captured

Let us snatch her knife from her
Her silver whistle too, if it is here.

– Tell, us, Maharit Charlès
How many poor people have you killed?
How many gentlefolk have you robbed?

– In my pockets are seven knives
And the very smallest among them
Would kill seven men a day.

– Tell, us, Maharit Charlès
How many children have you had?

– I had seven by my husband
Seven more by the outlaws.

Entre Montroulez a Karhaez	Between Morlaix and Carhaix
Eus eur puns a zo leun a dres	Is a well full of brambles
Poent he d'he perc'hen dond d'he rinsan	It is time its owner cleaned it out
Pevarzek bugel e meus henan.	I have fourteen children in it.
Maharit Charles a zo bet	Maharit Charlès was dressed
Gwisket deï eun invis roussinet	In a resined shirt
Eun tam koar allumet	With a piece of lighted wax
A deus ar potenç krouget.	And hanged from the gallows.

Provenance:

'Ar Jarlezenn', collected by Jean-Marie de Penguern from Jannet Puill, beggar-woman, Henvic (Léon), 1851. Bibliothèque nationale de France, Fonds des manuscrits basques et celtiques, ms. 89, 'Chants populaires de Léon (Bretagne) recueillis par M. de Penguern', fols 144–8. Published in *Dastumad Pennwern*, 'Gwerin 5', pp. 121–3.

Maharit Charlès does not, unsurprisingly, appear in the *Barzaz-Breiz*. The heroines of La Villemarqué's re-envisioning of Breton tradition are almost all, to a woman, tragic in a submissive mode, loving, maternal and filled with spiritual grace. Fortunately for the richness of the recorded tradition, however, other collectors had fewer problems with this extravagantly wicked female bandit-chief, who seems once again to offer another distant reflection of the lawless period of the Wars of the League – though she may also have been associated in popular imagination with the outlaw Marion Tromel, known as Marion du Faouët, who led a bandit gang in the mid-1700s in Cornouaille. Maharit Charlès, operating in the Lieue-de-Grève area of Trégor, also figures in another *gwerz* as mentor and guide to the infamous Rannou brothers – thus hinting at something like a 'cycle' of outlawry ballads clustered around a central character, as happens in other song traditions.

The theme of female transgression is strikingly signalled from the unusual opening challenge: *'have you ever heard that any good/came of hearing a girl whistle?'* The widely held superstition that women whistling are 'unlucky' has much to do with crossing gender boundaries (as revealed in the Anglo-American saying 'a whistling girl and a crowing hen/will always come to no good end'). In the *gwerz*, much of Maharit's power is physically embodied in the little silver whistle (sometimes made of gold or ivory) which she uses to summon her men or frighten her enemies, and the authorities make quite sure that it is taken away from her after her capture. Her renown as an outlaw is expressed in some versions by the fact that the king of Spain and an army of 500 men are required to bring about her arrest.

This is a *gwerz* of interestingly unstable perspectives, beginning in the voice of Maharit herself and eliciting some sympathy for this rejected girl who is 'treated like a dog' at home, and seeks refuge with the outlaws in the wood. The trick which lures her out of her retreat – asking her to stand godmother to a neighbour's new child – also suggests that she can still be reached at a human level. But all the rest conspires to make her a monster, from the pint of human blood she drinks in a version collected by Luzel to the consecutive and cold-hearted murders of her brother and father.[1] Her public confession at the end of the ballad adds, almost gratuituously, a whole sequence of infanticides to her list of crimes (see no. 27 for further discussion of this theme) and distances her still further from the sympathy of her listeners.

There is, then, a certain fundamental tension at work in the piece, which at least suggests the interpretation (and again, no. 27 is an interesting parallel) that 'unnatural' women are the product of violence against them. This seems to be the case in a very detailed version of this *gwerz*, some 50 couplets long, written down by Constance Le Mérer in Trégor.[2] Here Maharit's final words are chilling but also fiercely angry and unrepentant, and hark back again to her cruel treatment by her own family:

Me am eus ter c'hoar er gêr-man	I have three sisters in this town
Ter itron eus ar re vraouan	Three fine ladies, beauties all,
Ha ne brizont o fenn plegan	And they will not deign to bow their heads
'Vit sellout ouz ho c'hoar henan	And look at their elder sister
Ma dije ma lez-vamm roet	If my stepmother had given me
D'in dilhad hag eun tammig boed	Some clothes, and a bite to eat
Me na vijen ket bet kavet	I would not have been found
'Pad tri de korn a velaneg	For three days in the bushes of the broom
Etre Montroulez ha Tredrez	Between Morlaix and Trédrez
A zo eur c'hoad karget a drez	Is a wood full of brambles
Tri-c'hant penn maro 'zo ennan	Three hundred skulls lie therein
Me 'meus sikouret o lazan	I helped to kill them
Foiltr-forz da vervel ne rajen	I don't care about dying
Ma ve roet d'in ma goulen	If my final wish is granted
Me garfe kaout galon ma zad	To have my father's heart
Tre an douar ha seul ma zroad.	Between the earth and the sole of my foot.

Studies:
Mary-Ann Constantine, *Breton Ballads*, pp. 196–7.
Alain Croix, *L'âge d'or de la Bretagne*, pp. 68–9.
Désiré Lucas, 'La Lieue de grève en Trégor, un espace de légende'.

1   François-Marie Luzel, *Gwerziou Breiz-Izel: Chants et chansons populaires de la Basse-Bretagne. Gwerziou II*, pp. 74–9.
2   Collection Constance Le Mérer, cahier 13, p. 4. Published in Constance Le Mérer, *Une collecte de chants populaires dans le pays de Lannion*, pp. 142–6.

18. Love and leprosy: Iannik Kokard

Iannik Kokard a Blouilliau	Iannik Kokard from Ploumilliau
Braoa mab kouer 'zo er vro	Is the finest farmer's son in the land
Ar pabor euz ann holl baotred	Flower[1] of all the young men
Kalonik ann demezelled.	Darling of the girls.

Pa 'z ee Iann Kokard d'all Lew-Dreaz	When Iann Kokard went to the Lieue-de-Grève
Ar merc'hed koant 'lamme e-meaz	The pretty girls jumped up and ran out
Ann eill d'eben a lavare	Saying to each other
– Iannik Kokard 'zo vont aze.	– There goes Iannik Kokard.

Iannik Kokard 'n euz lavaret	Iannik Kokard said
Er ger, d'he dut, p'eo arruet	To his parents when he got home
– Ma zad, ma mamm, mar veoc'h kontant	– Father, Mother, if you don't mind
Me eureujfe ur plac'hik koant	I want to marry a pretty girl

Me eureujfe Mari Tili	I want to marry Mari Tili
Ur madou-braz 'roër gant-hi	They're giving a fine dowry with her
Reï 'reur d'ez-hi seiz komanant	They're giving her seven farms
Ha leiz ar bouezell a arc'hant	And a bushel full of silver

Leiz ar veol-vraz a neud-gwenn	A big tub of white yarn
Ur c'harr houarnet hag un denn.	A cart with iron fittings and a harness.
Ar C'hokard-koz a lavare	Old Kokard said then
D'he vab Iannik, eno neuze	To his son Iannik

– Mari Tili n'ho pezo ket	– You shall not have Mari Tili
Rag dac'h ha dimp 've rebechet	We, and you, would be blamed
Dac'h-c'hui ha dimp 've rebechet	We would be blamed and so would you
Rag ur gakouses ho pe bet.	For marrying a *kakouses*.

– Ma zad, ma mamm, da vihana	– Father, Mother, at least
Ma lest da vont da bardona	Let me go to the *pardon*
Ma lest da vont da bardona	Let me go to the *pardon*
D'ar Folgoat, pe d' Zantes-Anna.	To Le Folgoët or to Sainte-Anne.

---

1   *Pabor* literally means 'bullfinch'.

– Mar et d'ar pardon d'ar Folgoat
Doue ra reï dac'h beaj-vad
Doue ra reï dac'h beaj-vad
D'ho tud er ger kezelo mad.

Pa oa o tremenn Montroulez
Hag hen o kaout he Gakousez
– Iannik Kokard, ma c'harante
Na pelec'h et-c'hui er giz-se?

– Me 'ia da bardon ar Folgoat
Dilour, diarchenn, war ma zroad.
– Iannik Kokard, ma c'harante
Ma lest da vont ganec'h iwe

Da c'houlenn 'r c'hraz digant Doue
Ma kouskfomp er memeuz gwele
Kousket 'n ur memeuz gwelead
Debri er memeuz skudellad.

Euz a Vontroulez da Blouvorn
Ez int et ho daou dorn-euz-dorn.
Mari Tili a lavare
Toul porz hi zad pa dremene

– Iannik keiz gortoït un tamm
Ma'z inn en ti da gaout ma mamm
Da c'houlenn ha 'zo peadra
Da rei d'imb hon daou da goania.

– Ma merc'hik, me am euz klewet
Iannik Kokard 'zo dimezet
Pa vezo ouz taol o koanian
Ma merc'h, goulennit digant-han

Euz ma laro, mar eo kristenn
Roït d'ez-han he groaz-nouenn
Roït d'ez-han he groaz nouenn
Un arched a bewar flankenn.

– If you go to the *pardon* at Le Folgoët
May God grant you a pleasant journey
May God grant you a pleasant journey
And good tidings to your family at home.

As he was passing by Morlaix
He happened to meet his *kakouses*
– Iannik Kokard, my beloved,
Where are you going like that?

– I'm going to the *pardon* at Le Folgoët
Sockless, shoeless, and on foot.
– Iannik Kokard, my beloved,
Let me go with you too

To ask grace of God
That we might sleep in the same bed
To sleep in the same bed
And eat from the same bowl.

From Morlaix to Plouvorn
They went, hand in hand.
Mari Tili said
Passing the door of her father's house

– Iannik dear, wait a little
While I go in to find my mother
And ask her if she has anything
To give us both for supper.

– My daughter, I have heard
Iannik Kokard is married
When he's at table eating
My daughter, ask him then

From what he says, if he is a Christian
Give him his last rites
Give him his last rites
And a coffin with four planks.

– Iannik Kokard, ma c'harante
Anzaovit d'inn ar wirione
Anzaovit d'inn ar wirione
Ha c'hui 'c'h euz groeg ha bugale?

– Iannik Kokard, my beloved,
Admit the truth to me
Admit the truth to me
Have you a wife and children?

– Ia, me 'm euz groeg ha bugale
Me garrie beza 'r ger gant-he.
– Iannik Kokard, ma c'harante
Evit 'r banne diganin-me

– Yes, I have a wife and children
And I wish I was with them.
– Iannik Kokard, my beloved,
Drink a glass with me

Na roinn ket d'ac'h a winn-gwenn
Gant aouenn na zavfe d'ho penn
Me diskenno dac'h gwin-kleret
Wit ma roï dac'h nerz da gerzet.

I shall not give you white wine
In case it goes to your head
I shall pour you some fine red wine
To give you strength for walking.

P' iee Iannik Kokard da vouit dour
Na ouie ket ez oa klanvour
Na ouie ket ez oa klanvour
Ken a zellas ebars an dour.

When Iannik Kokard went to fetch water
He did not know he was ill
He did not know he was ill
Till he looked in the water.

Bars ar feuntenn dre ma selle
Gant al laournes e tispenne.
Iannik Kokard a lavare
D'he dad, d'he vamm, pa arrue

When he looked into the well
He was falling to pieces with leprosy.
Iannik Kokard said
To his father and mother when he arrived

– Ma zad, ma mamm, mar am c'haret
Un ti-newez d'inn a zavfet
Zavet-han d'inn en lez al lann
Tost d'ann hent a ia da Zant Iann

– Father, Mother, if you love me
Build me a new house
Build it on the edge of the moor
By the path which goes to Saint-Jean

Grit ur prennestr en he bignon
Ma welinn ar prosession
Ar baniel braz a Blouilliau
O vont etrezeg Sant Kado.

Make a window in the gable end
For me to watch the procession
With the great banner from Ploumilliau
Going towards Saint-Cado.

Ar baniel braz tro ar vered
Hag a wes am euz-han douget
Mar 'm euz-han douget lies-braz
N'hen douginn ken brema siouas.

How often I carried it
Around the churchyard, that great banner
Yes, I carried it many times
But not any more, alas.

He dad he vamm a lavare	His father and mother said
D' Iannik Kokard eno neuze	To Iannik Kokard then
– Iannik Kokard, d'in lavaret	– Iannik Kokard, tell us
Gant petra ez oc'h bet laouret?	What has given you leprosy?
– O eva gwinn, leiz ar werenn	– Drinking wine, a full glass
Digant ur plac'hik a garienn	Poured by a girl I loved
O eva gwinn ampouezonet	Drinking wine, poisoned
Gant ur gakouses milliget.	By a cursed *kakouses*.
Mari Tili a lavare	Mari Tili said
En Montroulez pa arrue	When she got back to Morlaix
– Trichouec'h kloarek am euz karet	– I have loved eighteen clerks
Hag ho zric'houec'h am euz laouret.	And given leprosy to all eighteen.
Iannik Kokard, ann diwesa	Iannik Kokard, the last
Laka ma c'halon da ranna	Has broken my heart
Ur strill-goad euz ma biz-bihan	One drop of blood from my little finger
A laourfe kant, koulz hag unan.	Could poison a hundred as easily as one.

Provenance:
Song collected by Prosper Proux from an unknown singer, Plouigneau (Trégor), 1863. Included in a letter sent to François-Marie Luzel and published in François-Marie Luzel, *Gwerziou Breiz-Izel: Chants et chansons populaires de la Basse-Bretagne. Gwerziou I*, pp. 252–8.

Iannik Kokard is both well represented and extremely localised. Over a score of versions collected from the mid-19th century onwards cover much the same area as the place names in the *gwerz*. This exceptionally clear version was sent to Luzel by the local poet Prosper Proux; it may have been tidied up by the latter, but the number and nature of the versions put its traditional origin beyond doubt.

The ballad could be historical; a Kokard family owned land in Ploumilliau from at least 1550, and the name Tili (Tilly) has been common in and around Morlaix for many centuries. Local place names such as Ar C'hlandi ('house of the sick') near Ploumilliau reflect the earlier presence of leper colonies, and there are well-documented exclusion trials from the 1470s. Though exact definitions of what may or may not constitute leprosy are famously contested, the disease is thought to have died out in Brittany by the end of the 16th century, suggesting that the ballad could be at least this old. The word *kakous* (fem. *kakouses*) does, however, have a complex history; after leprosy disappeared it was used to designate an 'unclean' social group, often barrel or rope-makers, the probable descendants of excluded leper communities – the barrel of *neud gwenn* ('white yarn') in Mari's dowry may refer to this. Yet the strong presence of the disease in the *gwerz*, coupled with the tight correspondence of names and places, is certainly intriguing. The song also refers to the *pardons*, or local pilgrimages, of Le Folgoët and Sainte-Anne-d'Auray, at the height of their importance in early modern Brittany, and often mentioned in the *gwerziou* (no. 4).

Historical or no, the event at the heart of this ballad has been thoroughly adapted to the genre. Mari is a demonic figure, the disease personified; her meeting with Iannik has the resonance of myth. In some versions Iannik asks *not* to be sent to the market where she sits waiting for him at a table piled high with food. The choice between life and death is made starkly iconographic, as in this example collected by Luzel from Mari-Yvonne Le Roy, a servant girl from Plouaret:

Gant-hi'n hi daou-dorn diou werenn	She holds two glasses in her hands
Unan gwinn-ruz, un' all gwinn gwenn.	One of red wine, one of white.[2]

The pivotal moment, when the girl's love turns to hate, is obscure. Here, Iannik's mysterious 'marriage' proves fatal; elsewhere Mari is motivated by an insult from his family. Both are clearly formulaic, that is, generic rather than realistic interpretations of events. Formulaic, too, are the 'eighteen' clerks or clerics whom Mari claims to have killed. The fears of blood, sex and contamination that haunt this *gwerz* are unusually relevant; a striking modern parallel appeared in Ireland in the mid-1990s, with reports of the Dungarvan 'Angel of Death', thought to have infected dozens of local men with the AIDS virus. She proved increasingly shadowy as focus turned from the details of the story to its source.[3] The dramatic potential of the *gwerz* was recognised by the writer Henry Bataille; his play, *La Lépreuse*, performed in Paris in 1896, was based on Luzel's text.

Stanzas from 'Iannik Kokard' surface in the gwerziou 'Mari Derrienig' and 'Ar C'hakous', both of which deal with leprosy. 'Mari Tili', perhaps coincidentally, is the name of another dark character in a ballad on the desecration of the Eucharist.

Studies:
Mary-Ann Constantine, 'Story and History in the Breton Ballads: the Case of *Iannik Kokard*'.
Mary-Ann Constantine, *Breton Ballads*, pp. 83–128.

---

2   François-Marie Luzel, *Gwerziou Breiz-Izel: Chants et chansons populaires de la Basse-Bretagne. Gwerziou I*, p. 264.
3   *The Times*, 13 September 1995.

19. Janedig the witch

Janedig koant hag he c'hamarad	Lovely Janedig and her companion
O vonet da bardon ar Ieodet.	Are going to the *pardon* at Le Yaudet.
Janedig koant oa ur plac'h kollet	Lovely Janedig was a fallen woman
Biskoazh na nevoa den gwelet	But no-one had ever realized this
Ken a oa he c'hompagnon o vont ganti	Until her companion travelled with her
Da bardon ar Ieodet.	To the *pardon* at Le Yaudet.
'Barzh ar Ieodet pa eo antreet	As they entered Le Yaudet
Daou barkad ed hi he deus gwelet.	She saw two fields of wheat.
Ar c'hentañ parkad ed he deus gwelet	When she saw the first field of wheat
D'he c'hompagnon hi he deus laret	She said to her companion
– Sell aze, 'me'i, ur parkad kaer a ed	– Look there, she said, at that fine field of wheat
'Benn a teufomp d'ar ger, eme'i ne vo ket	When we return, she said, it will no longer be here
Kar 'benn neuze a vo tout grilhet.	Because by then it will be burnt to a crisp.
He c'hompagnon ken souprenet	Her companion was so surprised
Netra 'bet de'i en 'eus respontet.	That he did not answer.
Ur pennad bihan duzhtu goude	A short moment later
Ar memestra hi a lavare	She was saying the same thing again
– Sell aze, 'me'i, ur parkad kaer a segal	– Look there, she said, at that fine field of rye
'Benn ma teufomp d'ar gêr 'vo aet tout, 'me'i, da bigal.	When we go home, she said, it will be all tares.
He c'hompagnon ken koleret	Her companion was so angry
En-dro d'ar gêr ganti eo duzhtu retornet.	That he took her straight back home.
– Hastomp buan 'ta Janedig, hastomp buan	– Let us make haste, Janedig, let us make haste
Dont d'ar gêr hom-daou	To return home, both of us
Me a wel arri glao, dared, oraj ha kuruno	I see rain and lightning, storm and thunder
Hastomp buan dont d'ar gêr en-dro.	Let us make haste to get home at once.

E-barzh ar gêr hi pa eo arriet
He zud a zo bet kalz estonet.

When she arrived at home
Her parents were very surprised.

– Pera 'sinifi 'ta kement-se
Pa oc'h deut d'ar gêr, 'ta ken prim-se?

– What does all this mean
That you are back home so soon?

– Gwel' a raen 'n amzer ken fall stummet
Donet d'ar ger a meump soñjet.

– I saw that the weather was turning bad
I thought it was better to come back home.

Pa oa Janedig gant he mamm e-barzh an ti
     antreet
He c'hompagnon d'he zad eñ en deus lâret

As Janedig went inside with her mother
Her companion spoke to her father

– Me, 'me'añ 'zo evidoc'h kalz poaniet
Me ma un' 'zo ivez koñtristet
'Welet peseurt merc'h a 'peus savet.

– I am, he said, very anxious for you
And deeply saddened for myself
When I see the kind of daughter you have raised.

Janedig 'zo ur plac'h kollet
Daou barkad ed he deus gwallet
En ur antren hent ar Ieodet.

Janedig is a fallen woman
She has spoiled two fields of wheat
Going along the road to Le Yaudet.

He zad pa glevas kement-se
D'he c'hompagnon en 'eus lâret

Her father, when he heard all this
Said to her companion

– Kerc'het duzhtu, 'me'añ, ar jañdarmed
Evit ma vo prim aretet.

– Go quickly, he said, fetch the *gendarmes*
So she can be arrested at once.

Pa eo arri ar jañdarmed deus he c'herc'het
Janedig zo n'em gav't estonet.

When the *gendarmes* came to fetch her
Janedig was surprised.

– Nimp, Janedig, 'zo deut d'ho kerc'het
'Vit an daou barkad ed ho peus gwallet
En ur antren hent ar Ieodet.

– Janedig, we have come to arrest you
Because of the two fields of wheat you ruined
Going along the road to Le Yaudet.

– Gwelet 'm eus, 'me'i, daou barkad ed gwallet
'Met na n'eo ket me en 'eus o gwallet.

– I saw, she said, two ruined fields of wheat
But I did not spoil them.

– Ho kompagnon oa ganeoc'h en 'eus gwelet
Hag 'velse eo deut da lâret dimp donet d'ho
     kerc'het

– Your companion was with you and saw it all
And he came and told us to arrest you

Ha ganimp d'ar prizon e teufet	And you will come with us to jail
Ken a 'po tout diwimp ansavet.	Until you have confessed everything.
'Pad eizh devezh eo bet prizoniet	For eight days she was kept as a prisoner
'Rok he deva netra 'bet anzavet.	And she did not confess anything.
An eizhvet devezh 'deus anzavet	The eighth day, she confessed
D'ar jañdarmed.	To the *gendarmes*.
Neuze p'he deus dionte anzavet	Once she had confessed
Neuze d'ar justis eo kaset	She was sent to the officers of justice
Neuze d'ar justis eo kaset	She was sent to the officers of justice
Aze neuze eo bet barnet	And there she was condemned
Nag evit beañ distrujet.	To be executed.
Ar juj en 'eus dionti 'ta goulet	The judge asked her
– Lâret dimp 'ta, Janedig	– Tell us now, Janedig,
Bremañ pa oc'h barnet, bremañ pa oc'h barnet	Now you are judged, now you are judged
Pelec'h ho poa disket	Where did you learn
E vije ed gwallet?	How to spoil wheat?
– E gant ur mesaer deñved	– With a shepherd
a oa bet savet e ti ma zad	Who had been raised in my father's house
Ha me ac'h ae gantañ bemnoz	And I went with him every night
Da glevet ar sabad	To hear the Sabbath
Da glevet ar sorserien	To hear the sorcerers
Nag ar sorserezed	And the witches
Ha me, 'me'i, a oa yaouank	And, she said, I was young
Allas din, am 'a desket.	And alas for me, I learnt.
– Lâret din neuze Janedig	– Tell us now, Janedig
Bremañ pa oc'h barnet, bremañ pa oc'h barnet	Now you are judged, now you are judged
Pera e vije ganeoc'h	What did you use
Pa pije an ed gwallet?	In order to spoil the wheat?
– Gant lagad kleiz ur malbran	– A raven's left eye
E nag kalon un toñseg	And a toad's heart

An had dimeus ar raden
Ha pa vije divraniet.

And a bracken seed
Taken when ready to fall.

– Lâret din neuze, Janedig
Bremañ 'ta pa oc'h barnet, bremañ 'ta pa oc'h
    barnet

– Tell us now, Janedig
Now you are judged, now you are judged

Pegoulz dimeus an amzer
A vez ar raden greuniet?

At what moment in time
Is bracken ready to drop its seed?

– En noz pardon Sant Yann
An eur an hanternoz, an eur an hanternoz
'N noz-se gant ur plad arc'hant
Me 'm 'a serret 'ne 'n ma boz

– During the night of Saint John's *pardon*
At midnight, at midnight:
That night, with a silver plate
I held it in the palm of my hand

An noz-se e c'hreuniont hag e tic'hreuniont
E nag e adc'hreuniont hag adarre
An hini 'n 'eus c'hoant d'ho daspign
Klask ane' an noz-se.

That night, they mature and drop their seeds
and bring forth new seeds immediately
Whoever wants to collect them
Must do it during that same night.

– Lâret din neuze 'ta Janedig
Bremañ 'ta pa oc'h barnet, bremañ 'ta pa oc'h
    barnet

– Tell us now, Janedig
Now you are judged, now you are judged

Pere eo ho kerio diwe'añ
A-raok ma vefet distrujet?

What are your last words
Before you are executed?

– Ma c'h on, 'me'i, 'ta bremañ na da ve'añ
    distrujet
Hag a vije bet well din birviken a vijen bet ganet

– If I must be executed now, she said
Better for me never to have been born

Peotramant e war-lerc'h ma badeiant
E oan diaset d'ar vered

Or, after my baptism
Better I had been taken straight to the graveyard

'Vit se vije ket ma zud e-war ma lerc'h
Gant ar galon rannet
'Vije ket ma zud 'war ma lerc'h
Gant an holl mepriset

That way my parents would not be
Broken-hearted after my death
That way my parents would not be
Despised by all, after my death

Kar ne n'eus nemerton, emezi, ma unan
Hag ken a zo kiriek.

Because, she said, I am the only one here
Myself alone, who is guilty.

Sell, nag eo ma ger diweañ	This, then is my final word
Ma c'h on da veañ distrujet.	If I must be executed.

Provenance:

Collected by Ifig Troadeg from Louise Le Bonniec, Pluzunet (Trégor), 1979. Published in Ifig Troadeg, *Carnets de route*, pp. 60–2, 'Jannedig koant'; and in *Tradition chantée de Bretagne. Les sources du Barzaz-Breiz aujourd'hui*, CD track 12.

CD:

Track 13. Same version.

Witchcraft, as opposed to divinely sanctioned manifestations of the miraculous, is a relatively rare phenomenon in the *gwerz* tradition. Three ballads mention it (see also no. 20), but this is the most widespread and the most precise in its description of the magic rituals concerned. It appears among the earliest collections, including those of Barbe-Émilie de Saint-Prix and of La Villemarqué – the latter notoriously identifying the miscreant girl as the 12th-century nun Héloïse, lover of Peter Abelard – and has continued to be sung and collected. The long and detailed version given here was collected in 1979 from a notable singer of *gwerziou*, Louise Le Bonniec (also known by her married name, Mme Riou) whose interpretation of the piece is remarkable both for the quality of the text and for its exceptional melodic approach. Every couplet offers a different variation on the tune, making it impossible to transcribe satisfactorily. Once again the action takes place on the way to a *pardon*, or local pilgrimage, this time at Le Yaudet, one of the key pilgrimage sites in Trégor.

Brittany was largely spared the wave of witch hunts and paranoia which swept through Europe in the 16th and 17th centuries, and so precise descriptions of would-be magical rituals or practices are thin in the written archives. Various forms of 'deviancy' were regularly condemned in a more general fashion by the missionaries who came into Brittany from the 1600s, and the zealous Jesuit leader Julien Maunoir was particularly preoccupied by what he felt was a widespread interest in 'demonism', reflecting the church's own anxieties about non-orthodox forms of religious behaviour. The ballad does in fact describe several practices mentioned in Maunoir's writings and in other treatises on witchcraft in this period. The most striking of these is the spoiling of wheat, partly accomplished through the power of fern or bracken-seed collected under the right conditions; comparing Louise Le Bonniec's account with other versions, it appears that the seed must be collected on St John's Eve (24 June) between eleven and midnight, and that the final mixture must crucially contain another plant which the young girl refuses to name. Folk belief in the magical properties of the mysterious 'fern-seed' (they actually propagate by spores) can be found right across Europe; as Shakespeare knew, it was thought to confer invisibility: 'we have the receipt of fern-seed', says one of Hal's friends, 'we walk invisible' (*Henry IV*, act 4).

Many versions of this *gwerz* contain a final curse spoken by the witch. This, collected by Luzel from the blind singer Garandel in 1849, is a particularly memorable example:

Me 'm euz ur c'houfik-bahut er ger, en ti ma zad	I have a strong-box at home, in my father's house
Hag ann nep hen digoro hen defo kalonnad	Whoever opens it, their heart will fail them
Ann hini hen digoro renko kaout kalon frank	Whoever opens it must have a strong heart
'Zo en-han ter aer-wiber o c'hori ur serpant	For inside there are three vipers, incubating a serpent
Ma deu ma zer aerik da ober bloavez-mad	And if my little snakes are to thrive
A renkont beza bewet gant ur boued dilikad	They must be fed with delicate meats
A renkont beza bewet gant ur boued dilikad	They must be fed with delicate meats
Ma eo gant kik glujar ha kik kefeleged	Like the flesh of the partridge or the woodcock
Hag iwe ar goad roïal euz ann inosanted	And also with the royal blood of innocents
Pa 'z aint wit beza badet, da doull dor ar porchet	When they are taken to be baptised at the porch
Ha kent ma vankfenn-me d'ober d'ez-he er-vad	Rather than see them go without
Me deufe da rei d'ez-he goad ma mamm ha ma zad.[1]	I would give them the blood of my mother and my father.

If a single one of these snakes escapes, she warns, it will set the firmament alight and upset the whole world. Various versions include details of Janedig's ability to prevent priests from saying mass or consecrating the host. Black magic concerning profanation of the host can be found in another *gwerz*, that of 'Mari Tili', who takes communion eight times and keeps the host hidden in her mouth, so that later she can shape them into the figure of a child and injure it; this is not a popular ballad, attested in only one orally collected version and as a broadside. It links in to a wider literature (and visual representation) of host-profanation, often linked to anti-Semitic texts, which ultimately derives from the sensational world of medieval Latin *exempla*.

Studies:

Yvon Le Rol, *La langue des 'gwerzioù' à travers l'étude des manuscrits inédits de Mme de Saint-Prix*, II, pp. 359–69.

Fañch Gourvil, *Théodore-Claude-Henri Hersart de La Villemarqué (1815–1895) et le 'Barzaz-Breiz' (1839–1845–1867)*, pp. 426–8.

Éva Guillorel, *La Complainte et la Plainte: Chanson, justice, cultures en Bretagne*, pp. 400–1.

---

1   François-Marie Luzel, *Gwerziou Breiz-Izel: Chants et chansons populaires de la Basse-Bretagne. Gwerziou I*, p. 52.

20. The wax child

Poularfuntun a houlenné
Deus a notro Bistigo eunn dé a voé
– Pelec'h a hoc'h bed pe a heo
Pe a heus esper da voned?

– Ma a ha da stal ma stal
Da choas eunn nétof incarnat
A dentelès or a ré arhant
Dam fennerès a zo eur plac'h coant.

– Ma ouïffec'h ar pés a houn mé
Birviquen habit na déffé
Honas a neus groet eur buguel coar
Do lémmel divoar an douar

Taër goech a dé a vé tommed
Taer goéch an dé a vé broudet
A nen brouder goech gand ar spillo
Otro, na diver ô coazeou.

– Poularfuntun, din a lered
Pelèc'h a hè ar buguel se badéet?
– Badéet è ar buguel coar
En ilis vras a Landréguar
Deus éôl golo a loar.

– Poularfuntun, din a lered
Ar gompèrien piou a hint bed?
– O mevel bras êo ar homper
Ac ar vatés vian ar gommer.

– Poularfuntun, din a lered
Piou a neus ar buguel badéet?
– Ehè eur bèlèguic ïoanq
Evit caod eur sommic arhant

Poularfuntun asked
Monsieur Bistigo one day
– Where have you been, where are you going
Where do you hope to go?

– I am going from shop to shop
To choose some scarlet material
With gold and silver lace
For my heiress, a beautiful girl.

– If you knew what I know
She would never have clothes again.
She has made a child of wax
To remove you from the world.

Three times a day it is heated
Three times a day it is pricked
And each time the pins are stuck in
Monsieur, your days are diminished.

– Poularfuntun, tell me
Where was the child baptised?
– The wax child was baptised
In the big church at Tréguier
In the light of sun and moon.

– Poularfuntun, tell me
Who were the godparents?
– Your head valet is the godfather
And the little serving maid the godmother.

– Poularfuntun, tell me
Who baptised the child?
– A young priest did it
In order to get a sum of money

Pevoar hant scoed enn arhant goën
A quemend all en or mélenn
A neus bed ar belec ïoanq
Evid ober ar vadéïant.

An otro Bistigo pa glévès
Da guair a hané a retornés

Da guair a hané a retornés
A de bénnéres a neus lared
– Roed din, ma merc'h, ô halhéô
Rac taédo an dud a zo dioaullo.

– Alhôè ma brés a zo colled
Ac alhoé ma gouf a zo torred
Alhoé ma faüdic bian
Ma a garjé enn creis an tan.

An otrou Bistigo pa clévès
Eunné hachik vian a groguès
Eunn é hachic bennec a hè crogued
Ac ar baüdik bian a neus torred
Ac ar buguel koar é neus caoed

Ac é ô retornan a daré enn kaër
Da glasq gendarmed dô hemer.

Cri a galon ma na voëlje
Enn Landréguer an neb a vijé
O voëled pevoar gorf a lesqui enn tan
Ac ar gleïer ô son ô hunan.

An otrou Bistigo a voelé tenn
Ac a denné bléô varr é benn
O voëled è bennérès o lesqui
Ac gué 'na néfoa buguel ne merti.

Ma guarjé Landrégueris
Béan zered clos dor ô hilis
Na vijé qued badéed ar buguel koar
En ilis vras deus êol golo ar loar.

Four hundred *écus* of white silver
And as much again in yellow gold
Is what the young priest got
For performing the baptism.

When Monsieur Bistigo heard this
He took himself off back home

He took himself off back home
And he said to his heiress
– My daughter, give me your keys
For the people have devilish tongues.

– The key to my wardrobe is lost
The key to my coffer is broken
And the key to my little chest
I wish it were in the middle of the fire.

When Monsieur Bistigo heard this
He grabbed a small axe
He grabbed a small-headed axe
And smashed the little chest
And he found the wax child

And he returned immediately to town
To fetch the *gendarmes* to arrest her.

Cruel the heart that would not weep
Being in Tréguier
To see four bodies burning in the fire
And the church bells ringing of their own accord.

Monsieur Bistigo wept hard
And tore the hair from his head
To see his heiress burning
And him with no other child but her.

If only the people of Tréguier
Had kept the door of their church tightly locked
The wax child would never have been baptised
In the big church in the light of sun and moon.

Provenance:

'Ar Buguel koar', collected by François-Marie Luzel from Marc'harit Fulup, Pluzunet (Trégor), 1867. Bibliothèque municipale de Rennes, ms. 1025, 'Chansons populaires de la Basse-Bretagne recueillies par des correspondants de Luzel', fol. 3. Our version follows the manuscript and differs in a few places from the published version, François-Marie Luzel, *Gwerziou Breiz-Izel: Chants et chansons populaires de la Basse-Bretagne. Gwerziou I*, pp. 146–9.

The ballad of 'The wax child' is linked by its dark subject to the previous *gwerz* about witchcraft (no. 19); but the two songs are also connected through place. Though collected more than a century before Louise Le Bonniec's 'Janedig ar Sorserez', Marc'harit Fulup's 'Ar bugel koar' comes from the same parish, and there are many similarities in the repertoires of the two, showing that the traditional repertoire of *gwerziou* has remained relatively stable in this area. Marc'harit Fulup (1837–1909) was easily the best-known singer of *gwerziou* in the 19th century (there is now a statue of her in her native village of Pluzunet). Though herself infirm, she acted as a 'hired pilgrim' on behalf of others, and covered most of Lower Brittany in her travels to various shrines and churches. Her constant journeying on foot gave her many opportunities to assemble a truly remarkable repertoire not only of songs (a notebook containing 259 song titles does not include all the songs she knew) but also of tales, legends, prayers and proverbs. She is one of Luzel's main sources, and her name appears regularly in the volumes of the *Gwerziou* and *Soniou*. Anatole Le Braz called her the 'mère aux chansons' and in 1900 François Vallée would capture her voice on phonograph – the first ever sound recording of a Breton-language song (see no. 12).

Luzel claimed in 1868 that this was not a widely sung ballad, and all the versions we have date from before the First World War; two tunes were recorded for it by Maurice Duhamel. As with 'Janedig Ar Sorserez' the principal character in the ballad is a young girl, but this time the black magic is directed specifically against her father, and sacrilege is a clearer underlying theme, since the 'child' is secretly baptised in the church with the help of a corrupt priest. In this version we hear very little from the young witch herself – the detailed accusation made by the mysterious Poularfuntun to the girl's father takes the place of a confession, and all is confirmed by the smashing open of the chest. The coffer or chest used (often by women) as a hiding place for dark secrets is another obvious link with 'Janedig ar Sorserez' though the motif really comes into its full metaphorical force in the troubling ballad of 'Mari Kelen' (no. 27). The ballad of 'The wax child' continues the story beyond this moment of revelation to describe the punishment of those involved in the affair – the girl, the corrupt priest and the 'godparents' of the wax child – who are burned at the stake in accordance with the statutes for witchcraft in France under the *ancien régime*.

A version collected by Prosper Proux develops this final section, allowing us to hear the voice of the repentant girl. She will herself carry the wood for her pyre, she declares; her father replies that she will be transported in a cart, like any other condemned person. The execution is described in more detail than the elliptical ending given by Marc'harit Fulup, and finishes with the striking image of the father obliged to watch the burning of his only child. The punishment for the priest is also more specific:

Ar bugel-koar, ar benherez	The wax child and the heiress
Ar paeron hag ar vaeronez	The godfather and the godmother
Ho fewar ez int bet losket	All four of them were burned
Dirag ann holl bopl dastumet	In front of the assembled crowd
Dirag ann holl bopl dastumet	In front of the assembled crowd
Ho fewar ez int bet losket	All four of them were burned
Ar belek iaouank disakret	The young priest was excommunicated
Ha kerkent goude dibennet.	And then his head was cut off.
Ann aotro-koz a oele stenn	The old man wept sore
Hag a ziframme he vleo-gwenn	And tore at his white hair
O welet he verc'h o leski	To see his daughter burning
Pa n'hen doa bugel nemet-hi.	He had no other child but her.[1]

Witchcraft and wax babies also appear in the Child ballad 'Willie's Lady' (Child 6) and its Scandinavian cognates, but in those ballads the context is far more explicitly linked to themes of childbirth. The hero's jealous mother casts a binding spell on her daughter-in-law to keep her from giving birth, but the couple make a wax child, pretend it is the real thing and so trick the witch into revealing her spell.

Studies:
Éva Guillorel, *La Complainte et la Plainte: Chanson, justice, cultures en Bretagne*, pp. 400–1.

---

1   François-Marie Luzel, *Gwerziou Breiz-Izel: Chants et chansons populaires de la Basse-Bretagne. Gwerziou I*, p. 144.

21. The fire in the lead tower

Kenta welaz ann tan enn tour plom	The first to see the fire in the lead tower
Oa eur bugel bihan var breac'h he vamm	Was a little child in its mother's arms
A lavaraz da Gemperiz	Who said to the people of Quimper
– Ema 'n tan enn hoc'h iliz.	– There is fire in your church.
Ema ann tan en daou goste	The fire is on either side
Siouaz e kreiz ema ive.	Alas, it is also in the middle.
Kriz vije 'r galoun na welje	Cruel the heart that would not have wept
En iliz Kemper neb a vije	To be in the church at Quimper
O welet ar zent ar zentezed	And see the saints come out
Deut tout en dro d'ar vered	All around the churchyard
Nen deuz manet hini ennhi	Nothing remained inside
Nemet imach ar grucifi	But the image of the crucifix
Ann tan violant en dro dezhi.	With violent flames about it.
Kriz vije ar galoun na welje	Cruel the heart that would not have wept
En porched Kemper neb a vije	To be in the porch at Quimper
O welet ar werc'hez vari	And see the Virgin Mary
O renkout kuitaat er meaz he zi	Forced to come out of her home
Ar groaz hag ar banier endro dezhi	The cross and banner around her
Ann tan violant endro d'ezhi.	The violent flames about her.
Kriz vije ar galoun na velje	Cruel the heart that would not have wept
E porched Kemper neb a vije	To be in the porch at Quimper
O welet eur beleg ha tregont	And see one and thirty priests
Hag hi tout oc'h en em respount	All of them questioning each other
Da c'hout pini oa ar savanta	To know which was the most learned
A bignfe en tour da genta.	Who would climb the tower first.
Persounn Kemper eo ann hardisa	The Quimper priest is the bravest
Ennhez a bign en tour da genta.	He climbs the tower first.

Persoun Kemper a lavare
Hag en tour na dre ma pigne

– Ann tour n'euz den evit mont ennhan
Gant ar ploum bervet o tivera
E leac'h ma kouez leski a ra

Ema ann aerouant war bek ann tour
Ema eno evel eur skour

Ema hen ru evel ar goad
Teuler a ra 'n tan euz he zaoulagad.

Persoun Kemper a c'houlenne
Dioc'h ann aerouant p'he conjure

– Petra glaskez var dro va zi
Me ne dan ket war dro da hini?

– Da iliz a zo interdizet
Gant eur plac'h fall ha daou gloarek
E kramp an tour enn noz nedelek.

Persoun Kemper a lavare
Dioc'h an aerouant pa gonjure

– Aerouant din leveret
Petra lavar ar brofeded?

– Miret oc'h ar zonerien da zon
Ha digas e Kemper an mission.

Kenta lazo ann tan enn tour ploum
Eo bara zegal ha leaz bronn

Leaz a zivron eur wrec'h triouac'h vloaz
Ne oufet ket biken kouet gwell tra.

The priest from Quimper said
In the tower, as he climbed

– No-one can go into that tower
For the boiling lead is dripping down
Where it falls, it burns.

There is a fiend on the tower spire
It is up there like a bird of prey

It is as red as blood
Fire darts from its eyes.

The priest from Quimper asked
The fiend, as he conjured it

– What are you doing on the roof of my house?
I don't go onto the roof of yours

– Your church has been deconsecrated
By a wicked girl and two clerics
In the chamber of the tower on Christmas night.

The priest from Quimper said
To the fiend, as he conjured it

– Fiend, tell me
What say the prophets?

– Stop the musicians playing
And send the Mission into Quimper.

The best thing to put out the fire in the lead
    tower
Is rye-bread and breast milk:

Milk from the breasts of an eighteen-year-old
    girl
You will never get anything better than that.

Provenance:
'Ann tour ploum', collected by Gabriel Milin from Perrine Poder (from Le Ponthou in Trégor), Brest (Léon), 1857. Collection Milin, ms. MVG 104, 7, published in Gabriel Milin, *Gwerin 2*, pp. 181–3.

It is unusual for *gwerziou* to record events which are also, as this one is, preserved in French broadsheets. The song tells the story of a fire in 1620 which destroyed the lead-covered wooden spire on Quimper cathedral, the seat of the bishopric of Cornouaille. A handful of versions were collected, all of them in the 19th century, by La Villemarqué in the area around Quimper, and by Penguern, Milin and Le Mérer in Trégor and Léon. Luzel, though he claimed to have looked for this song long and hard, never found it. The circulation of this type of news throughout Brittany was facilitated by a large itinerant population made up of low-skilled workers and beggars; Milin's informant, Perrine Poder, was a young beggarwoman from Trégor whom he had come across in Brest.

When dealing with this type of local event, ballad texts can vary considerably according to provenance. Thus the *gwerz* collected by La Villemarqué contains information not preserved elsewhere, including temporal details – the fire breaks out early in the morning on St Gregory's day – or the mention of a pauper who has sought refuge in the cathedral, or the description of the removal of certain precious objects from the building. The northern versions, on the other hand, are fuller in their descriptions of the processions, the attempts to vanquish the demon by deploying the sacred host, the dialogue between one of the priests and the demon (who reveals that the fire is the result of the profanation of the cathedral by a young girl and one – or two – clerics who committed sinful acts there on Christmas Eve) and finally in the extinguishing of the fire itself.

Comparing the *gwerziou* with the French printed prose account, it becomes apparent that the two sources narrate the same event from different perspectives. The broadsheet is contemporary with the period of the fire, a low-price print of the type sold at the beginning of the 17th century for the consumption of an urban, moderately literate public. Its title is *La Vision Publique d'un horrible & tres-epouvantable Demon, sur l'Eglise Cathedralle de Quimpercorentin en Bretagne.* (The Public Appearance of a horrible and most terrifying Demon on the Cathedral at Quimpercorentin in Brittany.) It was reprinted several times at Rennes and Paris during the year 1620, which suggests that it found favour with a non-Breton (and, indeed, non-Breton-speaking) public.

It is hard to say whether the song was inspired by the broadsheet, or whether both versions are separately based on oral accounts circulating in the wake of this exceptional event. Whatever the case, the written document makes much of the sensational nature of the fire and of the vision of a demon in the flames. The clergy, who banish the demon and extinguish the fire, are the principal actors. The religious dimension is perhaps less present in the ballads, which develop instead rather unorthodox and more magical aspects: the fire is put out not only by a consecrated host, but also, and mainly, by the breast milk of an 18-year-old mother nursing her first child – a counsel suggested by the 'prophets'. Indeed, in La Villemarqué's version this is the only solution offered. This is not a motif which appears in other ballads, although the healing breast and the rather obscure reference to 'prophets' might possibly echo the *gwerz* of Saint Henori (no. 2), but it can be found in a folktale collected by Luzel. Two Breton hymns circulated by the Jesuit missionary Julien Maunoir in the mid-17th century also make mention of the milk of the Virgin banishing demons. The *Pater en enor dan diuuron sacr ar Verc'hes* (*Pater* in honour of the sacred breasts of the Virgin) states:

Scuillit ur loumic eus ho laez	Pour a drop of your milk
Da gaçç an azrouant ermes.	To chase the demon out.[1]

The only known tune for this song was recorded by Constance Le Mérer in the region of Lannion in 1914: it is the four-line air known as 'Ker-Is', which became extremely popular during the 19th century, and was often used for *gwerziou* (see no. 5).[2]

Studies:
Gabriel Milin, 'La tour de plomb de Quimper'.
Éva Guillorel, *La Complainte et la Plainte: Chanson, justice, cultures en Bretagne*, pp. 158–70.
Éva Guillorel, 'La *gwerz* de la tour de plomb'.
Gwennolé Le Menn, *La femme au sein d'or*.
Thierry Rouaud, 'Gwerz an Tour Plomb. L'incendie de la cathédrale de Quimper en 1620'.

---

1   Cited in Gwennole Le Menn, *La femme au sein d'or*, pp. 108–9.
2   Constance Le Mérer, *Une collecte de chants populaires dans le pays de Lannion*, p. 158.

22. Cleric Laoudour and his sweetheart

– Na va mamic paour, grit va guele èz
Car va c'halonic a zo dies
Car va c'halonic a zo dies

Car va c'halonic a zo dies
C'hoant a meus da vont d'al leur nevez.

– Ha, va mabic qèz, mar am c'heret
Na d'al leur nevez c'houi ne yel qet

Tudchentil Lambal a vo ennàn
Hac o deus resolvet ho lazan.

– Bet mad pe bet fall nep a garo
Car d'al leur nevez me a yelo

Ha mar be sonnerrien me zanso
Ha ma na ve qet me a gano.

Cloarec al Laoudour a lavare
Bars e Keryaudet pa errue

– Debonjour ha joa bars er guêr-mâ
Ar pennerezic pelec'h e man?

– Emedé duont bars er gampr guen
Emâ e tiluya he bleo melen.

– Laqit prest hoc'h habit violet
Da vonet d'ar bal gant ar c'hloarec.

Ar c'hloarec joaüs a lavare
Bars el leur neve pa arrue

– Sonit-hu, sonnerrien, prest ur bal
Ma zimp va douç ha me da zansal

– Mother dear, make up my bed
For my poor heart is ready to break
For my poor heart is ready to break

My poor heart is ready to break
I want to go to the threshing floor.

– O, my dear son, if you love me
You will not go to the threshing floor

The gentry from Lambal will all be there
And they are determined to kill you.

– I don't care if it is for good or bad
I will go to the threshing floor

And if there are musicians I will dance
And if there are none, I will sing.

Cleric Laoudour said
When he arrived at Keryaudet

– Greetings and joy to all in this household
Where is the young heiress?

– She is there in her white bedchamber
Combing her yellow hair.

– Quick, put on your purple clothes
To go to the dance with the cleric.

Full of joy, the cleric said
As he arrived at the threshing floor

– You, musicians, play the dance-tune
So my love and I may go dancing

Sonet-hu demp prest un abaden
Ma zimp va douç ha me en dachen

Me a royo peb a louis aour
Ha na neo qet fall evit daou baour.

Tud chentil Lambal a lavare
– Erru ar c'hloarec d'al leur neve

Erru ar c'hloarec d'al leur neve
Hac e zouçic coant ous e goste.

Tud chentil Lambal a lavare
Da Gloarec al Laoudour en deiz-se

– Rubanet caer e zeo da zillat
Michanç c'heus c'hoant da vout hor c'hamarad?

– Otrou ar Baron, va excuset
Serret e voa ho yalc'h pa voent paet.

– Vit mont d'en em bilat na yemp qet
Da c'hoari ar zabren pez a guerfet.

Mes gante voa peb a zabren noas
Gant ar c'hloarec e voa ur pen-bas.

Criz vije ar galon na voelje
Bars el leur nevez nep a vije

O velet ar yêot glas o ruya
Gant goad an dud chentil o reda.

Penneres Keryaudet a vouele
Ha na gave den e c'honsole

Ha na gave den e c'honsole
Nemet ar c'hloarec, ennes a re.

Play us now a little piece
So my love and I can step out on the floor

I will give each one of you a golden *louis*
Not a bad reward for two poor folks like you.

The Lambal gentry said
– The cleric has arrived at the threshing floor

The cleric has come to the threshing floor
With his pretty sweetheart by his side.

The gentry of Lambal said
To Cleric Laoudour that day

– Your clothes are covered in fine ribbons
No doubt you wish to be among our friends?

– Forgive me, monsieur Baron
But your purse was not open the day they were
       paid for.

– We will not be beaten in a fight
A little sword-play, if you like.

Each one had a naked sword
The cleric had only his wooden staff.

Cruel the heart that would not have wept
To be on that threshing floor

And see the green grass redden
With the blood of gentlemen.

The heiress of Keryaudet wept
And found no-one to console her

She found no-one to console her
But the cleric, he did it.

Ennes a lavare dei bepret
– Tavit, Penneres, na vouelit qet

Tavit, Penneres, na vouelit qet
Qen a velfot va goad o redet

Pa velfot ar banne divezàn
Grit hoc'h aviou da vont gantàn.

Cloarec al Laoudour a lavare
Bars en Keryaudet pa arrue

– Cetu ho merc'h amàn, Derrien gos
Ma zê deut d'ar guêr, me a zo cos

Cetu hi amàn yac'h ha divlam
Vel en deiz m'oe ganet gant he mam.

Me a ya bremàn trezec Paris
Da gaout ar Roue, me meus avis.

Ebars en Paris pa errue
Pales ar Roue a c'houlenne.

– Debonjour ha joa bars er guêr màn
Pales ar Roue pelec'h e màn?

Debonjour, Roue ha Rouanes
Me a zeu yaouancq mad d'ho pales.

– Cloarec al Laoudour din leveret
Un torfet benac ho peus-hu grêt?

Torfet bras a voalc'h a meus-me grêt
Tud chentil Lambal a meus lazet

Trivac'h dijentil a meus lazet
Hac e veritàn sur beza crouguet

He said to her continually
– Hush, heiress, do not weep

Hush, heiress, do not weep
Until you see my own blood flow

When you see the very last drop
Make yourself ready to join the baron.

Cleric Laoudour said
Arriving at Keryaudet

– Here is your daughter, old Derrien
If she has come home, it is thanks to me

Here she is, as pure and spotless
As the day her mother brought her into the world.

Now I must go to Paris
I intend to go and find the king.

When he arrived in Paris
He asked the way to the king's palace.

– Greetings and joy to this household
Where is the palace of the king?

Greetings to you, King and Queen
I have come to your palace, though very young.

– Cleric, tell me
Have you committed a crime?

– I have committed a serious crime
I have killed the gentry of Lambal

I killed eighteen gentlemen
And I doubtless deserve to be hanged

Mes gante voa peb a zabren noas	But each one of them had a naked sword
Ganin ne voa nemet ur pen bas.	And I only had a wooden staff.
Mes ar Rouanez na c'houlle qet	But the queen did not wish
E vije ar c'hloarec punisset.	For the cleric to be punished.
– Va fagic bian, red, qerz d'an traoun	– Little page, run downstairs
Ha digassit din prest va scritoriou	And fetch me my writing desk
Mar scrifin en ru hac en guen	So I may write in red and white
Ec'h allo bale en pep tachen	That he may walk freely everywhere
Mar scrifân dezàn en ru hac en glas	So I may write in red and blue
Bale hardi gant ur pennat bas	That he may go freely with his wooden staff
Pa vezo arru en e ganton	And when he arrives in his own country
Deus eur baysantez ober un itron.	He will make a peasant girl into a lady.

Provenance:

'Cloarec al Laoudour. Var ton: Gouillaouic Calvez, din leveret', collected by Alexandre Lédan around Morlaix (Léon) from an unknown singer. Bibliothèque municipale de Morlaix, collection Lédan, ms. 2, 496–503. We here follow the spelling in the manuscript, rather than the later copy of 1852, which can be found in Laurence Berthou-Bécam and Didier Bécam, *L'enquête Fortoul (1852–1876): Chansons populaires de Haute et Basse-Bretagne*, II, pp. 692–4.

CD:

Track 14. Collected by Rudolf Trebitsch from Francis Gourvil, Morlaix (Léon), 1908. Published in *The Collections of Rudolf Trebitsch*, CD 2 track 36.

Over 60 versions of this *gwerz* about a fatal duel have been collected across all the Breton-speaking regions of Brittany. This version, preserved in the manuscript notebooks of the Morlaix printer Alexandre Lédan, is dated to 1815 and is the oldest of them all – indeed, it belongs to the very earliest known collections of Breton song. The version given on the CD is also among the earliest recording for any *gwerz*, and was made in 1908 by the Austrian ethnologist Rudolf Trebitsch as part of a research project on the Celtic languages undertaken by the Austrian Academy of Sciences.

The victim is usually called Laoudour, Lambol or Lamour, and the killer is sometimes the Marquis de Lamballe, or, more frequently, the Marquis de Guerrand. The three protagonists of this ballad take us to the very heart of the class rivalries of *ancien régime* Brittany. On one side, a penniless marquis, a classic example of an expanding class of impoverished nobility (the hereditary system was not favourable to younger brothers); on the other side, a *kloareg*, or cleric, the son of a relatively successful peasant family aiming to increase their social prestige by sending their children to study – often in the hope of them becoming priests. And between the two, a *pennhêrez*, the daughter and heiress of a wealthy farming family (see no. 13), for whose favours the two men are competing. The action (as in many other *gwerziou*) takes place on the *leur nevez*, or threshing floor, which acted as a hub of sociability in rural Brittany, bringing the activities of work, music and dance together.

The conflict between the cleric and the marquis stems from the confusion in their social rank. The former, indeed, appears richer and more respected than the noble, and upsets the usual stereotypes of hierarchy: he hands out golden coins to the musicians, wears fine ribbons and is popular with the ladies. In some versions of the ballad various tactless passers-by make a point of telling the marquis that his rival is better dressed than he is – making much, in a dozen or so couplets, of the cleric's rich attire. Others suggest that the disparity between the quality of the cleric's clothes and his commoner status can only end in tragedy. The conflict thus stems as much from the young cleric's temptation to overstep his rank as it does from the difficulties faced by the nobleman in keeping up appearances. Since he cannot compete with him economically, the marquis tries to redeem his honour by challenging his rival to a duel, reverting to an aristocratic practice which gives him the upper hand. Social difference is played out again in their choice of weapons, with the nobleman wielding a sword and the commoner a *penn-baz*, or metal-tipped staff. The versions vary in deciding whether the cleric kills or is killed by his rival, but the marquis always plays the role of unwelcome suitor and villain.

In a ballad already alive with different colours – from the blonde of the girl's hair to the rich gold and purple of the clothes – the description of the green grass reddened with blood is especially striking. The story usually finishes either with the cleric returning the heiress to her family '*yac'h ha divlam, vel en deiz m'oe ganet gant he mam*' ('as pure and spotless as the day her mother brought her into the world') or with the solitary return of the heiress, who takes to her bed never to rise again, and who will soon rejoin her cleric in the grave. Less typically, this version collected by Lédan has the duel followed by the young hero's journey to Paris, to ask for the king's pardon – a well-known ballad cliché (nos 15, 23 and 24). There he receives a letter (in our version, from the queen) written in coloured ink or tied up with coloured ribbons, an echo of the *lettres de rémission* handed out to certain classes of criminal under the *ancien régime*.

It may be that this ballad harks back to an episode in the turbulent youth of Vincent du Parc, Marquis de Locmaria in Plouégat-Guerrand, around 1626. In any case, all the elements in this song situate the events in the context of aristocratic violence and the height of the fashion for duelling in the first third of the 17th century. This particular marquis made a marked impression on oral tradition, appearing in other songs and narratives, perhaps most memorably as a reformed and benevolent old man in an astonishing *gwerz* which sets out his will and testament in minute detail, from the pious legacy promised to all the churches he has ever attended, to the construction of a hospital to accommodate the parish poor.

Studies:

Louis Le Guennec, 'La légende du Marquis de Guerrand et la Famille Du Parc de Locmaria'.

Éva Guillorel, *La Complainte et la Plainte: Chanson, justice, cultures en Bretagne*, pp. 325–31 and 423–32.

Anne Balland, *Littérature orale et noblesse bretonne: le cas Du Parc de Locmaria.*

Gabriel Milin, 'Kloarek Lambaul: La mort du marquis de Guerrand'.

23. The murder of Lord Pennanguer

An Autrou Pennangêr a Plouillau
Eo bravan map digentil zo er bro
Bravan map dengentil he caffet
Gant anvi ountan eo bet lazet.

An Autrou Pennanguer ha lavaré
En noblanz Keranvern an deiz a wouez
– M'ha mam, n'ha roet dim conge

D'ha vont d'ha Plouillau feté

Gant m'ha choar an dimesel ar Woas guen
Yello Guyonic a me d'ha offeren.
– N'hiet qued d'ha Plouillau feté
Rac ho tad zo clan, woar he gwelé.

Ed hu dha Plourec'h d'ha offern bred
Pe d'ha offern beure d'ha Yaudet
Disul éc'h hiet m'ar bei savet
R'he yauanc oc'h, ho tri, d'ha monet.

– Ennobstant, m'ar clean d'ac'h sentan
Eur graç digannac'h he choulennan
M'ar vo tolled eur bleunen, en avel
Ac er leac'h m'ha gello, m'he ha yell.

Pa heuz tollet eur bleunen, en avel
Eo bed conduet gant an drouc el
Da monnet en tresec'h Plouillau
Drouc chanc'h gant a nep ec'h heuillou.

An Autrou Pennanguer ha lare
En illis Plouïllau p'ha arrué
– Piou a neuz bed an effrontiri
D'ha alc'houéo m'ha scabell ouzi?

Lord Pennanguer from Ploumilliau
Is the finest son of a gentleman in the land
The finest son of a gentleman you could find
And he was killed out of pure envy.

Lord Pennanguer said
In the manor of Keranvern one day
– Mother, I pray you give me leave
To go to Ploumilliau today

With my sister, the demoiselle de Goasguen
Little Guyon and myself, we will go to mass.
– You shall not go to Ploumilliau today
For your father is ill, and in his bed.

Go to Plourec'h to high mass
Or to the morning mass at Le Yaudet
On Sunday you may go, if he is better

The three of you are too young to go there.

– Although I owe you my obedience
I ask this favour of you
That a feather be thrown up into the breeze
And where it goes, I go too.

When he threw a feather into the wind
It was guided by a bad angel
To go in the direction of Ploumilliau
Ill luck for whoever might follow it.

Lord Pennanguer said
In the church at Ploumilliau when he arrived
– Who has had the effrontery
To lock me out of my pew?

Person Plouillau a respontas
Ha troet hé c'heign d'an auter bras
– Ar scabell ze n'ha vo quet digoret
Nemet d'ha Delandan, ha d'he potret.

An Autrou Pennanguer p'ha neuz clevet
Woar ar marchepi eo daoulinet
Ho c'hortos clevet ar reson
Deuz ha beurz an autrou person.

Person Plouillau a lavare
D'he valet Sacrist an deiz se
– Ed, d'ha Lanascol breman buan
Ha leret d'an autrou Delandan

N'ha voquet offert ar sacrifiç
Quen n'ha vot aru bars en illis
Lert dezan he man pennanguer

Stouet woar he daoulin, penn an auter.

Sacrist Plouillau a neuz laret
En Lanascol pa voa arruet
– Eman en Plouillau Pennanguer
Ac aneuz coant d'ha gavout affer.

An autrou Delandan p'ha neuz clevet
Daou pe tri deuz e dud ha neuz galvet
– Quemeret habigou hernaget
Eur goal combat honneuz d'ha gavet.

An autrou Delandan ha lavare
En illis Plouillau p'ha arrue
– Autrou Pennanguer Sao a lezé
P'he m'he d'ha Lazo dirac doué.

– Gortos den cruel a violant
N'hem laz qued dirac ar sacramant
Mar ne neuz neimeid oud Delandan
N'ha laquit quet ac'hanon d'ha grenan.

The priest from Ploumilliau replied
Turning his back on the main altar
– That pew will not be opened
For any except Delandan and his men.

When Lord Pennanguer heard that
He kneeled down on the footstool
And waited to hear the explanation
From the mouth of the priest himself.

The priest from Ploumilliau said
To his valet-sacristain that day
– Go quickly now to Lanascol
And inform Lord Delandan

We will not offer the sacrifice
Until you have returned to the church
Tell him that Pennanguer is here

Down on his knees, beside the altar.

The sacristain from Ploumilliau said
In Lanascol when he arrived
– Pennanguer is in Ploumilliau
And he is in the mood to make a scene.

When Lord Delandan heard this
He called two or three of his people
– Fetch your tunics of chainmail
We are going to have a tough fight.

Lord Delandan said
In the church at Ploumilliau when he arrived
– Lord Pennanguer, get up from there
Or I will kill you in front of God.

– Wait, you cruel and violent man
Do not kill me in front of the sacrament
And if it is only you here, Delandan
You do not make me tremble.

P'ha sortias dré an dor bihannan	As he left through the smallest door
He woa tri cleize ous he treuzan	Three swords pierced him through
Daniel, Guianwarc'h ac ar merer	Daniel, Guianwarc'h and the tenant farmer
Ha woa bed muntrerrier Pennanguer.	Were the murderers of Pennanguer.
Person Plouillau a lavaras	The priest of Ploumilliau said
Ha distro he c'heing d'euz auter bras	Turning his back to the high altar
– N'ha quiteet den deuz an illis	– Let no man leave this church
Lest an tud gentil dober ho guis.	Let the gentlemen do as they please.
An dimesel ar Woasguen pa neuz clevet	The demoiselle de Goasguen, hearing this
Er verret querquen eo diredet.	Went straight to the graveyard.
Woar ar plaç eo bet Siouas Simplet	She fainted, alas, on the spot
Rey Sicour d'he breur n'he alle quet.	She could not help her brother.
Cri a vige ar c'halon n'ha gwouilgé	Cruel the heart that would not weep
En verret Plouillau nep a vige	In the graveyard at Ploumilliau
Ho vellet ar dimesel Woasguen	To see the demoiselle de Goasguen
Ho c'houlen d'he breur on absolven.	Begging for the last rites for her brother.
Ar person a zo bed arruet	The priest arrived
Hallas n'ha wouie qued an torfet	Alas, he knew nothing of the crime
– Eman zo testeni trist da bro	– It is a sad example for the country
Ha laka ma c'halon en canviou.	And puts my heart in mourning.
An Autrou Delandan a laverè	Lord Delandan said
En tall Maner Kerdu p'ha tremene	As he passed by the manor of Kerdu
– Quenavo maner ha coajou Kerdu	– Farewell manor and woods of Kerdu
Biquen, Biquen n'ho quelen m'hu	Never, never again will I see you
M'he a ya breman d'ha Rosambo	I will go now to Rosambo
D'ha commeret aze an avizou	To take counsel there
D'ha vellet m'ha yont an autro Creic'hriou	To see my uncle, Lord Creic'hriou
Evit goud ac hen, ame sicouro.	And ask him if he will help me.
An Autrou creic'hriou aneuz laret	Lord Creic'hriou said then
D'he niz Delandan phe neuzan guelet	To his nephew Delandan when he saw him
– Petra a neve a peuzte gred?	– What have you done this time?
M'he gwel gouad voar collier ta rochet	I see blood on the collar of your shirt

An autrou Delandan a neuz laret	Lord Delandan said then
D'he yont creic'hriou ep nac'h a bed	To his uncle Creic'hriou, denying nothing
– An autrou pennanguer a zo lazet	– Lord Pennanguer has been killed
Ac he maro zo d'him tamalet.	And I am blamed for his death.
– Mar hec'heust the lazet pennanguer	– If you have killed Pennanguer
T'he a renquo quitad ar c'hartier	You must leave the area
Woar douar Breiz n'ha franc n'he chomet muis	You must not stay any longer
Qued d'ha Montroules d'ha ambarquis.	Go to Morlaix and embark at once.

Provenance:
'Pennanguer', collected by Barbe-Émilie de Saint-Prix in the area of Callac (Haute-Cornouaille) in the 1820s or 1830s. Bibliothèque de l'Abbaye Saint Guénolé de Landévennec, manuscrit de Lesquiffiou, recueil 1, cahier 2, fols 55r–58r. Transcribed in Yvon Le Rol, *La langue des 'gwerzioù' à travers l'étude des manuscrits inédits de Mme de Saint-Prix*, II, pp. 289–99.

This dramatic ballad, describing the murder of the young Lord of Pennanguer, is only known from eight versions, all of them collected before 1865 in a small area of Trégor around the village of Ploumilliau where the action takes place. And these eight versions are found in the archives of only two collectors, François-Marie Luzel and Barbe-Émilie de Saint-Prix, one of the rare women song-collectors and an early 19th-century pioneer who passed on some of her material to various younger collectors, including La Villemarqué. One of her versions is given here. The most recent text was noted down by Luzel in 1863, and transmission of the song seems to have died out thereafter, since there are no further versions in spite of this being one of the most intensely collected regions well into the second half of the 20th century. There is no recorded tune.

The *gwerz* opens with the familiar commonplace, giving the name and residence of the main character, who is, inevitably, the 'finest gentleman in the land' (see no. 15). Much of the rest of the action is conveyed in a series of dialogues, taking us from the family home at Pennanguer to the scene of the murder in the church at Ploumilliau, and on to the manor at Lanascol. The striking motif of the feather thrown up into the air provides a nice metaphor for the random nature of the bad luck involved in this tragic encounter; it is not commonly found in the *gwerziou*, although it figures more often in Breton folktales.

This story of a quarrel between members of the local nobility can be grouped with other *gwerziou* relating to known historical events. As the historian Michel Nassiet showed, the events of the song correspond to a murder case dated to June 1649 and preserved in the trial records from the archives of the Parlement de Bretagne. The accounts match up well enough to suggest that here, once again, is proof that verifiable history can be transmitted over many generations; the ballad is especially rich in circumstantial details. The protagonists and the crime scene are the same in both sources. Both note that the killing takes place after Jacques de Kerret, the son of Lord Pennanguer, leaves the church at Ploumilliau through the small door – still visible today – and both agree that he is killed by Lord Lanascol's son; the others involved are also named.

The two families were in conflict over the acquisition of certain prerogatives and honours which would extend their influence in the parish. The ballad crystallises these, reducing them to a rivalry over rights to the best pews in the church. The written trial account is more detailed in its description of the wounds and the clothing of the victim; the *gwerz* is more informative on the altercation and the actual fighting, adding final couplets on the flight of the murderers. The song is also quite clear that this was a premeditated attack, an opinion supported by the written documents, which confirm that the murderer had put on a coat of chain mail to protect himself.

The *gwerz* naturally develops the psychological and emotional aspects of the encounter: the young man's mother is filled with foreboding; his younger sister holds him as he dies. The priest in this account is made an accomplice to the murder, and we hear at the end from the murderer himself, about to head into exile to escape arrest. In some versions, when they hear that the main culprit has escaped, the victim's family take their revenge, and retain their honour, by cutting down the mature trees which line the drive up to the château of Lanascol:

Ann dujentil pa glewjont se	When the noble family heard this
A dibenn holl gwez ann ale	They chopped down all the trees in the drive
A dibenn holl gwez ann ale	They chopped down all the trees in the drive
En dismeganz da Delande.	In order to insult Delande.[1]

Studies:
Michel Nassiet, *La France du second XVIIᵉ siècle*, pp. 109–10.
Daniel Giraudon, 'Penanger et de La Lande, Gwerz tragique au XVIIᵉ siècle en Trégor'.

1   François-Marie Luzel, *Gwerziou Breiz-Izel: Chants et chansons populaires de la Basse-Bretagne. Gwerziou II*, p. 208, sung by Garandel, Plouaret, 1844.

24. The reprieve of Contrechapell

Contrechapell breur dar Markis	Contrechapell, brother of the marquis
A zo prisonniet en Paris	Is held prisoner in Paris
A zo en Paris prisonniet	He is a prisoner in Paris
Balamour deun tolfet en deus gret	On account of a crime he has committed:
Brassa mignon en devoa ar roue	The greatest friend the king ever had
En deus lac'het gant e kleve	He has killed him with his sword
Brassa mignon en devoa Roue Franç	The greatest friend of the king of France
En deus lac'het en e presenç.	He killed him, in his presence.
Contrechapell a lavare	Contrechapell said
Er prison Paris pa entree	Going into the Paris prison
– Mam bige plun liou a paper	– If I had a quill, ink and paper
Em bige skrivet eur lizer	I would have written a letter
Em bige skrivet eur lizer pe zaou	I would have written a letter or two
Da verant a da vodillou	To Guérand and to Bodilio
Da verant a da vodillou	To Guérand and to Bodilio
En distro e teui da Rosambaou.	Returning, you will pass by Rosanbo.
Ne voa ked e hir peur lavaret	Scarcely had he finished speaking
Plum liou paper dean zo rentet.	When he was given quill, ink and paper.
Contrechapell a lavare	Contrechapell said
En prison Paris ag an de ce	In the Paris prison that day
– Ne kaffen ked eur messager	– Can I not find a messenger
A kasfe evidon eur lizer	Who will carry a letter for me
A kasfe evidon eur lizer	Who will carry a letter for me
Da laret dar varkizes dond en ker?	Telling the marquise to come to town?
Ar sollierez a respontas	The female gaoler replied
Da Contrechapell pa en c'hlevas	To Contrechapell when she heard him

– Skrivet o lizerou pa gherfet
Messager avoalc'h a vo kavet.

Vel ma voa skrivet ar lizer
E c'has ar zolierez da vessager

Na pa erruas en boudillo
E voa an danç e vond en dro

Nag ar sollierez a lavare
Dar Markizez pe sallude

– Dallet ta Markizez eur liser
Digant Contrechapell o breur kaer.

Ar Varkizez a lavare
Bars ar lizer pa lenne

– Va sonnerien cesset a son
Klac'har avoalc'h zo em c'halon.

A dre ma lenne al lizer
Ag i a c'halve e c'hocher.

– Na staghet deg marc'h deus ar c'haros
Me reng mont da Baris fenos

Me reng mont da Baris fenos
Hirness avoalc'h vo deus va c'hortos.

Ar Varkizes a lavare
Var ar pave Baris pa ziskenne

– Laket va roncet er merchossi
Golloete a tapissiri

Golloete a tapissou gloan
Rag bed on deont eun nosvez a boan

Pevar ughent leo eb laret ghir gaou
Zo entre Paris ha bodillaou

– Write as many letters as you like
We'll find a messenger for you.

When he had written the letter
He sent the female gaoler as a messenger

And when she arrived at Bodilio
They were in the middle of a dance

And the female gaoler said
To the marquise, greeting her

– Here, marquise, is a letter
From your brother-in-law Contrechapell.

The marquise said
As she read the letter

– Musicians, stop your playing
My heart is filled with great pain.

And still reading the letter
She called up her coachman.

– Harness ten horses to the carriage
This evening I must go to Paris

I must go to Paris this evening
It will have been a long wait.

The marquise said, stepping down
Onto the cobbled streets of Paris

– Take my horses to the stables
Cover them with fine embroidered cloth

Cover them with fine-worked woollen cloths
For they have had an arduous night

It is eighty leagues, in all truth,
Between Paris and Bodilio

Zo entre Paris ha bodillaou
A non deus bet repas nemet daou.

Kri a viche ar c'halon na voelche
En Paris an eb a viche

Ag o voellet ar markisez
O choas eun diou pe teir princess

O choas eun diou pe teir princess
Evit moned gati dar bales.

Ar varkisez a voujoure
En pales ar Roue pa arrie

– Sallud dec'h Roue a Rouanes
Me zo deud youankik do bales.

Nag ar Roue a houlene
Gant ar Varkisez ag an de ce

– Petore torfet a c'heus gret
Ma dorc'h deud ken yaouanq dam goellet?

Ar Varkisez a respontas
Dar Roue evel me c'hlevas

– Otro sire, va excuset
Me na meus gred torfed ebed

Da klasq va breur kaer Contrechapell
Braoa vab a march en Breiz Izel

Contrechapell breur dar markis
O c'heus prisonniet en Paris.

Ar Roue evel ma klevas
Dar varkisez a rezpontas

Between Paris and Bodilio
They have only been rested twice.

Cruel the heart that would not have wept
To be in Paris

And see the marquise
Choosing two or three princesses

Choosing two or three princesses
To accompany her to the palace.

The marquise made her greetings
Arriving at the king's palace

– Greetings to you, King and Queen
I have come to your palace, though I am very
        young.

The king asked
The marquise that day

– What crime have you committed
That you come to see me, and you so young?

The marquise replied
To the king when she heard him

– Sire, forgive me
I have not committed any crime

But I have come to seek my brother-in-law
        Contrechapell
The finest young man in Lower Brittany

Contrechapell, the brother of the marquis,
Whom you have imprisoned at Paris.

The king, hearing this
Replied to the marquise

– Evit Contrechapell no po ked
Rag var e varo me meus sinet.

Ar varkisez vel ma klevas
Na dar Roue a respontas

– Leket Contrechapell er valanç
Me roïo dec'h e boës a chevanç

A ma no po ked chevanç avoalc'h
Poëset va c'haross a va deg marc'h

Poëset va c'haross a va deg marc'h
Me a kred e ve chevanç avoalc'h.

Ar Roue evel ma klevas
Dar varkisez a respontas

– A pa roffer poës ar gher man
Markisez no pe ked a nean

Markisez a nean no pe ked
Rag var e maro me meus sinet

Rag var e varo me meus sinet
Mont eneb va sin ne allan ked.

Ar Varkizez vel ma klevas
Na ter goec'h dan douer a koueas

Na ter goëch dan douer a koueas
Ag ar Roue Franç a goureas

Nag ar Roue a lavare
Dar varkisez enon neuze

– Kaeran markisez a zo er vro
E oc'hu markisez Bodillo

– As for Contrechapell, you will not have him
For I have signed his death warrant.

The marquise hearing this
Replied to the king

– Put Contrechapell in the scales
And I will give you his weight in riches

And if that isn't enough treasure
Weigh my coach and my ten horses

Weigh my coach and my ten horses
That should be treasure enough.

The king hearing this
Replied to the marquise

– If you were to give me the weight of this town
Marquise, you shall not have him

Marquise, you shall not have him
For I have signed his death warrant

For I have signed his death warrant
I cannot go against my own signature.

The marquise hearing this
Fell three times to the ground

She fell to the ground three times
And the king of France raised her up

And the king said
Then to the marquise

– You are the most beautiful marquise in the
  land
You, the marquise of Bodilio

Ag ouspen Penerez Rosmadek	And you are also the heiress of Rosmadec
O refuzi me ne allan ked	I cannot refuse you this
O refuzi me ne allan ked	I cannot refuse you this
Va zad en tewoa o talc'het.	You were my father's protegée.
Diportet eun eur pe ziou en ker	Wait for an hour or two in town
Me a skrivo dec'hu o lizer	I will write you a letter
Me a skrivo dec'h o lizer	I will write you a letter
Da kaout Contrechapell o breur kaer	So you shall have your brother-in-law Contrechapell
Ed e ar Markisez dar gher	The marquise went into town
Ganti e vreur kaer Contrechapell	With her brother-in-law Contrechapell
March a rei hardi en Breiz Izel	He will walk bravely in Lower Brittany
Evid eur Pot brao a c'havalier.	Like a true fine cavalier.
Brava mab a march en breiz izel	The finest young man who walks in Lower Brittany
Eo an otro Contrechapell.	Is Lord Contrechapell.

Provenance:

'Contrechapell', collected by Jean-Marie de Penguern from an unknown singer near Taulé (Léon) in the mid-19th century. Bibliothèque nationale de France, Fonds des manuscrits basques et celtiques, ms. 111, 'Chansons, gwerz, Noëls bretons, recueillis par M. de Penguern', fols 64r–68v.

Contrechapell is an excellent example of the way historical fact and the aesthetic demands of the ballad genre simultaneously interact and pull against each other. This is one of very few Breton songs that deals with a story of national rather than local significance, referring as it does to an event that had repercussions across the whole of 17th-century France (see also no. 30). In 1627, François de Montmorency-Bouteville, one of the most powerful noblemen in the kingdom, fought a duel in the middle of Paris; he did so in direct defiance of a ban on duelling enforced by Louis XIII, who was attempting to curb the excesses of a highly disruptive nobility. This challenge to the king's authority was swiftly punished; the guilty nobleman was put on trial, condemned to death and decapitated. Both the duel and the ensuing trial were the subject of lively debate in broadsheets and pamphlets across France and, indeed, elsewhere in Europe, since what was at stake was nothing less than the monarch's ability to impose his will on the nobility.

The event also became the subject of a Breton *gwerz*. Montmorency-Bouteville, however, is not mentioned in the song at all; the protagonist here is his Breton cousin Count Des Chapelles (transformed in Penguern's version to Contrechapell), who acted as his second in the duel, fought alongside him and was also condemned to death. The versions of the ballad collected from oral tradition in the 19th century completely alter the story's denouement. Instead of closing with the expected scene of public execution (familiar from many other *gwerziou* relating to this period of history), *Contrechapell* unexpectedly stages an elaborate scene of family intercession and royal pardon, and has the hero return to Brittany a free man. A version collected by Barbe-Émilie de Saint-Prix even finishes with the resounding couplet:

Enan evim eurus pell deuz en Trone   There, we will be happy, far from the Throne
Leac'h a neuz nemet trahison.   Where there is nothing but treachery.[1]

Historians who have studied this song have read a political message into its wish-fulfilment ending, seeing it as a sign of support by Breton singers and audiences for local liberties and local lords against the central powers in Paris. It should be noted, however, that there was considerable support for the condemned men right across the provinces, as well as in the capital itself, particularly amongst the nobility. And it is worth remembering, too, that the endings of ballads are especially susceptible to change, and that it is not unusual to find versions of the same *gwerz*-type producing quite different narrative outcomes (see nos 5, 14, 22, 25, 26 and 32). The disparity between the historical event and its reimagining in ballad form tells us something about the nature of poetic justice within this genre. Here, the murder of the king's friend – and other versions make the victim his little page boy – is not, apparently, a heinous enough crime to condemn a respected Breton nobleman in the eyes of the singers and audiences of the *gwerziou*. Indeed, the historians' perception of this song as a piece of local or regional patriotism looks plausible enough, since this is quite definitely a view from the west. The king, who has resisted the increasing offers of fabulous wealth, finally gives in. His response to the marquise, naming and locating her in her Breton territory ('You, the marquise of Bodilio […] and also the heiress of Rosmadec'), makes it sound for all the world as if the king of France is bowing to the power of the provinces.

Ballad commonplaces provide ready-made building blocks with which to reconstruct the story. The king's audience with a family member seeking mercy for a relative is one such narrative block, as is the prisoner's request to write a letter, and the messenger's arrival during the course of a dance or celebration. The rapid gallop to Paris and the marquise falling three times to the ground when she hears the sentence of death passed on Des Chapelles are also episodes which can be found in other songs (nos 15 and 22).

1   Bibliothèque de l'abbaye Saint Guénolé de Landévennec, manuscrit de Lesquiffiou, I–2, fol. 9v–13v.

Studies:

François Billacois, *Le duel dans la société française des XVIe–XVIIe siècles*, pp. 247–75.

Yvon Le Rol, *La langue des 'gwerzioù' à travers l'étude des manuscrits inédits de Mme de Saint-Prix*, II, pp. 300–9.

25. Marivonnik abducted by English sailors

An de ken - ta deuz ar viz du Tis - ke - nas Zao -

zon en Dour - du, Tis - ken - nas Zao - zon en Dour - du.

An de kenta deuz a viz du	On the first day of November
Tiskennas Zaozon en Dour-Du	The English descended on Dourduff
Tiskennas Zaozon en Dour-Du	The English descended on Dourduff
En Dour-Du pa int diskennet	And when they descended on Dourduff
Eur plac'h yaouank o-deuz laeret	They kidnapped a young girl
Laered o deuz eur plac'hik koant	They abducted a young girl
Da gaz gant-he d'ho batimant.	And took her on board their ship.
Ar Varivonnik a ouele	Marivonnik wept
'Tremen ti he zad en de-se	Passing her father's house that day
– Kenavo ma mam ha ma zad	– Farewell my mother and my father
Biken n'ho kwel ma daoulagad	I will never set eyes on you again
Kenavo ma breur ha ma c'hoar	Farewell my brother and my sister
N'ho kwelin ken war an douar	I will not see you on this earth
Keno kerent ha mignoned	Farewell my relations and all my friends
Biken n'ho kwelin war ar bed.	I'll never see you more in this world.
Marivonik 'zo glac'haret	Marivonnik is in such distress
E c'halon 'zo kazi rannet.	Her heart is almost broken.
Ar c'habiten a lar dezi	The captain says
Neuze evit he c'honzoli	To console her then
– Tavit ma douz, na ouelet ket	– Hush my sweet, do not cry
Rag ho puez sur na golfet.	For you will certainly not lose your life.

– Otro 'n Anglez, d'in a lerfet
Evit petra 'peus ma laeret?

– 'Vi bean evuruz ganin
Ma oll vadou d'ec'h a roin

A pa vin arri 'bars em bro
Plac'hik koant me ho heureujo.

– Me 'zo wel ganin ma enor
'Vit kement tenzor 'zo er mor.

Otro 'n Anglez, c'hui am lezfe
War ar pont ive da vale?

– Pourmenet ar pez a gerfet
Mes laket ewez 'vec'h beuet.

Marivonik a bourmene
An eil pen d'ar pont d'eguile.

– Gwerc'hez Vari, leret-hu d'in
Pe me n'em veu, pe me na rin?

'Balamour d'ec'h, Gwerc'hez zantel
Me varvo hep pec'het marvel.

Oa ket he gir peur-lavaret
Ebars er mor eo 'n em dolet.

En fonz ar mor p'he arruet
Daou besk bihan a deuz kavet

Daou besk bihan a fonz ar mor
'Neuz he laket war c'hourre 'n dour.

Ar werc'hez 'neuz he zikouret
'Vit he c'harz da vezan beuet

Eur barad awel a zavaz
Da goste 'n aod he digassaz.

– Monsieur Englishman, tell me
Why have you kidnapped me?

– Be content and stay with me
I will give you everything I own

And when I return to my own land
My pretty young girl, I will marry you.

– My honour matters more to me
Than all the treasure in the sea

Monsieur Englishman, will you allow me
To walk a little while on the bridge?

– Walk as much as you like
But take care you do not drown.

Marivonnik took a walk
Up and down the bridge of the ship.

– Virgin Mary, tell me
Should I drown myself or no?

For your sake, holy Virgin
I will die without mortal sin.

Scarcely had she said the words
When she was thrown into the sea.

When she arrived at the bottom of the sea
She found two little fish

Two little fish at the bottom of the sea
Lifted her up again to the surface.

The Virgin heard her
And prevented her from drowning

A gust of wind arose
And blew her to the shore.

An Anglez bras a lavare	The big Englishman said
D'ar Varivonik p'en gwele	To Marivonnik when he saw her
– Ma karjes-te bean chomet	– If you had wanted to stay
Me a nije d'az heureujed.	I would have married you.
Ar Varivonik a lare	Marivonnik said
Kichen dor e zad en noz-se	At her father's door that night
– Ma zad paour digoret ho tor	– My dear Father, open the door
Marivonik 'zo 'c'houl digor	It is Marivonnik who asks you
Ho pugel a zo dec'h miret	Your child has been saved
Gant ar Werc'hez e savetet	Rescued by the Virgin
Savetet hon deuz fonz ar mor	I was rescued from the depths of the sea
A deut ganin-me ma enor.	And I kept my honour.
Taer zro d'an ti hi a deuz graet	Three times she circled the house
Ha war an treuzou eo marvet	And she died on the threshold
E toul an nor ec'h eo marvet	She died in the porch
Hag e zad en deuz he c'havet.	And it was her father who found her.

Provenance:
Noted by Constance Le Mérer around Lannion (Trégor). Collection Constance Le Mérer, cahier 1, p. 46. Published as 'Gwerz ar Varivonik' in Constance Le Mérer, *Une collecte de chants populaires dans le pays de Lannion*, pp. 66–7.

CD:
Track 15. Collected by Roland Laigo from Yann Ar Rouz and Fañch Ar Meur, Saint-Rivoal (Léon), 1974. Dastum NUM-21310.

This *gwerz* about a young girl kidnapped by English sailors has been collected many times across Brittany. Northern versions locate the scene of her capture at Dourduff, on the estuary at Morlaix. Southern versions place events at Pouldu in Basse-Cornouaille, where the river Laïta opens out into the sea. The similarity in sound between the two names (one means 'black water', the other 'black pool') has made it easy for singers to relocate this song, anchoring it in a place and a land-scape that bring the story alive for their listeners.

Although the coast of Brittany has been no stranger to British incursions over many centuries of hostilities, this is not a ballad which can be linked to a known historical event. There was, in fact, an invasion by British forces at Lorient, not far from Pouldu, in 1746; but given the shifting locality in different versions of the *gwerz*, the absence of specific details and the emotional and psychological focus on Marivonnik's dilemma, it would be difficult to make a case for that or any other known incursion. The *gwerz* does nonetheless express in general terms the very real fears of those living along the coast, and there are several written accounts in Breton relating to the long period of Anglo-French conflict between 1689 and 1815. The much less widely sung *gwerz* of 'Our Lady of Port-Blanc' (no. 35) gives those fears a different form again – an extremely striking one.

The account of Marivonnik's capture is undoubtedly the best example of an orally circulated song featuring the '*Zaozoun*' ('English') as enemies. This very full version of the *gwerz* was noted down by Constance Le Mérer in the Lannion area; the tune she gives is one often associated with it. The opening scene of the ballad makes much of Marivonnik's heartrending farewells to her parents, but its emotional centre lies in the question, common to several other *gwerziou* of female honour: should the girl lose her virginity or her life (no. 16)? The motif of lost honour is often developed in some quite curious directions, as in this version collected from Madame Cariou at Plounérin in 1979:

'Well eo ganin koueal er mor	I would rather fall into the sea
Evit aze koll ma enor	Than lose my honour
Kar an enor pa vez kollet	For once honour is lost
Ne vez ket kavet da brenañ	It cannot be bought back
Ne vez ket kavet da brenañ	It cannot be bought back
Evel an ed d'ar marc'hajoù	Like grain at market
Ne vez ket kavet kant ha kant	It can't be got by the hundredweight
Evel an ed e koc'hu Gwengamp.	Like grain in the market halls at Guingamp.[1]

Other versions stress the value of female honour by substituting grain with the even more ubiquitous potatoes, sold 'by the hundred' at market; virginity, declares the heroine, certainly does not come this cheap. In other songs at this point the threatened victim often asks for a knife to loosen her tight clothing, and plunges it into her own heart; Marivonnik solves her dilemma by throwing herself into the sea. In some cases she does simply drown. Many versions, however, prefer to see her saved by a miraculous little fish, who thoughtfully returns her to her father's house; more prosaically, as in a Léon version collected by Jean-Marie Perrot, she may be saved by a well-placed

1   Collection Serge Le Goic, Dastum NUM-03156.

fisherman.[2] As is often the case (no. 33), the same ballad type can be more or less accommodating of the miraculous, according to taste.

In most versions female honour triumphs: the young girl returns to her parents assuring them that she is still a virgin (her subsequent holy and, one cannot help feeling, rather gratuitous death in the text given here follows a familiar pious narrative arc). There is, however, a song from the *pays bigouden* which names the young woman as Chanig Manuel and which gives her story a rather different ending. She hesitates too long before throwing herself overboard and is forced to sleep with the captain; when she does try to kill herself, and is rescued by the little fish, she finds herself safely back at home but with *un tavañcher raid war c'horre* (an apron tight on the inside), signifying that she is pregnant.[3]

The song is known both as a typical narrative *gwerz*, and as a song for leading the popular round-dance: the version known as *En Anglezed boneteù ru* ('The red-capped English') is still used for dancing the *an-dro* in the Vannetais region. The version given on the CD, from the southern part of the Léon region, has been put to a similar use as a song for a *dañs ar podoù fer*. The piece is sung using the technique known as *kan ha diskan* (where two singers respond to each other in a rhythmic *a cappella*). In the final, ludic, part of the gavotte, the dancers have to turn right around and take up the dance in the opposite direction whenever the singers utter the words (half-Breton, half-French): '*dañs ar podoù fer, komer, tournez en arrière*' ('dance of the iron pots, old gossip, turn about').

Studies:

Youenn Le Prat, 'La mémoire chantée d'une frontière maritime au XVIIIe siècle: la menace britannique sur les côtes françaises vue d'en-bas'.

Laurence Berthou-Bécam and Didier Bécam, *L'enquête Fortoul (1852–1876): Chansons populaires de Haute et Basse-Bretagne*, II, pp. 760–1.

---

2   Collection Perrot, 'Barzaz Bro-Léon', Jean-Marie Perrot's personal notebook.
3   *Tradition familiale de chant en pays bigouden*, cassette and booklet, 30–1.

26. Sea-changes: Catherin An Troadec

Catherin 'n Troadec zo klevet	Catherin An Troadec can be heard
E fons ar mor tregont gouled	Under the sea, thirty fathoms deep
Tregont gouled e fons ar mor	Thirty fathoms deep under the sea
O c'houlen Doue d'hi zikour	Calling on God to save her
O c'houlen Doue d'hi zikour	Calling on God to save her
Ha sant Matelin Moncontour	And Saint Mathurin Moncontour
Ha sant Matelin Moncontour	And Saint Mathurin Moncontour
A c'houarn an avel hag an dour.	Who governs the wind and the water.
– Me rei en ho ti eur presant	– I will give you a gift, for your house
Eur c'haliç aour, eun en arc'hant	A chalice of gold, and one of silver
Eur c'haliç aour, eun en arc'hant	A chalice of gold, and one of silver
Ha d'ho seiz aoter guiskamant	And covering for your seven altars.
Me rei n'ho ti eur baniel gwen	I will give you a white banner, for your house
Vo seiz kloc'h arc'hant deus e ben	With seven silver bells on it
Hag a vo kaër de ho pardon	It will be lovely on your feast day
Dont arok ho prosision	At the front of the procession.
Eur c'houriz koër endro d'ho ti	A circle of votive wax around your house
Hag a vo kaër d'ho enori	Which will be fine in your honour
Skubei ho ti var ma daoulin	I'll sweep your house on bended knees
A gerc'ho dour en ho pinsin	And fetch the water for your font.
Skubei ho ti var ma daoulin	I'll sweep your house on bended knees
A gerc'ho dour en ho pinsin	And fetch the water for your font
A gerc'ho dour 'n ho pinsinaou	And fetch the water for your fonts
Setu aze ma vresanchaou.	These are my presents to you.
– Digoret frank kleud ar vered	– Open wide the graveyard gate
Arru Catherin an Tredec	Catherin An Troadec is here
Arru Catherin an Tredec	Catherin An Troadec is here
Debret c'hi jodaou gant ar pesked	Her cheeks eaten away by fish
Debret c'hi jodaou gant ar pesked	Her cheeks eaten away by fish
C'hoaz 'c'h e rouanez ar merc'hed	She is still queen among women
Rouanez var an oll verc'hed	Queen over all the women
Ha var an oll demezeled.	And over all young girls.

Provenance:

Collected by the Canon Besco from Mari-Job Merrien, Lanrivain (Haute-Cornouaille), 1920. Published as 'Catherin Troadec' by Henri Pérennès, 'Chansons populaires de la Basse-Bretagne', pp. 226–9.

This dramatic piece is a vividly condensed version of a ballad, or rather a whole interconnected complex of ballads, telling of a young woman who goes on a sea journey, encounters a storm, prays to the Virgin or Saint Mathurin of Moncontour and is rescued – or not. As is often the case with shipwreck ballads, this set of stories is fluid, and difficult to analyse, simply because the plot outcomes are so variable from one version to the next. The condensed version given here is thus not a bad example; striking, if enigmatic, it contains a number of potential subtexts.

The closest group tells the story of Katell (Catherin) An Troadeg being forced to go on a sea journey by her father (in some versions, she goes to collect kelp). As the boat sinks she says that she will offer many gifts to the church at Le Folgoët. She is instantly transported to the square, and her father calls for the door of the porch to be opened wide since his daughter has come. It is not clear, however, whether she is still alive, since we next hear of the old man 'cutting bread with his children':

Me gar ve real tou kreis ar ster	I wish my others were in the river
Me mech Katel ghenon er gher	And my daughter Katel with me at home
Me gar ve reel tou kreis ar mour	I wish the others were in the sea
Me mech Katellik toul ma dour	And my daughter Katellik on my doorstep

Me sadik paour pechi a ret	Father, dear, you sin
An dour ar mour so bennighet	The water of the sea is blessed
Ar steriou ret re zé nint ket.	The running rivers are not.[1]

That odd response is explained by one editor as referring to a belief that the sea is blessed because 'at the end of the world there must be as many corpses in the sea – plus one – as there are in all the graveyards on land'.[2] In one version only is the girl unambiguously rescued, when 'Mary of Folgoët' placed a stool beneath her feet, and Mary of Forwen 'swept the water from around her neck'. The other versions all suggest the more Gothic possibility that it is her corpse which arrives in the square or at the churchyard – 'her cheeks eaten away by fish'.[3]

A similar ambiguity runs through the second group of songs, which tell of a young woman obliged by her mother to go on a sea journey, 'to show the Marquis his son'. She and the baby go

---

1   'Katellik An Troadek', collected by La Villemarqué in the mid-19th century, published in Donatien Laurent, *Aux sources du Barzaz-Breiz. La mémoire d'un peuple*, p. 146.

2   Henri Pérennès, 'Ar pense/Le naufrage', *Annales de Bretagne*, 46 (1939), 300-3.

3   For the other versions in this group see Mary-Ann Constantine and Gerald Porter, *Fragments and Meaning in Traditional Song*, pp. 104–6.

down with the ship; she prays to Saint Mathurin to save the child, and while she drowns, his fate varies (he drowns in one, and is washed up 'on a plank' in the other). The third and largest group ties the story of mother and child into a different narrative context. Here, the ballad opens with parents *refusing* to let their pregnant daughter travel by boat to the *pardon* at Tréguier or Saint-Jean-du-Doigt. She goes anyway. As the boat sinks she prays to Saint Mathurin to save her unbaptised child, offering a rich litany of gifts. Virtually all possible outcomes seem then to be recorded: both are saved; only the child is saved; both are saved but the mother dies shortly afterwards. Or, as here, both die:

Kri vije er gallon na voelje	Hard the heart that would not have wept
En od er Yeodet nep a vije	To be on the beach at Le Yaudet
O voelet eur bughel ganet flam	And see a child, newly born
O vont da interiñ gant he vam.	Going to be buried with his mother.[4]

Connections between this group and other accounts of shipwrecks (with and without saintly interventions) on the way to *pardons* open out the network of plots still further. It is clear that, to an audience steeped in the *gwerz* tradition, the short and troubling ballad of Catherin An Troadec potentially holds a number of submerged narrative secrets.

Studies:

Mary-Ann Constantine and Gerald Porter, *Fragments and Meaning in Traditional Song*, pp. 101–21.

Daniel Giraudon, 'Tradition orale et feuilles volantes: Chroniques maritimes des Côtes-d'Armor en rimes bretonnes'.

Éva Guillorel, *La Complainte et la Plainte: Chanson, justice, cultures en Bretagne,* pp. 365–7 and pp. 410–13.

---

4   Bibliothèque nationale de France, Fonds des manuscrits basques et celtiques, ms. 111, 'Chansons, gwerz, Noëls bretons, recueillis par M. de Penguern', fol. 190v.

27. Infanticide and penance: Mari Kelen

Selaouet holl hag a kleofet
Eur zon a so newez savet
Eur son a so newez savet
Da Vari Gelen ez eo gret.

Da Vari Gelen ez eo gret
An euz d'hi mamm baour divoeret
Hi zad en euz-hi debauchet
Da vonet gant-han da gousket

Seiz bloas eo bet gan-han kousket
Seiz bugel 'n ez-han deûz ganet.
Ha Kelen–goz a lavare
D'he verc'h Vari, un dez a oë

– En bourk Burtul 'so eur retret
Me ho ped Mari da vonet
Me ho ped, Mari, da vonet
Ha marteze vefet zalwet

Ha marteze vefet zalwet
Rag ewit-on me na vin ket.
Mari Gelen, vel ma klewas
Da wisko hi dillad a ieas

Da wisko hi dillad ez eo eat
Da vont da vourk Burtul d'ar retret.

Mari Gelen a lavare
En bourk Burtul pa arrue
– Ez-ian da vonet d'ann daoulin
Dirag Jezuz, ma mestr divin

Hag a-raok mond da govesad
Ma c'houllin pardon euz ma zad.
Mari Gelenn a ia brema
Da goves gant ar joaussa

Listen, all, and you will hear
A newly composed song
A newly composed song
Made for Mari Kelen.

It was made for Mari Kelen
Who lost her poor mother
Her father debauched her
Made her sleep with him

Seven years she slept with him
Seven children she bore him.
Old Kelen said
To his daughter Mari, one day

– At Burtulet there is a retreat
I beg you, Mari, to go there
I beg you, Mari, to go there
And perhaps you will be saved

Perhaps you will be saved
As for me, I shall not be.
When Mari Kelen heard this
She went to get dressed

She went to get dressed
To go to the retreat at Burtulet.

Mari Kelen said
When she arrived in Burtulet
– I will go down on my knees
Before Jesus, my divine master

And before going to confession
I will ask pardon for my father.
Mari Kelen goes now
To confess to the most joyful

Da seiz bêlek deûz kovesaët
Heb kahoud absolvenn er-bed
Hinin anezhi n'absolvje
Diwar-benn 'lavar ar wirione.

Pa oa gand ann hent o tonet
Eur belêk iaouank 'deûz kavet
– Mari Gelen, d'in leveret
Pelec'h er giz-se ma'z oc'h bet?

Rag bet ez oc'h un tuz bennag
Pa 'ma n dour war ho taou-lagad
– Bet on 'n bourk Burtul er retret
Da seiz bêlek 'm eûz kovesêt

Da seiz bêlek 'm eûz kovesêt
Met hep kahoud absolvenn-bed.
– Mari Gelen, deut war ho c'hiz
'Wit ma z aimb hon daou d'ann iliz.

Hema so 'r bêlek iaouank
'N eûz gant-hi nec'h ha tourmant.
Barz en iliz p'eo arruet
Da Vari Gelen 'n eûz laret

– Mari Gelen, kovesaët
Ha na nac'het pec'het er-bed.
– Ar c'henta bugel a c'hânis
En krafenn ann tân hen pakis

En krafin ann tân 'm oa-han paket
Ha ma zad a so d'in kiriek
Hag ann eil bugel a c'hânis
Dindann ann oaled hen plantis

Ha ma zad o oë d'in kiriek
Grit ho polonte em andret
Ann drivet bugel a c'hânis
Dindan ma gwele hen lakiz

She confessed to seven priests
Without receiving any absolution
Not one of them would absolve her
Because she told the truth.

As she was coming along the road
She encountered a young priest
– Mari Kelen, tell me
Where have you been like that?

For you have been somewhere
Since there are tears in your eyes
– I have been to Burtulet, to the retreat
I have confessed to seven priests

I have confessed to seven priests
But without receiving any absolution.
– Mari Kelen, retrace your steps
So we may both go to the church.

This is a young priest
Who has great trouble and anguish with her.
When he arrived inside the church
He said to Mari Kelen

– Mari Kelen, confess
And do not hide a single sin.
– The first child I bore
I buried in the ashes of the fire

In the ashes of the fire I buried him
And my father is the cause
And the second child I bore
Below the hearth I planted him

And my father was the cause
Do as you will concerning me
The third child I bore
I placed underneath my bed

Dindan ma gwele 'm boa-han laket
Ha ma zad a so d'in kiriek
Grit ho polonte em andret
Pa ve 'n tân larfac'h d'in monet.

– Mari Gelen, deportet c'hoas
Ma torchin 'r gliz euz ma bisaj
Ma torchin 'r gliz euz ma bisaj
Wit ma c'halon 'so fatik braz.

– 'R bevare bugel a c'hâniz
En leur-ann-ti hen a blantiz
En leur ann ti 'm eûz-han plantet
Ha ma zad a so d'in kiriek.

Ar bempved bugel a c'hâniz
Indann troad ann daol hen plantiz
Ar c'houec'hvet bugel a c'hâniz
Dindan ann treuzou hen plantiz

Ar seizvet gasis d'ar jardin
Hep biskoas na c'houvesas dên.
– En han' Doue, deportet c'hoas
Ma torchin 'r gliz eûz ma bisaj

Ma torchin 'r gliz euz ma bisaj
Rag ma c'halon 'so fatik braz.
– Grit ho polonte em andret
Ma c'hovesion a so gret.

– Mari Gelen, d'in-me laret
N'oc'h eûz ket un arc'h alc'houezet?
– Eo, duma so 'n arc'h alc'houzet.
– En hounès, Mari, ez iefet

En hounès, Mari, ez iefet
Ha na larfet da zên er-bed
A-benn eur bloas me arruo
Neuze, Mari, m'oc'h absolvo.

Under my bed I placed him
And my father is the cause
Do as you will concerning me
Even if I should have to face the fire.

– Mari Kelen, wait a little
Let me wipe the sweat from my face
Let me wipe the sweat from my face
For my heart is heavy indeed.

– The fourth child I bore
I buried in the floor of the house
In the floor of the house I buried him
And my father is the cause.

The fifth child I bore
I buried beneath the table legs
The sixth child I bore
Under the threshold I buried him

The seventh I took into the garden
Without a soul knowing.
– In the name of God! Wait a little
Let me wipe the sweat from my face

Let me wipe the sweat from my face
For my heart is heavy indeed.
– Do as you will concerning me
My confession is done.

– Mari Kelen, tell me
Do you have a chest with a lock?
– Yes, at home there's a chest that locks.
– Into it, Mari, you will go

Into it, Mari, you will go
And say not a word to anyone
In a year's time I will arrive
Then, Mari, I shall absolve you.

Hema 'so eur bêlek iaouank	This is a young priest
Hen euz gant-hi nec'h ha tourmant	Who has great trouble and anguish with her
Ha pa oa ar bloas achuet	And when the year was up
Hema da welet 'so deuet.	He did indeed come to see her.
Ann arc'h war-n-ez-hi p'eo digored	When the chest was opened
Netra en-hi na so kavet	Nothing was found inside
Med un tamik eûz hi c'halon	But a little piece of her heart
Marteze 'vel boued eur graouenn	Perhaps as big as a hazelnut
Marteze 'vel boued eur graouenn	Perhaps as big as a hazelnut
Un dra derrupl 'oa da gomprenn.	A dreadful thing to consider.
'N he vouchouer 'n eûz-han laket	He put it in his handkerchief
Da vourk Burtul gant-han eo eat	And took it to Burtulet
Da vourk Burtul gant-han eo eat	And took it to Burtulet
War vur 'r vered 'n eûz-han laket	And placed it on the graveyard wall
War vur 'r vered 'n eûz-han laket	On the graveyard wall he placed it
D'ofernia wit-hi ez eo eat.	And went to say a mass for her.
Bêlek bourk Burtul a lare	The priest of Burtulet said
D'ann aotrou ar fleur en de-se	To Monsieur Ar Fleur that day
– Mar treac'h al mal-bran war ar goulm-wenn	– If the raven wins over the white dove
Ez aï Mari ha te d'ann ifern.	Mari, and you, will go to hell.
Dre c'hras Doue hag ann Drindet	Through the grace of God and the Trinity
Ar goulmik wenn 'n eûz gonezet	The little white dove was victorious
Ar goulmik wenn 'n eûz gonezet	The little white dove won it
'N aotro ar fleur so delivret	And Monsieur Ar Fleur was saved
'N aotro ar fleur so delivret	Monsieur Ar Fleur was saved
Ho daou d'ar Baradoz int eat	And both of them went to Paradise
Eat int ho daou dirag Doué	Both of them went before God
Ha gras d'imb oll da vont iwe.	By grace, may we all go there as well.

Provenance:

'Mari Gelen', collected by François-Marie Luzel from the beggar-woman Mari-Ann An Noan from Duault (Haute-Cornouaille). Bibliothèque municipale de Rennes, collection Luzel, ms. 1021, notebook 7, pp. 155–60. We follow the manuscript version rather than the version published in Luzel's *Gwerziou Breiz-Izel: Chants et chansons populaires de la Basse-Bretagne. Gwerziou I*, pp. 88–95.

This powerful story of an infanticide mother and her confessor have counterparts in the figures of Mary Magdalene and Christ ('The Maid and the Palmer' of Child 21) in an international ballad found from Scandinavia to France. But these structural and thematic parallels are buried deep, for where most of the international ballads retain the legendary feel of the characters, 'Mari Kelen' is thoroughly, deeply, naturalised. Two of the known versions place the ballad in the little hamlet of Burtulet, in the parish of Duault, in the wooded hilly interior of Brittany. The isolated settlements and the lonely road up to Burtulet church are an appropriate landscape for the grim events of the *gwerz*.

A handful of versions have been found to date, most from the mid or late 19th-century, but there are also a couple recorded in the 1980s. The complete version given here was sung to Luzel by the beggar-woman Mari-Ann An Noan, herself from the Burtulet area. Lacking some of the grotesque details of the others, it is finely structured and hints at a more complex relationship between the girl and her father: she prays for him in the churchyard, and later, through the tussle between the raven and the dove for the piece of shrivelled heart, his salvation appears to be ultimately linked to hers (that is, if one assumes he is to be equated with the otherwise mysterious Monsieur Ar Fleur, although the name could refer to the young priest, whose soul also hangs in the balance). As a result, the ballad seems, infanticide notwithstanding, almost sympathetic to Mari, a victim both in the original incest and in the strangeness of her penance. This is not the case in the other versions, which contain an additional, violent, episode, given here in a version sung to Anatole Le Braz by Marc'harit Fulup between 1895 and 1905:

Barz er ger p'e arriet	When she arrived home
Da gichen ar c'houf hi a zo êt	She went up to the chest
Ar c'houf he unan zo digoret	The chest opened by itself
Seiz porc'het diouthan zo dilampet.	Seven piglets leapt out of it.
– Bonjour me mamm gri ha dinatur	– Greetings, oh unnatural mother
C'hui peuz lac'het seiz crouadur	You have killed seven children
C'hui peuz lac'het seiz innosant	You have killed seven innocents
Hep oleï na badeïant	Without last rites or baptism
Zo privet deuz guelet Doué	They are denied a view of God
Etre pad an éternité.	For the length of eternity.
Ganthi ho seiz hi zo dilampet	She is torn to pieces by the seven
Beteg he c'halon ho deuz tennet	Even her heart is torn out
Ha gant ar goad he deveuz scuillet	And with the blood that she sheds
Deuz he bugale badéet.	Her children are baptised.[1]

---

1   Archives at the Centre de Recherche Bretonne et Celtique, Brest, collection Anatole Le Braz, notebook EF, pp. 64–8.

Marc'harit's is a harshly moral version; the girl is unequivocally sinful and there is a vicious logic in the bloody 'baptism' accomplished by the piglets, who reverse, unpleasantly, the already unpleasant image of the sow eating her farrow. (One 20th-century version opts for seven less poetically apt wolves and seven utterly bizarre 'lions'.)[2] The chest or coffer where Mari undergoes her transformative penance recalls the secret locked chests of other transgressive women (the witch Janedig and the daughter in 'The wax child', nos 19 and 20). The undertow of dark sexuality and the extreme abuse inflicted on the female body in this piece make it one of the most troubling of all the *gwerziou*, and it is almost surprising to find it surviving in repertoires as long as it did. In another 19th-century version, sung by Perrine Poder to Gaël Milin, an episode at the end makes it clear that the young priest's act is a bold, even hubristic one, and that he risks his own damnation if Mari is not ultimately saved.[3]

That Perrine Poder's version has Mari seek redemption not in the 'retreat' but at the 'mission', may point to a specific socioreligious context for this *gwerz*. Like many places in Europe, Brittany experienced the far-reaching Jesuit programme of religious education, characterised by its vivid, highly pictorial depictions of the joys and (more often) torments of the hereafter. Jesuit teaching took hold in the 17th century, and the imagery of 'Mari Kelen' is suggestive of their first, zealous wave of didacticism; as similar missions continued to Brittany in succeeding centuries, however, it is not possible to be certain that the *gwerz* took its current form around then. Part of the ballad's power to disturb lies in the tension between the very plausible nature of the characters and the acts assigned to them, and the type-based characterisation of the religious material from which it probably derives. The human suffering of the *exemplum* figure seems (but perhaps only for modern taste) too strong to be resolved by the proffered final salvation.

Studies:

Mary-Ann Constantine, 'A Breton Mary Magdalene: the gwerz of Mari Kelenn'.

Mary-Ann Constantine, *Breton Ballads*, pp. 129–70.

Éva Guillorel, *La Complainte et la Plainte: Chanson, justice, cultures en Bretagne,* pp. 365–7 and pp. 390–404.

---

2   '*Seizh lion dezhi a zo bet lampet*'. Version collected by Daniel Giraudon, from Maryvonne Le Grouiec in 1981. We are grateful to the collector for sharing this text.

3   Gabriel Milin, *Gwerin 2*, pp. 191-3.

28. The murdered servant girl

Mar plij ganac'h selaouet hag e klewfet kana
Ur zon a zo kompozet a-newe 'wit ar bloa
Grêt d'ur vinores iaouank a oa o serviji
Bars ar gêr a Lanhuon, en un hostaleri.

Listen, and you will hear me sing
A new song composed this year
About a young person who was a servant girl
In Lannion, working in an inn.

Ann noz goel ar Rouane, 'wit ar bloa tremenet
Arruout daou valtoutier da c'houlen bea lojet
Goullet ho d-eûs da debri hag iwe da eva
Ar vates Perinaïg ewit ho servija.

On Twelfth Night, last year,
Two customs men arrived asking for lodging
They asked for food, and they asked for drink
And the little servant Perinaïg to wait on them.

– Salv-ho-kraz, 'me 'nn hostizes, ewit se na reï
    ket
Seiz bloaz 'zo 'man em zi, biskoaz potr n' d-eûs
    servijet.
P'oa 'r vates Perinaïg 'tiservija 'nn daol d'he
Kalon ar valtouterienn diout-hi a domme.

– By your leave, said the hostess, she will not do
    that
She has been seven years in this inn and never
    waited on a man.
But while the little servant girl Perinaïg waited
    on them at table
The hearts of those customs men grew warm for
    her.

Pa oe debret ho c'hoanio, ha poent mont da
    gousket
Ur goulaou hag ul letern ho deveus goulennet
D-eûs goulennet ul letern hag en-han goulaou
    sklêr
Ar vates Perinaïg da dont d'ho c'has d'ar gêr.

When they had eaten and it was time to go to
    bed
They asked for a lantern with a bright light
They asked for a lantern with a bright light
And the servant Perinaïg to guide them back
    home.

Homan 'zo ur vroeg vad, karget a vadeles
'Allum goulaou el letern ewit roï d'he mates.
– Setu aman ul letern, hag en-han goulaou sklêr
Et brema, Perinaïg, d'ho c'hondui d'ar gêr.

The hostess is a kind-hearted woman
And she lights up the lantern to give her servant.
– Here is the lantern, with a bright light inside
Go now, Perinaïg, and take these men home.

P'oant arru ur pennadig gant-hi di-ouz an ti
Unan ann daou valtoutier a zistroas out-hi.
– Mouchet-hu ho letern, lac'het ho koulaou
    sklêr.
– Ha penoz hec'h alliin monet neuze d'ar gêr?

As soon as they were a little way from the house
One of the customs men turned to Perinaïg.
– Put out your lantern, put out your bright light.
– But how will I be able to return home?

– Deut ganimb, Perinaïg, deut-c'hui ganimb
    d'hon zi
Me a roï d'ac'h da danva diouz a dri seurt gwinn.
– Ho trugare, aotrone, diouz ho kwinn gwella
'N ti ma mestres 'zo pewar, pa garan, da eva.

– Come with us, Perinaïg, come into our house
I will give you three different kinds of wine to
    taste.
– I thank you, sirs, for your best wine
But my mistress has four types and I may drink it
    when I like.

– Deut ganimb, Perinaïg, deut da vordig ar c'hè
Ewit ma refomp d'ac'h herve hor bolante.
– Sal-ho-kraz, maltouterrienn, salv-ho-kraz, na
    inn ket
Peb den onest 'zo breman en he wele kousket

– Come with us Perinaïg, come down by the
    quay
That we may do with you as we see fit.
– By your leave, customs men, I will not go
All honest men are now asleep in their beds

Me am eûs bars ar gêr-ma kendirvi bêleienn
Pa arruin dirazhè, penoz sevel ma fenn?
Homan 'zo ur vroeg-vad, karget a vadèles
'Chomm ann noz war ar bâle, da c'hortos he
    mates.

In this town I have cousins who are priests
When I visit them, how could I hold up my
    head?
The hostess is a kind-hearted woman
And she walks up and down all night waiting for
    her servant.

Sonet dek hag unnek heur, hanter noz tremenet
Ar vates Perinaïg er gêr na arru ket.
Mont 'ra neuze ar vroeg-ma da wele he fried
– Aotro Doue ma fried, c'hui a gousk disoursi
Ho mates Perinaïg er gêr n'eo ket arri.

Ten, eleven o'clock has struck; it is past midnight
Perinaïg the servant girl does not come back.
This woman goes to her husband's bed
– God in heaven my husband, you sleep soundly
And the servant, Perinaïg, has not come home.

– Aotro Doue, eme-han, n' gouskan ket disoursi
Me am eûs ur breur bêlek a offernio 'wit-hi
A offernio 'wit-hi dirag aoter 'r rozer
Ma vô bolante Doue ma arruo er gêr.

– By the lord God, he says, I do not sleep
    without anxiety
I have a brother who is a priest, he will say a
    mass for her
He will say a mass with a rosary at the altar
So by God's grace she will come home.

Sevel 'ra euz he wele da vale ar ruio
Kement-ha-ken-bihan m'arruas er butto
Hag hen 'klewet ur vouez 'vel o tont euz ann
    env
– Kers da bont Santes Anna, hag eno hi c'havi.

He left his bed to go through the streets
And finally he arrived at the Mounds
And he heard a voice as if it came from the sky
– Go to St Anne's bridge, you will find her
    there.

Arruet 'tal ar pont, 'n eûs hi c'havet maro	He arrived at the bridge, and found her dead.
'N he c'hichenn al letern, hag en-han ur goulaou	Beside her was the lantern with the light inside
Hag hen 'komanz da grial, da skoï war he galon	And he began to cry out, and beat himself on the heart
– Aotro Doue, eme-z-han, Perinaïg 'r Mignon!	– O lord God, he said, Perinaïg Ar Mignon!
Aotro Doue, eme-z-han, Perinaïg 'r Mignon	Oh God, he said, Perinaïg ar Mignon
Te oa seiz vloaz 'zo em zi, te 'oa 'r plac'h a-feson!	You were seven years in my house, you were an honest girl!
M'ho suppli, tado, mammo, re a vag bugale	I beg you, mothers and fathers bringing up your children
Iwe mestro, mestrezed, kement d-eûs domestiked	And you also, masters and mistresses, and all who have servants
N'ho lezet ket en noz da vonet da vale	Do not let them walk at night
Da vonet hoc'h unan, ispisial merc'hed.	And go out alone, especially the girls.

Provenance:
'Perinaïg Ar Mignon', collected by François-Marie Luzel from Marc'harit Fulup, Pluzunet (Trégor). Published in François-Marie Luzel, *Gwerziou Breiz-Izel: Chants et chansons populaires de la Basse-Bretagne. Gwerziou II*, pp. 146–9.

CD:
Track 16. Collected in the early 1960s by Jo Guilleux from François, Henri and Yvon Morvan, Saint-Nicodème (Haute-Cornouaille). Dastum NUM-08003.

This *gwerz* about the murder of a Lannion servant girl in 1695 is widespread across Lower Brittany, with dozens of orally collected versions and (unusually, since there is not a great deal of cross-over between the two traditions) at least one 19th-century printed ballad. Today it is still frequently performed. Words and tunes are, as so often, fairly interchangeable, but this song has a disconcertingly wide range. Besides being sung to various slow and serious melodies appropriate to the subject matter, the words are also set to much livelier airs and used to lead dances in Central Brittany. Rhythm and tune are paramount in the dancing, and the rather startling narrative content of the *gwerz* seems not to disturb the participants (see also no. 25). The *kan ha diskan* version of this song (CD track 16) used to lead a gavotte by François, Henri and Yvon Morvan showcases both the festive ambiance of the dance and the impeccable rhythmic discipline of the singers. The three brothers, all farmers from Saint-Nicodème, are among the best-known *fest-noz* singers of the second half of the 20th century. They are often seen as the male equivalent of the Goadec sisters, who lived some 15 miles away (see no. 1).

The story of the *gwerz* unfolds through a sequence of dramatic and psychologically acute scenes. The actual murder is the dreadful invisible centre of the song; it remains unspoken, undescribed, with everything leading to it, or dealing with its aftermath. As a servant, Perinaïg is completely trapped by the demands of people she cannot disobey: the men who are customers at the inn, and her mistress, the innkeeper's wife. The latter seems a surprisingly complex, not to say contradictory, character, at once intensely protective (initially refusing to allow the girl to serve the men, waiting in agony for her return) and almost wilfully rash (allowing her to serve them at table, and sending her off to guide them home). Yet Perinaïg herself is given some agency in the ballad, parrying the men with three sharp answers when they tell her to blow out the lantern light, enter their house to drink wine and come down to the dock-side. In Marc'harit Fulup's fascinating version, the repeated insistence on the brightness of the lantern seems freighted from the start with a significance that comes clear when the girl's body is found; her life is extinguished, the little lantern burns on.

Gwerziou are noted for their careful localisation of events. This song, set unusually in an urban context, is even more detailed than most. When all the versions are brought together, their combined information about the streets, bridges, churches and landscape features of Lannion actually make it possible to map the course of events on the night of the murder. The parish registers note that 'Perrine Le Mignon' was discovered 'by the river' on 5 January 1695 between eleven and midnight; the ballad tells us it was by St Anne's bridge on Twelfth Night (*nos gouel ar Rouane*). It may be that this level of detail reflects a closer relationship with the printed ballad; and there are stylistic features of Marc'harit Fulup's version which, though difficult to define precisely, make it feel different to other *gwerziou*. Explicit or extensive reference to emotions is one of them; or rather, perhaps, the expression of emotion in a non-formulaic fashion: the men's hearts 'warming' with lust, the anxiety of the mistress, the chest-beating despair of the innkeeper, all of these have a novelty – almost a realism – about them that sets this *gwerz* apart. The 13-syllable quatrains are also a format not found in the older *gwerziou*.

As is frequently the case, the richness of local detail fades out in versions collected further away from the epicentre of the event (see also nos 15 and 29). Versions from Cornouaille and the Vannetais are shorter and sparser. And where minute knowledge of Lannion's streets and bridges no longer signifies, other names take their place. A version collected from Mari Faro in the *pays bigouden*, in the extreme south-west of Brittany, sets the crime in nearby Landudec. Other transformations give the song renewed meaning in different social or political contexts. A version collected from the coastal region of Ploemeur makes its two murderers sailors, not customs men. And a Vannetais text published by François Cadic adds a local political twist: the final moral warns innkeepers against allowing their female servants to accompany republican soldiers '*rac en darn muian ha n'hé n'en dint meit Bouriarion*' ('for most of them are thugs and killers').[1] The song is thus openly siding with the insurgent Chouans, who remained loyal to king and church in the 1790s, involving the Vannetais area in terrible episodes of retribution and violence (see nos 30 and 34).

---

1   François Cadic, 'La jeune fille de Lannion', *Mélusine* 7, 127–31.

A century on, the violent death of the servant girl from Lannion is renewed, revisited and used to express contemporary political anxieties.

Studies:
Gwendal Ar Braz, 'Gwerz Perinaig ar Mignon'.
Éva Guillorel, *La Complainte et la Plainte: Chanson, justice, cultures en Bretagne*, pp. 146–58.

29. The drowning of Toussaint de Kerguézec

Gla - c'ha - ret 'vo Pleu - sa - lis, koulz pin - wig 'vel peo - rien, Na

gant keuz d'un den - jen - til, na - tif deus ar c'han - ton.

Glac'haret 'vo Pleusalis koulz pinwig 'vel peorien	The people of Ploëzal are distressed, rich and poor
Na gant keuz d'un den jentil, natif deus ar c'hanton.	They are mourning for a gentleman, a local man.
Ha pa en devoa leinet un de eus taol e dad	When he had dined at his father's house
Hag eñv o voned neuse da glask e gamarad.	He set off then to look for a companion.
E gamarad a oa 'n ur plass all okupet	The companion was busy
En deus respontet deañ ne c'halle ket moned	And replied that he could not go with him
Derc'hel a ra da vont gant an hent penn-da-benn	So he set off and travelled the road to the end
Souden ez eo arriet war vord ar stank Vijen.	When suddenly he found himself at Bizien pool.
Na pan eo bet arriet war vord ar stank Vijen	When he arrived at the edge of Bizien pool
Eno en deus remerket ur bagad signed gwenn	He noticed a flock of white swans
Ha pa en deus e denn deus e fusuilh laosket	And when he fired his gunshot
Ar bagad signed gwenn en aer toud zo savet	The whole flock of white swans rose into the air.
Toud a savjont en aer nemed unan, siwazh	All flew into the air, except for one, alas
Honnezh deuas da goueañ da greis ar skornenn vras.	That one fell into the middle of the thick ice.
Ar chass a oa gantañ na oant ket c'hoazh desket	The dogs who were with him were not yet trained
Da vont d' daped ar preizh pa vije warnañ tennet.	To go and collect the game when it had been shot.
Deus 'daleg deg eur hanter da vont beteg kreiste	From half past ten to midday
E oa en bord ar stank, soñjal e tostaje	He stood by the pool, thinking how to get near.

An desir bras en devoa da daped aneañ
Da vont ober ur regal pa vije o koaniañ.

He had a great desire to get hold of it
To make a great feast for his dinner.

Diwiskañ 'ra an Aotrou jusdekor ha vestrenn
Lesen, en bord ar stang, fusuilh ha jibierenn

The gentleman took off his jerkin and his jacket
Leaving his gun and his game-bag by the edge of
the pool

Ober 'ra sin ar groas kent 'wid mont war an dour
Pediñ 'ra a wir galon Mamm Jesus d'henn sikour.

He made the sign of the cross before going on to
the water
Praying with a true heart for the Mother of Jesus
to save him.

Na oa ket arri c'hoazh deus ar bord tregont
gourhed
Allas! ar skornenn vras dindañ zo torret.

He had not left the edge more than sixty yards
behind
When alas! the thick ice broke beneath him.

Ober 'ra sin ar groas kent 'wid koueañ en dour
Pediñ 'ra a wir galon, Mamm Jesus d'henn
sikour

He made the sign of the cross before he fell in
the water
Praying with a true heart for the Mother of Jesus
to save him

Pediñ 'ra a wir galon, Mamm Jesus d'henn
sikour
Pe an assistans deus re bennaket d'henn tennañ
deus an dour.

Praying with a true heart for the Mother of Jesus
to save him
Or the help of anyone who would pull him out
of the water.

Un den a oa er velin, e hano Koad An Noan
Pa'n deus 'hañ klewet o krial e teredas buan.

There was a man at the mill, called Koad An Noan
When he heard him shout he ran quickly.

Pa oa arriet war ar chossel e oa kaoch't gant an
dour
Allas! ma na c'helle ket mont da reiñ deañ sikour.

When he reached the path he had gone under
the water
Alas! So he could not go and rescue him.

Daoust piw ez eo an den, en devo kalon vad
A hay d'anoñs ar c'heloù da Geriku d'e dad?

So who is the man, with a strong enough heart
To go to Kéricuff to his father, with the news?

Ma eontr Koad An Noan hardi hag efrontet
A ha d'anoñs ar c'heloù d'an Aotrou 'Gergwezeg

Uncle Koad An Noan is brave and bold
And goes to announce the news to Lord
Kergwezeg

Ha pan eo bet arriet en penn an antre hir
Eno a eo bet lampet ar gwad demeus ar fri.

– Deboñjour deoc'h, emeañ, Aotrou a
    Gergwezeg
Gant ur c'heloù trist bras eh on deut d'ho kweled

Setu aman ar botoù, an arm hag an dilhad
Un den zo beuet er stank a lerer eo ho mab

Un den zo beuet er stank a lerer eo ho mab.
– O, ya, sur, Koad An Noan, ar re-mañ zo da'm
    mab.

An Aotrou had an Itron hag an Dimeselled
Teir gwech d'al leurenn sal eh int bet fatiket

Teir gwech d'al leurenn sal eh int bet fatiket
Ma eontr Koad An Noan en deus nehe savet.

An Aotrou 'Gergwezeg pan eo bet divatet
Da skrivañ ul lizher eh eo 'n em lakaet

Da gass de Bontrew na da gerc'had ur vag
Da deass 'barzh stank Vijen 'wid degemer e vab.

'N Aotrou Person Hengoad, An Esklav a lare
A oa beuet an Aotrou er stank en e goste

A oa beuet an Aotrou er stank en e goste
Hag a vije interet en Hengoad en ur be.

– Med 'n ilis a Bleusal eh eo bet badeet
Hag eno meump esperañs, 'wid ma vo interet.

And when he arrived at the great entrance
The blood gushed from his nostrils.

– Good day to you he said, Lord Kergwezeg
I have come to see you with sad and terrible
    news

Here are the shoes, the gun and the clothes
Of a man drowned in the pool; they say he is
    your son

A man drowned in the pool; they say is your son.
– O yes, indeed, Koad An Noan, those are my
    son's.

The lord and the lady and the young ladies
Fell three times to the floor of the hall

Three times to the floor of the hall they fell
But Uncle Koad An Noan he picked them up
    again.

Lord Kergwezeg, when he came to,
Set about writing a letter

To send to Pontrieux to fetch a boat
To go to the pool to collect his son.

The priest of Hengoat, An Esklav, said
That the gentleman had drowned on his side of
    the pool

That the gentleman had drowned on his side of
    the pool
And that his tomb would be at Hengoat.

– But he was baptised at Ploëzal
And that is where we hope he will be buried.

– Gant se 'ta, Koad An Noan, gret ho tever ervad
Rak ni ranno hon c'halon marg a barzh en
    Hengoad.

– Therefore, Koad An Noan, do your work
    carefully
For our hearts will be broken if he goes to
    Hengoat.

Stignet eh eo ar vag, laket warni roejoù
Er c'hoste deus Pleusal eo savet an Aotrou.

The boat is pulled ashore and fixed up with
    wheels
The gentleman is brought to the Ploëzal side.

Ken kàer hag ur ros ru, petramant ros skarlet
A oa bisaj an Aotrou, pa oa deus 'r stank savet

As beautiful as a red rose or a rose of scarlet
Was the face of the young nobleman when he
    came out of the pool

A oa bisaj an Aotrou, pe oa deus 'r stank savet
Ken ma lare an dud, e oa ressussitet.

Was the face of the young nobleman when he
    came out of the pool
So that people said he was resuscitated.

Na kri vije ar galon, na kri ma na ouelje
A oant toud war vord stank Vijen ur merc'her da
    greiste

Cruel the heart that would not have wept
Amongst those at the edge of Bizien pool one
    Wednesday at midday

O weled ar c'horf paour, na war ar prad savet
'C'hortos lien d'henn lieniñ, ha douar benniget.

To see the poor corpse placed in the field
Waiting for the shroud and for sacred ground.

Konduet eo gant enor, d'an ilis a Bleusal
Hag alumet dirazañ, un triwec'h pilad koar.

He was driven with honour to the church at
    Ploëzal
And eighteen candles were lit before him.

– Me ho ped, Aotrou Person, e fin ho sakrifiss
Da gaout sonj aneañ, e-barzh en hoc'h ilis

– I beg of you, monsieur priest, when you finish
    mass
To remember him in your church

Da gaout soñj aneañ, en fin hoc'h oferenn
Ha ni ho rekompenso, beañ a vo moien.

To do something in his memory during your
    mass
And we will recompense you; we have the
    means.

Glac'haret eo Pleusalis, koulz pinwig 'vel peorien
Ha galloud 'reont beañ, maro eo o c'habiten.

The people of Ploëzal are distressed, both rich
    and poor
And they have reason to be, for their captain is
    dead.

Provenance:

Collected by Daniel Giraudon from François Richard, Ploëzal (Trégor), 1980. Published in Daniel Giraudon and Donatien Laurent, 'Gwerz an Aotrou Kergwezeg', pp. 19–23.

CD:

Track 17. Same version.

This long and richly detailed *gwerz* recounts a tragic local event that took place some 270 years before this version was collected. In January 1709, when the whole of France was in the grip of an especially cold winter, the 19-year-old Toussaint de Kerguézec (in its Breton spelling, Kergwezeg), from the noble family of Kéricuff, drowned while out shooting swans. During his exhaustive research into this song, Daniel Giraudon found note of the young man's death in the parish records at Ploëzal, thus providing the *gwerz* for the first time with a secure historical context. Versions of the *gwerz* can be found in the early 19th-century collections of Barbe-Émilie de Saint-Prix and Théodore de La Villemarqué, and it continued to be collected into the 20th century. As with the ballad of Perinaïg Ar Mignon (no. 28), the *gwerz* was also printed as a *feuille volante*, a rare occurrence for orally transmitted songs in circulation before the French Revolution.

The Trégor versions, collected near the scene of the tragedy, are, like this one, full of telling and often moving incidental detail; names of people and places tie the action into a specific place, a known community. Bizien lake, where the young man drowned, is still identifiable in the landscape, although it has now dried up. It marks the border between the parishes of Ploëzal and Hengoat, which explains the concerns expressed in the *gwerz* about where Kerguézec would be buried.

François Richard's version, first collected by Daniel Giraudon, has 40 couplets, using the longer, 13-syllable verse form, sung to a simple tune. The narrative arc is also very simple, with relatively little in the way of plot, but the piece is striking for its combination of stylised motifs and painfully realistic details. The initial premise of the story – a young nobleman shoots a swan – seems to trail a cluster of legendary associations foretelling tragedy (many cultures see swans as otherworld birds, or suggest that killing them is taboo), and the flurry of birds rising from the lake is an especially vivid image. But the song is also very clear that this is a practical act, rooted in a lived reality, and that the dead swan is destined for the dinner table – if the dogs had been more experienced, it says, their master would not have risked his life. It is that 'ghosting' of the specific and the everyday with the poignancy of myth which, as so often in the *gwerziou*, gives them a kind of extra dimension. When the elderly Koad An Noan breaks the news to the family, 'blood gushes from his nostrils' in a stylised motif used in similar situations; but he also brings with him 'the shoes, the clothes and the gun' which identify the drowned man as an individual. We learn, again on a practical note, that the boat used to retrieve the body had to be fitted up with wheels; but that the corpse brought ashore is astonishingly 'like a rose'. A version collected by Madame de Saint-Prix notes an ironic detail not mentioned elsewhere: close to his heart the young man carried a religious image, intended to protect him.[1]

As with the ballad of the murdered servant girl (no. 28), or La Fontenelle (no. 15) versions of this song alter as they move further and further from the story's heartland at Ploëzal. In southern Trégor and in Central Brittany, place names are changed, and the drowned man has become not a young nobleman but a *kloareg* – a student at a seminary, training for the priesthood. Further south still, in the Vannetais region, the song is radically reduced in length and detail, becoming the equivalent of a brief pencil sketch, with an unnamed protagonist out shooting ducks. This Vannetais tendency towards creating shorter, more lyrical versions of the richer northern ballads is one of the reasons that the area was relatively little explored by 19th-century collectors more interested in the 'big' historical ballads. Although, as versions in this anthology show, a minimal ballad narrative can have a powerful poetic impact (no. 34), the 'idea' of the *gwerz* as necessarily long and detailed was an important factor in shaping the recorded tradition.

Studies:
Daniel Giraudon and Donatien Laurent, 'Gwerz an Aotrou Kergwezeg'. Republished in Donatien Laurent, *Parcours d'un ethnologue en Bretagne*, pp. 279–307.
Daniel Giraudon, 'Un distro war werz an Aotrou Kergwezeg'.

---

1   Bibliothèque de l'Abbaye Saint Guénolé, Landévennec. MS Lesquiffiou, vol. 1, notebook 2, fols 14v–17v.

30. The execution of the Marquis de Pontcallec

Kohha iou - ank   me   che - le - uet, o Koh ha iou - ank me che-e-le - uet,   Ergannen-

men   e zo sa - ùet,   You li you   la fon la   ri   da - re, You li   you   la fon la - ri   da

Koh ha iouank me cheleuet, o	Listen to me, young and old, o
Koh ha iouank, me cheleuet	Listen to me, young and old
Er gañnen-men e zo saùet	This song was composed
You li you la fon la ri dare	*You li you la fon la ri dare*
You li you la fon la ri da	*You li you la fon la ri da*
Er gañnen-men e zo saùet	This song was composed
De varkiz bras er Pontkelleg	About the great Marquis de Pontcallec
De varkiz bras er Pontkelleg	About the great Marquis de Pontcallec
E oè éon un dén kri ha kalet	Who was a man, cruel and hard
E oè éon un dén kri ha kalet	Who was a man, cruel and hard
Hag alkent oè bet dibennet.	Yet he was executed all the same.
Éon e noè bet én him zigizet	He had disguised himself
Un abid liañn e noè laket	Putting on rough garments
Un abid liañn e noè laket	He had put on rough garments
Eit ne vehè ket bet anaùet	So as not to be recognised
Eit ne vehè ket bet anaùet	So as not to be recognised
Kèr éon e zoutè é vezè klasket	For he knew they were hunting him
Kèr éoñ e zoutè é vezè klasket	He knew they were hunting for him
Ba borh en Ignôl noè én him guhet.	He hid in the village of Lignol.
– Bonjour d'oh-hui otrou person	– Good–day to you, monsieur priest
Azil genoh e houlennan	Grant me asylum, I beg of you

Ma plij genoh, reit azil d'ein
O ma vè és de andurein.

– Taùet, taùet, otrou markiz
Na me rei doh-hui lonjeris

Na me e rei d'oh-hui lonjeris
Na kuh dohtè e zo rekis.

Na barh é ganbr pe oè laket
Er markiz ne noè ket dihoallet

Er markiz ne noè ket dihoallet
Étal er fenestr noè én him laket

Étal er fenestr noè én him laket
Hag aben oè bet remerket

Nag ur paorig a Laouelan
En noé éoñ guélet ba ér ganbr.

Ur miz arlerh, é klah é voued
Ba borh en Ignôl noè arrestet

Ba borh en Ignôl noè arrestet
Bar presbitoér noè antréet

Bar presbitoér p'oè antréet
Nag er markiz noè remerket

Nag er markiz noè remerket
E oè doh en daul éh évet

E oè doh en daul éh évet
En dé-se noè éoñ anaùet.

– Bonjour d'oh-hui otrou person
Hui e rehè d'ein en alézon?

– Mein e rei d'oh-hui kant dinér
Ur péh bara barh hou poch-kerh

I beg of you, give me asylum
Of a kind I can endure.

– Enough, enough, monsieur the marquis
I will give you lodging

I will give you lodging
You must hide from them.

Once he was settled into his room
The marquis was not cautious

The marquis was not very cautious
He stood near the window

He stood near the window
And there, someone spotted him.

A poor beggar from Langoélan
Saw him in his room.

A month later, begging for his bread
He stopped in the village of Lignol

He stopped in the village of Lignol
And went into the presbytery.

When he entered the presbytery
It was then that he noticed the marquis

It was then that he noticed the marquis
Drinking at the table

He was drinking at the table
And that was the day he recognised him.

– Good-day to you, monsieur priest
Will you give me alms?

– I will give you a hundred *deniers*
And a big hunk of bread in your pack

Ur péh bara barh hou poch-kerh	A big hunk of bread in your pack
Mein hou supli, na laret ket gér.	And I beg of you – say not a word.
– Otrou person, n'én him chifet ket	– Monsieur priest, do not fret
Me e zo ur paor é klah é voued	I am a poor man who begs for food
Me e zo ur paor é klah é voued	I am a poor man who begs for his food
Mein me e oui goarnein ur sekred.	I know how to keep a secret.
Un dé arlerh d'en abradé	The following day, late afternoon
É oè er paorig ba Gemené	The poor beggarman was at Guémené
É oè er paorig ba Gemené	The poor beggarman was at Guémené
Arlerh En Doaron éoñ e glaskè.	And he was trying to find En Doaron.
– Bonjour d'oh-hui otrou Doaron	– Good-day to you, monsieur En Doaron
Kauzal dohoh e houlennan.	I beg a word with you.
– Paorig bihan, d'ein e laret	– Tell me, poor beggar
Émen er markiz ho pes kavet?	Where did you find the marquis?
– Na me e larei d'oh me sekred	– I will tell you my secret
Otrou Doaron, ma me féet	Monsieur En Doaron, if you pay me
Otrou Doaron, ma me féet	Monsieur En Doaron, if you pay me
Me e houlen genoh daou gant skoéd.	I'm asking for two hundred *écus*.
– Na goarnet hou sekred genoh	– Keep your secret to yourself
Mé ne rein ket blank ebet d'oh	I won't give you a penny
Mein ne rein ket blank ebet d'oh	I won't give you a penny
Kèr me 'ouia kenkoulz èldoh.	For I know quite as much as you do.
Nag en dé arlerh é-rauk kuh-hiaul	The following day, before sunset
É oè En Doaron barh borh en Ignol.	En Doaron was in the village of Lignol.
Barh borh en Ignôl p'oè arriùet	When he arrived at Lignol
Bar presbitoér oè antréet	He went into the presbytery
Bar presbitoér oè antréet,	He went into the presbytery
Ag er markiz ou-doè kavet.	And they found the marquis.

En Doaron bras a Gemené
Bozé é zorn ar é ziskoé

– Deit-hui genein otrou markiz
Ha mein hou kasei de Bariz

Na de Bariz pé de Nañned.
– Kaset-mein dré er Pontkelleg

Kaset-mein dré er Pontkelleg
De glah me abid alaouret

Me e fauté d'ein bout guisket braù
Eit mont dirak er bouro bras.

Madam markiz a-pe gleùas
E zichen béañnik mat d'en nias

E zichen béañnik mat d'en nias
Lak hé harros ar en hent-pras

Lak hé harros ar er paùé
Pemp marh antier doh pep kosté.

– Na bout é krevehè unon sel ér
Me e vo ba énoñ aben dek ér.

Meit hé hoché e laras dehi
– Madam markiz, neh zo d'oh-hui

Ne dalv ket d'oh mont de Nañned
Kar pen er markiz e zo koéhet

É ma é ben ar er paùé
É hoari jeu d'er vugalé.

The great En Douaron of Guémené
Placed his hands on his shoulders

– Come with me, monsieur the marquis
And I will take you to Paris

To Paris or to Nantes.
– Let me go through Pontcallec

Let me go through Pontcallec
That I may fetch my suit of gold

I wish to be well-dressed
When I go before the executioner.

Madame the marquise, hearing the news
Comes down in haste.

In great haste she comes
And has her carriage made ready for the highway

She has set her carriage on the road
With five stallions on either side.

– If one should perish every hour
I will still be there in ten hours.

But her coachman said to her
– Madame the marquise, sad news for you

It is no good going to Nantes
For the head of the marquis has fallen

His head is on the cobbled street
A plaything for the children.

Provenance:

Collected by Donatien Laurent from Véronique Broussot, Kernascléden (Vannetais), around 1960, Archives du Centre de Recherche Bretonne et Celtique, Université de Bretagne Occidentale, Brest. Published in Joël Cornette, *Le Marquis et le Régent: Une conspiration à l'aube des Lumières*, pp. 224–30 + CD track 7; and in Éva Guillorel, *La Complainte et la Plainte: Chanson, justice, cultures en Bretagne*, CD track 23.

CD:

Track 18. Same version.

Like 'Contrechapell' (no. 24), this is one of the few *gwerziou* rooted in a historical event of not just local but national significance. At the beginning of the 18th century, a small group of Breton noblemen conspired against the Regent of France; Chrisogone-Clément de Guer, marquis de Pontcallec, was among them. He was arrested and executed in 1720 along with three of his fellow conspirators.

Alongside a rich fund of French-language archives recording this event – including, most notably, the court proceedings in their entirety – various traditional songs in Breton have been collected, particularly in those areas of the Vannetais where the marquis himself lived and was captured. This lengthy version, which lasts over 15 minutes, was collected from Véronique Broussot at Kernascléden and is a good example. The broad story is generally the same: hunted by the king's soldiers, Pontcallec, disguised as a peasant, takes refuge in a presbytery; he is betrayed by a beggar, judged at Nantes and beheaded. The portrayal of Pontcallec himself, however, varies considerably. In some of the versions he is presented as a cruel and immoral villain who thoroughly deserves his fate. In others, he is a pious and courageous nobleman, denounced despite the fact that his actions were for the glory of his native Brittany. This is the interpretation taken by La Villemarqué in his *Barzaz-Breiz*; in a rhythmical version marked by the refrain, 'You who have betrayed him, be cursed, be cursed!', he portrays a young martyr who has sacrificed himself for his country.[1] This characterisation went on to become especially popular in nationalist circles, where even today Pontcallec is treated as something of a hero of the Breton cause – although historically speaking his role was far more limited, and primarily concerned with defending the interests of the nobility.

The death of the marquis on the scaffold is a particularly intense moment in the ballad. In some versions, Pontcallec takes a heartrending farewell of his loved ones and his country; even the soldiers who arrested him are in tears, while the citizens of Nantes weep and cry that 'it is a sin to kill the marquis!'. The climax comes when the severed head rolls across the cobbles to serve as a football for children. These motifs are not exceptional in themselves; many are clichés which make up the poetic grammar of the *gwerziou*. Thus the description of the death of Pontcallec is, pretty well word for word, the same as that used for the death of La Fontenelle, another nobleman

---

1   Théodore Hersart de La Villemarqué, *Barzaz-Breiz*, 2nd ed. (1845), II, pp. 152–3.

executed more than a century earlier, and whose memory is also preserved in Breton oral tradition (no. 15). It is these building blocks of the tradition – reusable, stereotyped motifs – which permit singers to inflect their depiction of Pontcallec more or less negatively. For example, though certain versions introduce him as 'the best man in the world', others begin with him as 'the worst man in the world'; with the alteration of a single word, the entire interpretation of the song changes.

The *gwerz* on the death of Pontcallec is also a very good example of the way a historical event can be renewed over time and through oral transmission. Although the arrest of the marquis took place in 1720, several songs relocate the story to the period of the French Revolution (see also no. 28). Pontcallec is no longer arrested by the king's soldiers, but by counter-revolutionary Chouans, engaged in the civil war which ravaged western France from 1793. In one of these versions, he is not merely executed but specifically guillotined. It is not surprising to find that these revived and renewed versions are concentrated in the Vannetais, the Breton region most profoundly marked by the Chouan uprising. Refiguring earlier *gwerziou* in a more immediate political context instils them with new meanings, and keeps them powerfully relevant for both singers and audience. In this way they keep their place in a living oral tradition.

Studies:
Éva Guillorel, 'La complainte du marquis de Pontcallec, les *gwerziou* bretonnes et l'histoire'.
Éva Guillorel, *La Complainte et la Plainte: Chanson, justice, cultures en Bretagne*, pp. 468–81.
Brice Evain, *Deux héros de Bretagne. Le marquis de Pontcallec et Marion du Faouët*.
Philippe Jarnoux, 'Pontcallec ou les métamorphoses de la mémoire'.
Joseph Loth, 'La chanson du marquis de Pontcallec'.

31. Loeiz Er Ravalleg murdered by his friends

Didosteit olle tut iaouang ac a re gous ive
Evit glevèt eur guerse compozed e nève
So savet eun den yaouyank eus pares langonet
A neus collet i vuhé vont guelti vionnet.

Come close, people young and old
To hear a newly composed *gwerz*
About a young man from the parish of Langonnet
Who lost his life going to see his friends.

D'en trisec de vis avril a voa de goelliou pask
Va deut e vrasson mignonet de di i tad d'en clask.
— Deut guenè me mignon bras loisic à rawallec
A ni iello deur pardon St fiarc ar faoet

On the thirteenth of April during the Easter
  holidays
His best friends came to collect him from his
  father's house.
— Come with me, my friend Loisic Er Ravallec
And we'll go to the *pardon* of St Fiacre at Le Faouët

Ni vuello rei eur bouquet deur curé langonet

We'll see them give the bouquet to the curate of
  Langonnet.[1]

— Tremallet ma mignonet, tremallet nen taon ket
Me so bet ober me fask bar eur bord langonet
Me so bet ober me pask gant curé langonet
Congé ma mam a me sat a rei d'hi men cahouet.

— You go on, my friends, go on, I'm not coming
I went to the Easter service in the village of
  Langonnet
I went to the Easter service with the curate of
  Langonnet
And I need to have permission from my father and
  mother.

— Bonjour moric rawallec a hui mari fraoa
Lescet o mab zont ghénoni d'a ober eur vala
De guello rei eur bouquet d'eur churé langonet.

— Good-day to you Moris Er Ravallec, and to you
  Mari Fraoa
Let your son come with us for a walk
To see them give the bouquet to the curate of
  Langonnet.

— Tremallet ta me mignon, lorsket e vo guenech
Meis roc e vo cueuet n'heol è vo rentet d'eur
  gerk.
— Tevet moric ravallec tevet na chiffet ket
Tri fortr à neus m'an honni à neffeur drouc e bet.

— Go along then, my friend, we'll permit him to
  go with you
But he must be back at home before the sun sets.
— O hush, Moris Er Ravallec, be quiet and do not
  fret
Three fine lads like us, we'll come to no harm.

---

1   *Rei eur bouquet* ('to give the bouquet') refers to a tradition at some local *pardons* of bringing a posy of flowers to lay at the feet of the priest. Placed on the altar, they were thought to help protect the giver from illness and bad luck.

Pe oant deru St fiacr evint d'an dut eur pig

Ac e evont boutaillat kentorr vont d'an ilis

A ei zeit da zaoulina dirac ar sacrific.

Pe voa achu an offeren bret ac ive ar sermon

Ié laret vont degant è de guerli ar faoet

When they arrived at St Fiacre

They drank several bottles before going to church

And they went and kneeled before the sacrament.

When the mass was done and the sermon too

They told him to come with them to Kerli at Le Faouët

De vuel i zouç mari ann ac e vuion caret.

– Tremallet ma mignonet, tremanet nan daon ket

Gar me vo divuet dan gher a me vo scandalet.

To see his sweet Mari Ann, his beloved.

– Leave it, my friends, leave it; I will not go

Or I'll be late getting back, and there will be trouble.

– Tevet loisic ravallet, tevet na chiffet ket

Kentorch a vo cueuet 'n heaul ni vo d'en gher rentet.

Kemet neus groet var n'hezan, kemet neus consentet

Voet eo loisic a ravallet de Kerlis faoet

– Be quiet, Loisic Er Ravallec, be quiet and do not fret

We'll be back at the house before the sun sets.

They insisted so much that he agreed

Loisic Er Ravallec went to Kerli at Le Faouët

Loisic ravallec voellé cost en dol bar Kerli.

– Tro doué, n'em zicouret, petra emeus me groet?

Song ema but abred d'an gher a chetu me divuet.

Loisic Er Ravallec wept beside the table at Kerli.

– My God, help me, what have I done?

I thought to be home early, and I am late.

– Tevet, loisic ravallec tevet ne ouellet ket

Tri fotr a so guet homni, na nom ket drouc e bet

Loisic ravallet vouelle etc.

– Kentorc a erruen gher mon sur da but lazet.

– Be quiet, Loisic Er Ravallec, be quiet and do not weep

Three fine lads like us, we'll come to no harm.

Loisic Er Ravallec wept.

– Before I get home, I am sure to be killed.

– Tevet moric ravalec tevet ne ouellet ket

Chomet guenonhi pen nos a ne po drouc e bet.

– Be quiet [Loisic][2] Er Ravallec, be quiet and do not weep

Stay this night with us, you'll come to no harm.

Demeus enon retournan mont e ran mes an ty

Mont beteg croes penfel ac an etaillerie

Pe voant eru croes Penfel e chomint en e sao

Ac e rein tol pous d'hezan ac en tol en e fos.

And with that they turn round and leaving the house

Go as far as the cross at Penfel and the [...][3]

When they arrived at Penfel cross, they stopped.

They struck him down and threw him in the ditch.

---

2   The Breton text erroneously gives the name of Loisic's father here.

3   The end of this line is unclear.

A pe vant tollet gant hé en clevet en hom benec.
Èchappet voa lois ravallec a voet è vandalec
Ac hi de mont voar i lech ghis daou blei arrajet.
– Tevet loisic ravallec, tevet na redet ket
Eno plac ma, ma mignon bras, dra sur a farviet!

When they had thrown him in there they heard
    someone.
Loisic Er Ravallec escaped and ran off into the
    broom bushes
And they followed him like two raging wolves.
– Be quiet, Loisic Er Ravallec, be quiet and do
    not run away
In this place, my friend, you are indeed going to
    die!

Trisec tol contal d'ezan, commancet an peorsec
Neus reit an dut maleurus da loisic ravallec.
– Me kèr me cas, mignonet, Bord Sceul en ti me
    sat
Me pardono d'hor kemet d'hor hu eur galon vat

Thirteen stabs with a knife these wretches gave
Loisic Er Ravallec, and began a fourteenth.
– If you take me, my friends, to my father's at
    Porsqueul
I will forgive you with all my heart

Me ker me cas ma mignonet deun tu all d'ar
    pont guen
Me pardono d'hor kemet d'or hu breman a ben.
– Ler kenavo lois ravallec à d'ho mam a d'ho tat
    à de kemet gherfet
Gar, birviken tam bara e bordsceul ne zebfet.

If you will just take me, friends, to the other side
    of the white bridge
I will forgive you all immediately.
– Say goodbye, Loisic Er Ravallec, to your
    mother, your father and all the others
For you will never again eat a morsel of bread at
    Porsqueul.

– À sa ta ma mignonet pe ma reit dhé mervel
Tenet curun St Barbar à so bar doublabur ma zé
A me a farvo neusé mar pligeo gant doué.

– Well then, my friends, if I must die
Remove the Crown of Saint Barbara from the
    pocket of my shirt
And then if God wills, I will die.

A pe va lazet ganthé hi en eus hon scluget
A hien neuse en caset gant hè de ster bras eur
    faoet
Pe vant digouet gant an dour e bars en hon tollet.

And when they had killed him, they dragged
    him
And carried him to the great river at Le Faouët
When they reached the water they threw him in.

Moric ravallec goellè, a goellè gant glaharch
Cas cahouet i vab loisic ler benach voar zouar.
– Tevet moric ravallec tevet ne goelet ket
Dontet è rei vuech eun amzer o mab e vo cavet

Moris Er Ravallec wept, he wept with pain
Looking for his son Loisic somewhere on earth.
– Be quiet, Moris Er Ravallec, be quiet, do not
    weep
The time will come when your son will be
    found

Donnet e rei eur justic an autrou Senechal
Cavet vo corf mab loisic ouar an dour o nungial.

The law will come, monsieur Seneschal
The body of your son Loisic will be found,
    floating in the water.

Cri vis calon na ouelè bar pardon ar faoet
Guellet loisic ravallec ouar i kein bar eur prat
Diflappet i bleo melen ebars ni zao lagat.

Cruel the heart that would not have wept at the
    pardon of Le Faouët
To see Loisic Er Ravallec on his back in the field
His blond hair dishevelled over his eyes.

Dre teir guech e voa galvet moric a ravallec
Dont de zao i vab lois dor prajou eur faouet
Voa enon na mam na tad à nac car ligné bet
Kemet zè d'en savè met curé langonet.

Three times they called Moris Er Ravallec
To come and identify his son in the field at Le
    Faouët
No-one – no father, no mother, kith nor kin –
Would come to identify him, except the curate
    of Langonnet.

Curé langonet larrè, ié larrè gant glaharc
– Adeo loisic ravallet mont e res dant douar
Me oa chortos diout dirriou e langonet
Mes broman e verch laket e bered eur faoet.

The curate of Langonnet said, he said with
    sorrow
– Adieu, Loisic Er Ravallec, you are going under
    the earth
I was expecting you today at Langonnet
But now you will be buried in the graveyard at
    Le Faouët.

M'ho ped langonetiss ger, pe iefet deur faoet
Mont de larrè o pater ar bé lois ravallec
Mont de larrè ou pater ouar bé lois ravallec
A neus collet i bué vont de guel y mignonet.

I beg you, people of Langonnet, when you go to
    Le Faouët
Go and say a prayer on the grave of Loisic Er
    Ravallec
Go and say a prayer on the grave of Loisic Er
    Ravallec
Who lost his life going to see his friends.

Provenance:
Collected by Théodore Hersart de La Villemarqué around 1835, Cornouaille. Collection La Villemarqué, first notebook, pp. 69–73. Published as 'Loisik Rawallek' in Donatien Laurent, *Aux sources du Barzaz-Breiz: La mémoire d'un peuple*, pp. 86–8.

CD:
Track 19. Collected by Loeiz Le Bras from Louise Vally, Melrand (born at Bubry, Vannetais), 1980. Dastum NUM-20425.

This powerful *gwerz* is frequently used as a kind of textbook case to demonstrate the fact that oral tradition can sometimes preserve the memory of an event more fully, and more meaningfully, than the written record. The crime described in this song is the subject of a thick legal dossier held at the archives of the court of royal justice at Hennebont, and concerns the death of Loeiz Er Ravalleg at Le Faouët (Cornouaille) in 1732. The trial lasted for four years, and, as the victim's father tried unsuccessfully to point out, was riddled with irregularities. Key witnesses were not called, the judge allowed the affair to drag on and the accused parties were ultimately acquitted.

The first known version of the *gwerz* is the one given here. It comes from the notebooks of Théodore Hersart de La Villemarqué. Seen here in its rough uncorrected form, with all its orthographical eccentricities and gaps, one gets an idea of the kind of tidying-up required before publication in the *Barzaz-Breiz*. Many other versions were subsequently collected in the 19th and 20th centuries, mostly from villages close to the events in the ballad, including the version sung by Louise Vally (CD track 19). In the 1960s, in the course of a thorough investigation of the background to this song, Donatien Laurent interviewed some 50 local people capable either of singing the *gwerz* or able to add some piece of information to the story. Knowledge of the event was, over two centuries later, still very much alive in the area, and Laurent was able to bring together different oral testimonies and add many new versions of the song to those already recorded. Taken all together, the oral testimony brings out a number of features that do not appear in the written records, some of them standing in direct contradiction to the findings of the court. A key role is played by a young woman from the village, widely believed to be an accomplice to the murder. Her name does not appear at all in the written archives, but Laurent's informants claimed that she belonged to a highly influential family with long-standing connections to the local magistrates. The song's clear identification of those involved in the death of Loeiz Er Ravalleg thus acts as a kind of redress, a slow-burn justice, keeping the memory of the tragedy alive. As with so many of the *gwerziou* in this anthology, the witness borne by oral tradition is intimately linked to, and reliant upon, the places where the events happened. On the ground, it is not difficult to follow the three young men between the villages – Langonnet, the church, Kerli, the cross at Penfel. The Ravallegs' house at Porsqueul still stands, as does the house where Loeiz was persuaded to stay for what would be his final drink – the place was still known in the 1960s as the *ti milliget* (the cursed house).

La Villemarqué's version, though elliptical and slightly mysterious in places, is also possessed of a terrible immediacy. This is a story, a lads' night out gone wrong, that translates too readily into our own time. There are some striking details – the wounded Loeiz escaping briefly, uselessly, into the bushes; the brutality of the attack, and the dead body lying in the field, with 'blond hair dishevelled across his eyes'. The structure of the piece is also intensely poignant, with the repetition of the injunction to be quiet and not fret or weep reappearing in radically different contexts – in the cheerful bluster of the friends to Moris Er Ravalleg, in their soothing of the anxious Loeiz, and, cruelly, in the moments before they attack. It appears also at the end of the *gwerz*, as a different voice tells the boy's father not to weep, because the truth will finally be known. Other versions bring their own details to the story; sometimes, instead of the mysterious 'Crown', it is an image of Saint Barbara which protects him (or rather, horribly protracts the business of the killing). Elsewhere, a sense of the miraculous is evoked through the image of the corpse's arm pointing upwards, accusatory, from a pile of dead leaves.

Studies:

Donatien Laurent, 'La gwerz de Louis Le Ravallec'.

Donatien Laurent, 'La gwerz de Louis Le Ravallec: Enquête sur un crime de 1732'.

Natalie Anne Franz, *Breton Song Traditions and the Case of the Gwerzioù: Women's Voices, Women's Lives*, pp. 221–64.

Philippe Guilloux, *Qui a tué Le Ravallec?*.

32. The twice-married woman

Pa z is me davit dour da feunteun ar c'hoat aleg
Me rankountras va dous hag hen gwisket e
skarleg

Hag hen goulenn diouzin ha me a ioa dimezet
Dre ma oan yaouankig ne greden ket lavaret.

– Ha c'houi zo dimezet? livirit din me ho ped.
– Salv ho kras, Aotrou ker, dimezet choaz nen
oun ket.

Hag hen kregi em dourn ha rei din e vizaoued
Hag eur mouchouer kaër a ioa ennan pemp
boked.

– Va list da vont d'ar gear, ember me vô skandalet
M'em euz eur goall lez-vamm, goasa oufet da
welet.

– Livirit d'ho lezvamm ar feunteun oa strafuillet
Gant marc'h eun den jentil, o tizrei euz an
Naoned

Liviret d'ho lezvamm ez oc'h hizio dimezet
Gant eur marc'heg yaouank o tizrei euz an
Naoned.

Benn teir zizun aman, me zizroio d'ho kwelet
Hag a gaso ganen klujiri, keveleged

Hag a gaso ganen klujiri, keveleged
Hag eur banne gwin dous, ar gwin demeuz hon
eured.

When I went to fetch water at the fountain of
Coatalec
I met my love dressed in scarlet

And he asked me if I was engaged to be married.
Because I was very young, I didn't dare to tell
him.

– Are you engaged? Tell me, I beg of you.
– With all due respect, sir, I am not yet engaged.

And he took me by the hand and gave me his
rings
And a fine handkerchief with five embroidered
flowers.

– Let me go home now, or I will be in trouble
I have an unkind stepmother, the worst you ever
saw.

– Tell your stepmother that the well was
disturbed
By the horse of a gentleman returning from
Nantes.

Tell your stepmother that today you became
engaged
To a young rider returning from Nantes.

Three weeks from now, I will return and see you
And with me I shall bring partridge and
woodcock

And with me I shall bring partridge and
woodcock
And a little sweet wine, the wine for our
wedding day.

Hag hi d'ar gear dioc'htu ho sellet ouz he bizou

Bizou he breur-mager oa gantan 'n e zourn deou

Teir zizun 'dremenas, eur miz a oa tremenet

Hag ar marc'heg yaouank ne oa ket c'hoaz
  dizroët.

— Red eo deoc'h dimezi, sonjal 'm euz great em
  c'halon

Ha kavet am euz deoc'h va merch eun den a
  feson.

— Salv-ho kras, va lez-vamm, 'm 'euz ezom a zen
  ebed

'Med euz va breur mager, a zo er gear digouezet

Bet am euz digantan gwalennig aour va eured

Dont a raï dizale, laouen ha skanv d'am
  cherc'het.

— Gant gwalenn hoc'h eured, me ho ped, serrit
  ho peg

Pe me dapo eur vaz hag a zesko deoc'h prezeg

Pe dre gaër pe dre heg red e vo deoc'h dimezi

Da Jobik al Loarek, da botrik ha marchossi.

— Da Jobik, nan biken, mervel 'rin gant ar
  c'hlac'har

Va mamm, va mammik paour, ma vijez var an
  douar!

— It d'en em glemm er porz, klemmit kement ma
  karfot

Kaër ho po benn eiz dez, dimezet mat e vefot.

And she went home at once, gazing at her ring

Her foster-brother's ring, which she wore on her
  right hand.

Three weeks went by, a month went by

And the young rider had still not returned.

— You must get engaged, I have thought it over

And I've found you, my girl, just the man you
  need.

— With all respect, stepmother, I have no need of
  anyone

But my foster-brother, who came to the house

He gave me the little gold ring for my wedding
  day

He will come for me soon enough, joyful and
  light-hearted.

— Hush, and don't mention that wedding ring again

Or I shall find a stick which will teach you to
  make speeches

Like it or not, you must get married

To Jobik Al Loarek, the stable boy.

— Jobik? No, never, I would die of sorrow

O mother, dear mother, if you were still alive!

— Go and complain in the yard, complain all you
  like

There is no use moaning; in eight days you will
  be married.

P'edon e Keridon en avis mont d he gwelet
E klevis sonerien o seni en he banked

When I reached Keridon, intending to go and see her
I heard the musicians playing for her wedding feast

E klevis sonerien o seni en he banket
Mont rin betek eno pa oufen beza lazet.

I heard the musicians playing for her wedding feast
And up to the house I went, kill me though it might.

– Digorit din an nor, c'houi plac'h nevez eureujet
An avel a zo kriz, va daou zorn a zo kropet

– Open the door, newly-married woman
The wind is bitter cold, my hands are numb

Digorit an nor din, va daou zourn a zo kropet
O terc'hel penn va marc'h ha va mantell alaouret.

Open the door to me, my hands are numb
With holding the bridle of my horse and my golden cloak.

– 'N zigorin ket an nor, va fried a zo kousket
Ha mar hen dihunan sur e vezin skandalet.

– I will not open the door, my husband has gone to bed
If I wake him, he will scold me for sure.

– Digorit an nor din, c'houi plac'h diou wech eureujet
War ho tourn deou ema gwalenn genta hoc'h eured.

– Open the door, twice-married woman
On your right hand is your first wedding ring.

P'oa digoret an nor hag elumet ar goulou
P'en em weljont o daou e rannas o c'halonou.

She opened up the door and lit the lamp
When they saw each other, their hearts broke.

Provenance:
'Ar breur-mager', collected by the theatre group Potred Sant Nouga in Saint-Vougay (Léon), 1910, and written down in a notebook belonging to Jean-Marie Perrot. Collection Perrot, 'Barzaz Bro-Leon'.

CD:
Track 20. Collected by Donatien Laurent from Monsieur Coïc, Loctudy (Cornouaille), 1968, Archives du Centre de Recherche Bretonne et Celtique, Université de Bretagne Occidentale, Brest. Dastum NUM-a77630.

The song of the twice-married woman is an excellent example of the way Breton songs can absorb and adapt themes and plot motifs from other traditions, in this case French (see also no. 10). It is an amalgamation of two well-known songs. The first is light-hearted in style and tells of a young girl sent to fetch water from the well, where she is seduced by a young man. It usually ends with the girl explaining her late arrival home through a series of implicitly sexual metaphors – the water of the well was muddied, or troubled, by birds or by a horse come to drink. Widespread and frequently attested, the earliest published version of this song dates back to 1586. The second song, probably later and quite different in tone, is about a woman who marries a young man called up to the army on his wedding day. When he returns, usually after seven years, he finds that his wife has given him up for dead and is newly remarried.

Dozens of versions of the story of the twice-married woman have been recorded, and it can often still be heard in the form of *kan ha diskan* – the call-and-response singing used in dances in Central Brittany (see nos 25 and 28). It offers a striking demonstration of some of the fundamental differences between the French and Breton song traditions. In French, even narrative songs tend to be shorter and lighter with generalised, stock characters. In Breton the songs tend to be much longer, embedded in a local landscape, and are often imbued with a sense of tragedy.

In French these two songs are quite separate. Breton tradition, however, frequently melds them together, with the girl at the well marrying either her seducer or another man, who is subsequently called up to fight – as in the version collected from Monsieur Coïc in Basse-Cornouaille (CD track 20). The multiple, exceptionally fluid versions of the *gwerz* expand and develop this basic narrative from a number of different perspectives. The introduction of place and personal names anchor it in local Breton landscapes, but little else is stable. The end often takes on a tragic, and occasionally melodramatic note: sometimes the newly remarried bride and her first husband die broken-hearted in each other's arms; elsewhere the first husband challenges the second to a duel and threatens to kill his wife. In some versions the girl herself has a child, who also dies. A lengthy version collected by François-Marie Luzel from Marc'harit Fulup goes even further, adding a score of couplets filling in the story of the young woman during the years her soldier-husband is away – a period usually passed over swiftly and in silence. Rejected by her parents after losing her honour, she finds refuge with her godmother, who arranges for her to marry the original seducer; in Fulup's version, all these people are named.[1]

Perhaps the most intriguing adaptation of this highly malleable song appears under the title *Ar Breur Mager/ Le Frère de Lait* ('The Foster-Brother') in La Villemarqué's *Barzaz-Breiz*. Here, added to the familiar elements of the unhappy girl, the stepmother, the encounter at the well, the forced marriage and the lover's return is a new dimension. The returning rider (who is the girl's betrothed, and also her foster-brother) is in fact a ghostly revenant, with ice-cold hands, come to claim his bride. They ride through the night to an island of apples, where the girl's dead mother and sisters are waiting. The following day the girl is found dead. In extensive notes to the piece, La Villemarqué – with typical disingenuity – compares his Breton text favourably with a range

---

1   Archives at the Centre de Recherche Bretonne et Celtique, Brest. Collection Anatole Le Braz, ALB4 M70, pp. 200–3.

of European parallels, including a Greco-Serbian ballad translated in Fauriel's *Chants populaires de la Grèce moderne* (1824–5) and one of the most popular literary ballads of the Romantic period, Gottfried Bürger's *Lenore* (1774). The latter poem, itself derived from a folk narrative widespread across Europe, vividly dramatised the night-ride with the dead lover. It is hard not to believe that the unforgettable phrase *die Toten reiden schnell!* ('the dead ride swiftly') was running through the young Breton author's mind as he 'restored' this *gwerz* to its supposedly 13th-century orginal.

Studies:

Éva Guillorel, *La Complainte et la Plainte: Chanson, justice, cultures en Bretagne*, pp. 135–45.

Mary-Ann Constantine, 'Ballads Crossing Borders: La Villemarqué and the "Breton Lenore"'.

33. The recruit: Garan Ar Briz

Ten - net eo ar so - ort gant Plou - be - riz,   Les - tet re - o du gant Ka - wa - niz.

Tennet eo ar sort gant Plouberiz
Lestet reo du gant Kawaniz

Lestet reo du gant Kawaniz
Digoue'et ar bilhed d' C'haran Ar Briz.

Garanig Ar Briz a lere
E n'hag ar bilhed du pa denne

– Me na rojen forzh 'vit partiañ
Panevet ma mamm baour a zo klañv

Emañ war he gwele seizh vloaz zo
Na deus ket ur c'hristen nemedon.

Garanig Ar Briz a lavare
Barzh ar ger d'e vamm pa n'arrie

– Sevel ma mamm baour ha deuit er-maez
Ma rin ho kwele c'hoazh ur wech.

Hag ar vamm pa glevas kemend-mañ
Respontas d'he mab eus n'en ouelañ

– O ma bugel te a gomañs skuizhañ
Pa n'out seizh vloaz zo deus ma bevañ.

– Ajen forzh na pa vijen pevarzek
Partiañ ma mamm baour a zo red

The boys from Ploubezre all drew lots
The boys from Cavan ended up with the black

The boys from Cavan ended up with the black
The lot fell to Garan Ar Briz.

Garanig Ar Bris said
Pulling out his black ticket

– I would not mind going away
If my poor mother were not so ill

Seven years she has been in bed
And I am all she has in the world.

Garan Ar Briz said
When he came to his mother's house

– Get up, mother dear, and leave the room
That I may make your bed one more time.

And his mother, when she heard that
Replied weeping to her son

– Oh child, you have had enough of this
Though you have cared for me only seven years.

– And if it were fourteen it would be all the
    same to me
My dearest mother, I have to go

O tennañ ar bilhed me zo bet
Hag ar bilhed du me 'm eus tennet.

I have just drawn lots
And I pulled out the black ticket.

Na oa ket e c'her peurachuet
Ur jendarm en ti zo antreet.

Scarcely had he said the words
When a *gendarme* entered the house.

– Allons 'ta Garanig, eme'añ
Allons 'ta hast buan, depechañ.

– Come along Garanig, he said
Come along, hurry now, make haste.

Garanig Ar Briz pa neus klewet
Er vriad e vamm e eo kroget

Garan Ar Briz, hearing this
Took hold of his mother's arm

Ha tri bok d'e vamm a neus roet
Hag er–maez an ti eo sortiet.

And he gave his mother three kisses
And he went out of the house.

Garanig Ar Briz a lavare
Barzh ar presbitor pa n'arrie

Garan Ar Briz said
When he reached the presbytery

– Dalc'h, matez ar person, ma alc'houezioù
Aet da welet ma mamm baour a-wechoù.

– Here, priest's maid, take my keys
Go and see my poor mother now and again.

– Lakaet anezhañ, emezi, lec'h ma gerfet
Ar garg deus ho mamm na n'oulan ket.

– Put them where you like, she said
I do not want to take on the care of your mother.

Garanig Ar Briz pa neus klewet
'N iliz parroz eo antreet.

Garan Ar Briz, when he heard this
entered the parish church.

– Aotro Sant Garan ma vaeron
Graet evidon mar plij un donezon

– Monsieur Saint Garan, my godfather
Grant me, if you please, one gift

Lakait ho kleier da son glas
Ar reo vunut hag ar c'hloc'h bras

Toll all the bells in your towers
The small ones and the great bell

Lakaet anezhe da son kañvo
Na d'am mammig paour pa vo marv

Ring the knell
For my poor mother when she dies

Na d'am mammig paour pa vo marv
Ha ma o c'hlewan me day d'am bro.

For my poor mother when she dies
And if I hear them, I will come home.

Garanig Ar Briz a lavare
N'hag e war ar bord e lestr nevez

Garan Ar Briz said
On the bridge of his new ship

– Me a glev ar c'hleier o son glas
Ar reo vunut hag ar c'hloc'h bras

Klevet a ran anezhe o son kañvo
O, kleier Kawan, kleier ma bro.

Hag e gabiten pa neus klewet
Da C'haranig Ar Briz a neus laret

– O, 'me'añ, me na gredan ket se
Klevfes kleier Kawan alese

Klevfes kleier Kawan alese
Te ve'añ pemp kant lev dioute.

– Lakaet ho troad dehou war ma hini
Ha c'hwi klevo ma mestr kenkoulz ha me.

E droad war e hini pa neus lakaet
Hag kenkoulz hag eñ a neus klevet.

Hag e gabiten pa neus klevet
Da C'haranig Ar Briz a neus laret

– Me a sino dit war baper gwenn
C'halli vale hardi en peb tachenn

Garanig a zo ur gwir kristen
Sort neus hini war ma batimant

Sort neus hini war ma batimant
Ur sort na n'on ket me ma unan.

Garanig Ar Briz a lavare
Barzh en bourg Kawan pa n'arrie

– Na laret c'hwi din-me Kawaniz
Pera zo a-newez 'n ho iliz?

– I hear the bells tolling
The small ones and the great bell

I hear them ringing the knell
O, bells of Cavan, o bells of my home.

And his captain, when he heard him
Said to Garan Ar Briz

– Ah, he said, I do not believe
That you can hear the bells of Cavan from here

That you can hear the bells of Cavan from here
When you are five hundred leagues away.

– Put your right foot on mine
And you will hear, master, as well as I do.

He placed his foot on the other man's
And heard [the bells] as clearly as he did.

The captain, when he heard them
Said to Garan Ar Briz

– I will sign for you on white paper
So that you may go anywhere without trouble

Garanig is a true Christian
And there are few of them on board my ship

There are few of them aboard my ship
And I am not one of them either.

Garan Ar Briz said
When he arrived at Cavan

– Tell me, you who live in Cavan
What is new in your church?

– Evit nimp, eme, na n'ouzomp ket se
'Mañ ar c'hleier o son noz ha deiz

Emaint noz ha deiz o son kañvo
Na zo kristen c'hanet war o zro.

Garanig Ar Briz pa neus klewet
'N iliz parroz eo antreet.

– Aotro Sant Garan ma vaeron
Graet evidon mar plij un donezon

Seset ho kleier da son kañvo
Arri eo ho filhor e-barzh ar vro.

Na oa ket e c'her peurachuet
Ar c'hleier da son zo poezet.

Pa n'eo antreet e-barzh an ti
Oa teir gwerc'hez deus he lienniñ

Unan oa terc'hen mat d'ar golo
Hag un all oa konduiñ he spilho.

Garanig Ar Briz pa neus klewet
Er vriad e vamm e eo kroget

Er vriad e vamm e eo kroget
E galon e-greiz a zo rannet.

Hag emaint o daou war ar varv-skaoñv
Doue da vardonno an anaoñ

Aet int o daou en peb a vez
Doue da viro gant o ene.

– We simply do not know, he said
The bells ring night and day

They ring the knell night and day
Though no-one is touching them.

Garan Ar Briz, when he heard this
Went into the parish church.

– Monsieur Saint Garan, my godfather
Perform a miracle for me, if you please

Tell your bells to stop tolling
Your godson has come home.

Scarcely had he said the words
Than the bells ceased to ring.

When he went into his house
Three maidens were wrapping her in a shroud

One held firmly to the sheet
Another plied the needle.

Garan Ar Briz, when he heard this
Took hold of his mother's arm

He took hold of his mother's arm
And his heart broke in two.

And both will be laid on the bier
God have mercy on all dead souls

Both are in the tomb
God preserve their souls.

Provenance:
Collected by Claudine Mazéas from Jeanne-Yvonne Garlan, Minihy-Tréguier (Trégor), around 1960–1. Dastum, NUM-2832.

CD:
Track 21. Same version.

The corpus of Breton printed ballads contains several songs about young men being called up to the army, or attempting to desert. Many of these date from the 19th century, and have found their way into the oral tradition. But there is also a well-attested body of earlier songs which clearly derive from the prerevolutionary period, and within this group two main song types focus on the experiences of new recruits. These are usually known by the names of their protagonists, *Garan Ar Briz* and *Silvestrig*, and they describe forms of recruitment characteristic of the *ancien régime*, notably the drawing of lots practised by the local militia set up under Louis XIV. All the young men old enough to join up are summoned, and those who draw the *bilhed du* (black ticket) or a designated unlucky number are obliged to undertake a long period of service. Most of the songs refer to a seven-year stint – a symbolic figure, but also in reality the average length of time soldiers spent in their regiments in the 18th century. The version of *Silvestrig* given in La Villemarqué's *Barzaz-Breiz* does not, therefore, as he claimed, evoke the departure of a young Breton nobleman joining William the Conqueror on his way to Hastings in 1066.[1]

The version given here, performed by the Trégor singer Jeanne-Yvonne Garlan, is unusual in situating Garan Ar Briz on board a ship, rather than fighting on a battlefield. A 'raw' version of *Silvestrig* collected by La Villemarqué has the same maritime context: after three years, the young man's father sees a sinking ship filled with soldiers who are all dying of scurvy (reminiscent of the 'death ship' in some versions of no. 10, 'Seven years at sea', which also features the drawing of lots).[2] The usual ending for this song is rather different, with the anxious father sending a little bird with a letter for his son, as in this version collected in 1979 by Yann-Fañch Kemener in Haute-Cornouaille:

Na 'barzh lein montenn Treger, didost da doull ma dor	On the Trégor hilltop, right by my door
Me 'glev an eonig bihan 'kano, me greda 'ma en gor.	I hear a bird singing, I think it is nesting.
Kano a ra ken mignon, kano a ra ken gê	It sings so prettily, it sings so gaily
Me 'garje 'm 'ize bet ur galon evel-se.	How I wish I had a heart like that.

---

1   'Le retour d'Angleterre', Théodore Hersart de la Villemarqué, *Barzaz-Breiz* (Paris: 1867), pp. 141–5.
2   Collection La Villemarqué, notebook 1, fol. 43. Published in Donatien Laurent, *Aux sources du Barzaz-Breiz: La mémoire d'un peuple*, p. 70.

Diskennit 'ta, eonig bihan, eonig a diw askell	Come down then, little bird, little bird with two wings
Ha c'hwi a nijfe 'vidon betek bordig ar brezel?	Will you fly for me all the way to the battle?
Ha c'hwi a nijfe 'vidon betek bord an arme	Will you fly for me over to the army
Da welet Jelvestr ar Moal m'emañ 'n e vuhe?	To see if Jelvestr Ar Moal is still alive?[3]

The bird accomplishes its task, and by the time it returns, the young man is already back on the doorstep of his home.

That same idea of miraculously linking two people who have been forced apart great distances is also at the heart of 'Garan Ar Briz'. Here the pain of separation from family is intensified by the fact that the young recruit's mother is chronically and seriously ill, and that no one else will look after her. There is an added emotional dimension of *mal de pays*, an intense attachment to place, with the hero summoned to his mother's deathbed by the bells of his local church, though they are ringing 500 leagues away. The focus of these *gwerziou* is thus less on the experiences of the men who are called up than on the theme of separation itself – set, in this case, within an edifying Christian context of filial piety and devotion to the local saints. The most arresting image of the entire ballad, however, is one which vanquishes distance and separation through a lovely moment of physical contact: 'Lakaet ho troad dehou war ma hini' ('place your right foot on mine') says Garan to his captain, and then you will hear the bells, and let me go home. That literal embodying of the miraculous is characteristic of the world of the *gwerziou* at its most imaginatively compelling.

Studies:

Henri d'Arbois de Jubainville, 'Note sur une chanson bretonne intitulée *Le Retour d'Angleterre* et qu'on croit supposée'.

Stéphane Perréon, *L'Armée en Bretagne au XVIIIᵉ siècle*, pp. 182–91.

Éva Guillorel, *La Complainte et la Plainte: Chanson, justice, cultures en Bretagne*, pp. 349–50.

---

3   Sung by Élise Magourou, Kerpert. Yann-Fañch Kemener, *Carnets de route*, pp. 262–3.

34. The death of the Chouan Jean Jan

Da houil Ie-hann dé a – veid dé-é Da houil Ie-ha-ann dé a – veid dé Ha jan-dar-

med Baod a–ar va-lé Ti la rou la lir lir Ti la la ti la rou lan lir, Ti la rou lan la.

Da houil Iehann dé aveid dé	On St John's Eve, day for day
Da houil Iehann dé aveid dé	On St John's Eve, day for day
Ha jandarmed Baod ar valé	The *gendarmes* of Baud went out walking
Ti la rou la lir lir	*Ti la rou la lir lir*
Ti la la ti la rou lan lir, Ti la rou lan la	*Ti la la ti la rou lan lir, Ti la rou lan la*
Ha ré Pondi e oé eùe	And those from Pontivy, they were there too
'Paréz Melrand kosté Kerlé.	In the parish of Melrand, over by Kerlé.
– Bonjour doh hui groagé Melrand	– Good day to you, women of Melrand
Ne huès chet guélet er chouan?	Have you seen any Chouans?
– Chetu en eih dé treméned	– It is eight days gone
N'ès chet guéled chouan erbet.	Since we last saw a Chouan.
– Geù e laret, groagé Melrand	– You lie, women of Melrand
Kèr déh hui poé gi hoah guéled.	For you saw one yesterday.
Fanchon Er Saoz 'dès achaped	Fanchon Er Saoz slipped away
De avertiss er chouaned.	To warn the Chouans.
– Paotred, achapet mar karet	– Boys, you had better run
Kèr ariù er soudarded.	The soldiers have arrived.
Marù é Jean Jan ha Lavinci	Jean Jan is dead, the Invincible too
Ha veint ket kaset da Bondi	They have not been taken to Pontivy
E mant duhont ér bounaleù	They are down there in the broom bushes
Goèd édandé a bouladeù.	Bathed in their own blood.

Lavinci 'gost ma oé ur braù

'Zo intèred é Sant Derhiaù

The Invincible, since he was so brave

Was buried at Saint-Thuriau

Chervij e hrei é relègeù

De frotein er chapelèteù.

His relics will serve

To finger like rosary beads.

Provenance:

Collected by Loeiz Le Bras from Joachim Le Clainche, Baud (Vannetais), 1960s. Dastum, NUM-20782. Published in Éva Guillorel, *La Complainte et la Plainte: Chanson, justice, cultures en Bretagne*, CD track 24; and in François Cadic, *Chansons populaires de Bretagne publiées dans la Paroisse bretonne de Paris*, CD track 20.

CD:

Track 22. Same version.

A number of *gwerziou* composed during the troubled years of the French Revolution were subsequently absorbed into the oral tradition: most of these songs were collected by members of the clergy, and tend to reflect a counter-revolutionary perspective. They frequently praise the refractory priests who refused to take the oath of allegiance to the Civil Constitution of the Clergy in 1790, or, as here, recount the exploits and ordeals of the Chouan leaders who fought, from 1793, in defence of religion and the monarchy.

Though fewer in number there are several revolutionary songs reflecting a republican point of view. The geographical distribution of songs clearly demonstrates the painful divisions between 'blue' (republican) and 'white' (monarchist) sympathies in the very heart of Breton-speaking Brittany. Counter-revolutionary songs and stories were principally collected in Léon and the Vannetais region – the latter area was most closely involved in the Chouan uprising (see nos 28 and 30). The opposite camp held sway in the *pays bigouden* in Lower Cornouaille, which voted solidly republican in the 19th century and communist in the twentieth, and where as late as 1985 collectors recorded fragments of a Breton song about a naval combat from the revolutionary period, with the stirring French refrain: *Vive la République! Vive la liberté!*

The song on the death of Jean Jan is a fine example of the extremely attenuated narrative style of the Vannetais region – it is typical, too, of those ballads which make heroes and martyrs of the Chouan leaders by focusing on their deaths. Jean Jan was killed at the side of his companion Claude Lorcy ('the Invincible') during a surprise attack by a republican column at Melrand on 24 June 1798; his sweetheart Fanchon Er Saoz, wounded in the fight, tried and failed to save him. The *gwerz* has remained in circulation locally, with all known versions collected in close proximity to the area of the events described. A version collected in 1911 by Jean-Yves Le Diberder from Marie-Louise Le Pallec in the neighbouring village of Baud even preserves the names of the people who denounced the Chouans, who were hiding in the village.[1] All the characters mentioned in the song are well known. Jean Jan, born in 1771, was the son of a farmer from Baud, who became a student at the same time as his neighbour Claude Lorcy. Both joined the rebels from the very first counter-revolutionary uprisings in 1793, and Jean Jan held several key positions in the Chouan command over the following years. As for Fanchon Er Saoz, she died at the age of 88, some 60 years after the events of the song, and possibly helped to keep Jean Jan's memory alive locally.

The memory of the Chouan leader was also kept alive in the region by the local clergy. At the end of the 19th century, the abbé Guilloux rediscovered bones in the chapel of Saint-Thuriau, believed to be those of Claude Lorcy and wrote an account of the life of Jean Jan. From 1914 the abbé François Cadic published a number of Chouan songs in his Paris-focused journal *La paroisse bretonne de Paris* – a collection of these would appear in 1949 under the title *Chants de chouans*.

These highly politicised songs can, however, be put to ironic use by oppositional factions. During the campaigns for local elections, for example, the socialists used 'Chouan songs' to make fun of the rebels' heroically tragic fates. This is the context for the version of 'Jean Jan' sung by Joachim Le Clainche well into the 1970s (CD track 22). The collector, Loeiz Le Bras, recalls hearing his great-aunt singing this song; it became part of his own repertoire and he sings it to this day. Historical memories of Jean Jan and Claude Lorcy have thus been kept alive into the 21st century, through the songs, as well as through objects and a continuous association with the places where they fought.

The case of Jean Jan is not unique. It is still possible to find different forms of popular memorialisation of the French Revolution in Brittany and across western France. There are the 'tombes de mémoire' (unofficial commemorative graves), often situated in forests and associated with the victims of both sides: they are especially prevalent in the Vannetais region, and are frequently the focus of localised popular cults. Anecdotes and legends are still in circulation, enriched both by oral tradition and by an increasing number of publications. Regular commemorative events – the bicentenary notable amongst them – also help to keep local knowledge of this turbulent period alive at a local level.

Studies:

Roger Dupuy, 'Le Barzaz Breiz et la production poétique orale dans la société rurale bretonne à la fin du XVIIIe siècle ou: Les choix d'un vicomte'.

François Cadic, 'La mort de Jean Jan', *Paroisse Bretonne de Paris*. Republished in François Cadic, *Chansons populaires de Bretagne publiées dans la Paroisse bretonne de Paris*, pp. 407–10 + CD track 20.

François Cadic, *Chants de chouans*, pp. 153–72.

Jean-Marie Guilloux, 'Mort de Jean Jan et de l'Invincible'.

1   Yves Le Diberder, *Chansons traditionelles du pays vannetais*, vol. 2, pp. 789–90.

Youenn Le Prat, "*Vive la République!*". *Ar Volonter*, récit de combat naval et chant républicain'.

Éva Guillorel, *La Complainte et la Plainte: Chanson, justice, cultures en Bretagne*, pp. 482–3.

Éva Guillorel, 'Folksongs, Conflicts and Social Protest in Early Modern France'.

Alain Croix, *Mémoire de 93: Sur les traces de la Révolution en Bretagne*, film and booklet, pp. 18–19.

Révoltes, Résistances et Révolution en Bretagne, CD track 4 and booklet, pp. 28–31.

35. Our Lady of Port-Blanc

Seiz lestr partijont assambles	Seven ships together they set off
Partijont a goste Londres	They set off from near London
Ma teujont war du Breiz-Izel	And came to the coast of Brittany
Wit massacri ar bobl fidel.	To slaughter the faithful people.
Med Itron Varia ar Porz-Gwenn	But our Lady of Port-Blanc
E-man e zi war an dossenn	Has her house on the hill
E-man e zi war an dossenn	She has her house on the hill
A wel ar Zaozon deuz a bell.	And sees the English from afar.
Itron Varia ar Porz-Gwenn	Our Lady of Port-Blanc
A ra zoudarded gant radenn	Makes soldiers out of bracken
A ra zoudarded gant radenn	Makes soldiers out of bracken
D'ampich ar Zaozon da diskenn	To stop the English landing.
Kerkent, hi a deuz permitet	Instantly she granted
M'aje ar radenn da zoudarded.	That the bracken should turn to soldiers.
Etre Porz-Gwenn ha Crec'h-Marted	Between Port-Blanc and Crec'h Martet
A oa kant mil a zoudarded	There were a hundred thousand soldiers
Ha pa zellent er c'hoste all	And when they looked at the other side
A welent mui pe gement all	They saw more, or just as many
Tre Plouvouscant hac ar Porz-Gwenn	Between Plougrescant and Port-Blanc
Holl a oant formet gant radenn	All were created from bracken
Zoudarded vaillant, armet mad	Valiant soldiers, thoroughly armed
Prest da rei d'ar Zaozon combat.	Ready to battle with the English.
Kement garrek a oa war drô	Every rock in the area
A oa n'em chanchet en forjô	Was turned into a fortress
A oa n'em chanchet en forjô	Was turned into a fortress
En forjô leun a ganonô.	A fortress full of cannon.

Krec'h ar Gontess, war an huël	Crec'h ar Gontess, upon the heights
Weler anezhan diabell	Can be seen from afar
Biscoaz sur ar Zaoz na welaz	Never for sure had the English seen
Kement demeuz a bopulaz	Such a massive crowd
P'oant en dro d'ar vaz-pavillon	As they stood around the main-mast
E clewent ar musik o sôn	They could hear the music playing.
Tafêk, Perroz ha Louannek	Tomé, Perros and Louannec
A oa leun gouch a zoudarded.	Were stuffed full of soldiers.
Gentiles Rouzic ha Bono	The Seven Isles, Rouzic and Bono
Oa fortifiet trô war zrô	Were fortified in every direction
Gant moguerio incomprénabl	By ramparts, astonishing
D'ho spered ha d'ho daoulagad.	To their minds and eyes.
Tud Breiz-Izel, hed a coste	The people of Brittany, along the coast
A zo en spourôn noz ha de	Are in dread day and night
A zo en spourôn noz ha de	Are in dread day and night
Gant aon na da goll ho buhe.	For fear they will lose their lives.
Mouez ar c'hanonô a groze	The voices of the cannon rumbled
Ken a sklake tout ar c'hontre	So it shook the whole country
Gant an drouz démeuz an tennô	The noise from the blasts
A goueze ar vugaligô.	Made the little children fall down.
Paour ha pinvik, iaouank ha coz	Poor and rich, young and old
A bartijont a greiz an noz	Left in the middle of the night
Kwitâd ho zi hac ho mado	Left their houses and possessions
Ha décapi er foréjô	And made for the woods
'N eur bedi ar Werc'hez Vari	Praying to the Virgin Mary
Jezuz he mab d'ho frezervi.	And Jesus her Son to preserve them.
Ar Zaozon a lamp en Gweltraz	The English leapt onto the Isle of Gildas
Prest da ziskenn an Douar-braz	Ready to descend on the mainland

| Imajô 'r Zent deuz bruzunet | They shattered the images of the saints |
| Cloc'h ar chapel ho deuz laêret | And stole the bell from the chapel |

| Laket deuz-han er wern-gestel | They hung it from the mainmast |
| Da zôn wit ober an appel | To ring out the call to arms |

| Kouet ê digant-hê er mor dôn | But it fell from them into the deep sea |
| Eur veach bep seiz la e sôn | Once every seven years it rings |

| Ewit ma lavaro tud Breiz | And so the people of Brittany say |
| – 'Man cloc'h Sant Gweltraz er Ger-Eiz. | – St Gildas is ringing in Ker-Is. |

| Pa 'c'h ê partiet ar Zaozon | When the English left |
| Oa rejouisset ho c'halon. | People's hearts rejoiced. |

| Pa int retornet d'ho c'hontre | They went back to their lands |
| Deuz savet eun iliz newe | And built a new church |

| Prenet eur gaer a gurunenn | And bought a most beautiful crown |
| Da Itron Varia ar Porz-Gwenn. | For our Lady of Port-Blanc. |

Provenance:
Collected by Anatole Le Braz from Lise Bellec, Penvénan (Trégor), 1894. Published in Anatole Le Braz, *Rapport sur une enquête relative aux saints bretons, à leurs légendes, à leurs oratoires*. Republished in Mary-Ann Constantine, 'Notre-Dame de Port-Blanc. Itron Varia ar Porz-Gwenn', pp. 411–15.

This intriguing *gwerz* was noted down by the writer and collector Anatole Le Braz in the northern coastal village of Port-Blanc. In his manuscript account of the song's discovery (which may be one of the fictional *mises-en-scène* he often devises for his published works of folklore), he claims that it had been a long search. Luzel apparently knew of a single couplet, encapsulating the miracle at the heart of the story:

| Itron Varia ar Borz Wenn | Our Lady of Port-Blanc |
| A ra soudarded gant radenn. | Made soldiers out of bracken. |

The song itself, however, remained elusive until Le Braz 'heard a woman singing to herself' in the sacristan's house in the village. She turned out to be one of his regular and most productive informants, the seamstress Lise Bellec. Le Braz sent the text 'with all its gaps and inconsistencies'[1] (he had not recorded the tune) in a report prepared for the Ministry of Public Instruction.

English attacks along the north coast of Brittany were a regular occurrence over many centuries: as with the ballad about the descent of English forces at Dourduff (no. 25), this *gwerz* describes what would be a continually renewed threat over many centuries. One commentator has suggested that it refers to an attack as early as 1492, when the English did apparently land on St Gildas, but retreated in the face of staunch local defence. The construction of Port-Blanc's beautiful chapel to the Virgin, which dates from the 16th century, may have been in commemoration of this defeat; it is still there, hugging the slope, with a huge roof that drops almost to ground level, as if wanting to protect as many people as possible. On the other hand, the reference to the bell of St Gildas tolling in 'Ker-Is' (the underwater kingdom, corresponding to the Welsh *Cantre'r Gwaelod*) looks to be much later, since there is very little evidence for widespread knowledge of this story before the 19th century. This allusion to Ker-Is, and the style of the ballad generally, along with the fact that the text collected by Le Braz remains the only known version, suggests that this is a later composition, reflecting perhaps the detailed historical and geographical knowledge of a local 19th-century poet.

Whatever its circumstances of composition, and whether or not it recalls a particular event, the ballad certainly evokes a wonderfully precise local landscape, and pays homage to what is effectively a *local* saint. In a reversal of the process which hides or replaces 'smaller' saints with more widely culted national or international figures (see no. 6), Breton worship of the Virgin is often intensely localised, and she 'splits' readily into different selves. Le Braz's report to the Ministry also contains an anecdote about two fishermen who see 'Notre Dame de Port-Blanc' in the form of a shining light gliding over the sea, on her way to visit her 'first cousin, Notre Dame de la Clarté, at neighbouring Perros-Guirec'.

The ballad also captures in a few memorable phrases what war means to civilians. The noise of the cannon shakes the entire region, and knocks little children to the ground; the villagers abandon everything and flee into the woods at night, praying for deliverance. That deliverance, when it comes, is superbly apposite. The granite coast around Port-Blanc is all jagged outcrops and, from early summer, tall bracken. Anyone who has seen bracken unfurling will appreciate the image – both helpless and brave – of tightly clenched fists, and ranks of soldiers, facing the threat from the sea.

Studies:

Anatole Le Braz, *Rapport sur une enquête relative aux saints bretons, à leurs légendes, à leurs oratoires (août–septembre 1894)*.

Mary-Ann Constantine, 'Notre-Dame de Port-Blanc. Itron Varia ar Porz-Gwenn'.

Bernard Lasbleiz, 'Itron Varia ar Porzh-Gwenn'. Republished in Bernard Lasbleiz, *Ma'm bije bet kreion: Chroniques musicologiques du Trégor et autres pays de Bretagne*, pp. 100–4.

1   'La voici, avec ses incohérences et ses lacunes', cited in Mary-Ann Constantine, 'Notre-Dame de Port-Blanc. Itron Varia ar Porz-Gwenn', p. 412.

Bibliography

Ar Braz, Gwendal, 'Gwerz Perinaig ar Mignon', *Enklaskoù Klas Termen*, Lise Diwan 2 (Carhaix: Embanna-durioù an Hemon, 1999), 5–26.

Arbois de Jubainville, Henri d', 'Note sur une chanson bretonne intitulée *Le Retour d'Angleterre* et qu'on croit supposée', *Revue Archéologique*, 17 (1868), 227–40.

Atkinson, David, *The English Traditional Ballad. Theory, Method, and Practice* (Aldershot: Ashgate, 2002).

—— *The Anglo-Scottish Ballad and its Imaginary Contexts* (Cambridge: Open Book Publishers, 2014).

—— and Steve Roud (eds), *Street Ballads in Nineteenth-Century Britain, Ireland, and North America: The Interface between Print and Oral Traditions* (Aldershot: Ashgate, 2014).

Balcou, Jean and Yves Le Gallo (eds), *Histoire littéraire et culturelle de la Bretagne*, 3 vols (Brest, Paris and Geneva: Champion, Slatkine, 1987).

Ball, Martin J. and James Fife (eds), *The Celtic Languages* (London: Taylor & Francis, 1993).

Balland, Anne, 'Littérature orale et noblesse bretonne: le cas Du Parc de Locmaria', unpublished Master's thesis (Nantes: Université de Nantes, 1999).

Belmont, Nicole (ed.), *Aux sources de l'ethnologie française: L'académie celtique* (Paris: Comité des travaux scientifiques et historiques, 1995).

Becker, Roland and Laure Le Gurun, *La Musique Bretonne* (Spézet: Coop Breizh, 1994).

Belz, Jorj and Fañch Desbordes, *Sonamb get en Drouzerion. 100 sonenn a vro-Gwened*, 2 vols (Lesneven: Hor Yezh, 1985).

Bénichou, Paul, *Nerval et la chanson folklorique* (Paris: José Corti, 1970).

Berthou-Bécam, Laurence, 'Après Luzel et La Villemarqué … Gabriel Milin', *Musique Bretonne*, 139 (1996), 14–19.

—— 'Enquête officielle sur les poésies populaires de la France', unpublished doctoral thesis, 3 vols (Rennes: Université Rennes 2, 1998).

—— and Didier Bécam, *L'enquête Fortoul (1852–1876): Chansons populaires de Haute et Basse-Bretagne*, 2 vols (Paris and Rennes: Comité des travaux scientifiques et historiques, Dastum, 2010).

Billacois, François, *Le duel dans la société française des XVIᵉ–XVIIᵉ siècles: Essai de psychologie historique* (Paris: EHESS, 1986).

Blanchard, Nelly, *Barzaz-Breiz: Une fiction pour s'inventer* (Rennes: Presses universitaires de Rennes, 2006).

—— (ed.), *Jean-Marie de Penguern (1807–1856): Collecteur et collectionneur breton* (Brest: Centre de recherche bretonne et celtique, 2008).

Bourgault-Ducoudray, Louis, *Trente Mélodies populaires de Basse-Bretagne* (Paris and Brussels: Lemoine, 1885).

Boyd, Matthieu, 'The Female Jailer: Commonplaces in the gwerziou', in Joseph Harris and Barbara Hillers (eds), *Child's Children: Ballad Study and Its Legacies* (Trier: WVT Wissenschaftlicher Verglag, 2012), pp. 186–204.

Brett, Caroline, 'Breton Latin literature as Evidence for Literature in the Vernacular AD 800–1300', *Cambrian*

Medieval Celtic Studies, 18 (1989), 1–25.

Broudic, Fañch, *La pratique du breton de l'Ancien Régime à nos jours* (Rennes: Presses universitaires de Rennes, 1995).

—— *Parler breton au XXIᵉ siècle* (Brest: Emgleo Breiz, 2009).

Brown, Terence (ed.), *Celticism* (Amsterdam and Atlanta: Rodopi, 1996).

Buchan, David, *The Ballad and the Folk* (London: Routledge & Kegan Paul, 1972).

Buhez Association (ed.), *Parlons du breton* (Rennes: Ouest-France, 2001).

Buléon, Mathurin, *Chansons traditionnelles du pays vannetais* (Vannes: Archives départementales du Morbihan, Dastum Bro-Ereg, 2012).

Cadic, François, 'La jeune fille de Lannion', *Mélusine,* 7 (1893), 127–31.

—— 'Le Sire de Villaudrain', *Paroisse bretonne de Paris* (1905), 8–10.

—— 'La mort de Jean Jan', *Paroisse Bretonne de Paris* (1915).

—— *Chants de chouans* (Geneva and Paris: Slatkine, 1981, repr. 1949), pp. 153–72.

—— *Chansons populaires de Bretagne publiées dans la Paroisse bretonne de Paris (1899–1929)* (Rennes and Brest: Presses universitaires de Rennes, Dastum, Centre de recherche bretonne et celtique, 2010).

Calvez, Ronan, 'Du breton mondain', *Annales de Bretagne et des Pays de l'Ouest,* 115 (2008/3), 135–53.

Cambry, Jacques, *Voyage dans le Finistère, ou Etat de ce département en 1794 et 1795,* 3 vols (Paris, 1797–98).

[no author], 'The Carmichael Watson Project'. Available at: http://www.carmichaelwatson.lib.ed.ac.uk/cwatson/.

Carné, Gaston de, 'L'héritière de Keroullas', *Revue Historique de l'Ouest,* 3 (1887), 5–24.

Carrington, Henry, *Breton Ballads Translated from the Barzaz-Breiz* (Edinburgh: Turnbull and Spears, 1886).

Castel, Ifig, *Amzer vat* (Kreizenn sevenadurel Lannuon, 2004), CD.

Charles-Wurtz, Ludmila, 'Le lyrisme de *La Guzla*', in Antonia Fonyi (ed.), *Prosper Mérimée: Écrivain, Archéologue, Historien* (Geneva: Droz, 1999), pp. 99–110.

Chassé, Charles, 'Les charivaris d'Hennebont', *Le Fureteur breton,* 55 (1919), 12–14.

Child, Francis James (ed.), *The English and Scottish Popular Ballads,* 5 vols (1882–1898, repr. New York, 1965).

Constantine, Mary-Ann, 'Story and History in the Breton Ballads: the Case of *Iannik Kokard*', *Reading Medieval Studies,* XX (1994), 13–35.

—— 'A Breton Mary Magdalene: the gwerz of Mari Kelenn', in Eyðun Andreassen (ed.), *Visions & Identities. Proceedings of the 24th International Ballad Conference* (Tórshavn: Tungulist, 1996), pp. 73–93.

—— *Breton Ballads* (Aberystwyth: Cambrian Medieval Celtic Studies, 1996).

—— 'Ballad Crossing Borders: La Villemarqué and the "Breton Lenore"', *Translation and Literature,* 8 (1999), 197–216.

—— 'Saints Behaving Badly: Sanctity and Transgression in Breton Popular Culture', in Jane Cartright (ed.), *Celtic Hagiography and Saints' Cults* (Cardiff: University of Wales Press, 2003), pp. 198–215.

—— 'Neither Flesh Nor Fowl: Merlin as Bird-man in Breton Folk Tradition', *Arthurian Literature,* XXI (2004), 95–114.

—— *The Truth Against the World: Iolo Morganwg and Romantic Forgery* (Cardiff: University of Wales Press, 2007).

—— 'Notre-Dame de Port-Blanc. Itron Varia ar Porz-Gwenn', in Fañch Postic (ed.), *Bretagnes, du cœur aux lèvres: Mélanges offerts à Donatien Laurent* (Rennes: Presses universitaires de Rennes, 2008), pp. 409–15.

—— '"Impertinent structures": a Breton's Adventures in Neo-Gothic Wales', *Studies in Travel Writing,* 18 (2014), 134–47.

—— (ed.), *Ballads in Wales-Baledi yng Nghymru* (London: FLS Books, 1999).

—— and Gerald Porter, *Fragments and Meaning in Traditional Song: from the Blues to the Baltic* (Oxford: Oxford University Press, 2003).

Cornette, Joël, *Le Marquis et le Régent: Une conspiration bretonne à l'aube des Lumières* (Paris: Tallandier, 2008).

Costello, Louisa Stuart, *A Summer Amongst the Bocages and the Vines* (London: Richard Bentley, 1840).

Cox Jensen, Oskar, *Napoleon and British Song 1797–1822* (London: Palgrave Macmillan, 2015).

Croix, Alain, *La Bretagne aux 16ᵉ et 17ᵉ siècles: La vie, la mort, la foi* (Paris: Maloine, 1981).

—— *L'âge d'or de la Bretagne* (Rennes: Ouest-France, 1993).

—— *Mémoire de 93: Sur les traces de la Révolution en Bretagne* (Rennes, 1997). Film and booklet. Available at: https://www.canalu.tv/video/universite_rennes_2_crea_cim/memoire_de_93.14527.

—— (ed.), *La Bretagne d'après l'itinéraire de monsieur Dubuisson-Aubenay* (Rennes: Presses universitaires de Rennes, Société d'Histoire et d'Archéologie de Bretagne, 2006).

[no author], *Dastumad Pennwern, Chants populaires bretons de la collection de Penguern* (Rennes: Dastum, 1983).

Doncieux, George, *Le romancéro populaire de la France* (Paris: Émile Bouillon, 1904).

Duhamel, Maurice, *Gwerziou ha soniou Breiz-Izel: Musiques bretonnes: Airs et variantes mélodiques des 'chants et chansons populaires de la Basse-Bretagne' publiés par F. M. Luzel et A. Le Braz* (Paris: Lerolle, 1913, repr. Rennes: Dastum, 1997).

Dupuy, Roger, 'Le Barzaz Breiz et la production poétique orale dans la société rurale bretonne à la fin du XVIIIᵉ siècle ou: Les choix d'un vicomte', in Heikki Kirkinen and Jean Perrot (eds), *Le monde kalévaléen en France et en Finlande, avec un regard sur la tradition populaire et l'épopée bretonnes* (Paris and Helsinki: Klincksieck, 1987), pp. 281–7.

Evain, Brice, 'Deux héros de Bretagne. Le marquis de Pontcallec et Marion du Faouët', unpublished Master's thesis (Rennes, 2009).

Fauriel, Claude, *Chants populaires de la Grèce moderne*, 2 vols (Paris: 1824–5).

Favereau, Francis, 'Phonologie des rimes et des vers dans la poésie chantée à Poullaouen', *Klask*, 3 (1996), 35–41.

Fox, Adam, *Oral and Literate Culture in England, 1500–1700* (Oxford: Oxford University Press, 2000).

Franz, Natalie Anne, *Breton Song Traditions and the Case of the Gwerzioù: Women's Voices, Women's Lives* (Rennes: Tir, 2011).

Fréminville, Chevalier de, *Antiquités des Côtes-du-Nord* (1837, repr. Paris, Geneva, Gex: Slatkine, 1980).

Friedman, Albert B., 'The Oral-Formulaic Theory of Balladry – A Re-rebuttal', in James Porter (ed.), *The Ballad Image: Essays Presented to Bertrand Harris Bronson* (Los Angeles: Center for the Study of Comparative Folklore & Mythology, University of California, Los Angeles, 1983), pp. 215–40.

Gauter, Jean, *Mémoire contée et chantée du chemin de saint Jacques en Bretagne* (Brech: Association bretonne des amis de Saint-Jacques-de-Compostelle, 2015).

Gemie, Sharif, *Brittany 1750–1950: The Invisible Nation* (Cardiff: University of Wales Press, 2007).

Giraudon, Daniel, 'Chansons de langue bretonne sur feuilles volantes et compositeurs populaires: Un chanteur-chansonnier du Trégor. Yann ar Gwenn', unpublished doctoral thesis (Brest: Université de Bretagne Occidentale, 1982).

—— 'Un distro war werz an Aotrou Kergwezeg', *Planedenn*, 11 (1982), 29–46.

—— *Chansons populaires de Basse-Bretagne sur feuilles volantes* (Morlaix: Skol Vreizh, 1985).

—— 'Une chanson de conscrits en langue bretonne: Chanson Paotred Plouillio', *Mémoires de la Société d'Émulation des Côtes-du-Nord*, 116 (1987), 39–63.

—— 'Tradition orale et feuilles volantes: Chroniques maritimes des Côtes-d'Armor en rimes bretonnes',

La mer et les jours, XVe siècle–1940. 5 siècles d'arts et cultures maritimes en Côtes-d'Armor (Saint-Brieuc: Les Presses Bretonnes, 1992), pp. 170–2.

—— 'Penanger et de La Lande, Gwerz tragique au XVIIe siècle en Trégor', *Annales de Bretagne et des Pays de l'Ouest*, 112 (2005), 7–42.

—— *Traditions populaires de Bretagne: Du soleil aux étoiles* (Spézet: Coop Breizh, 2007).

—— 'Drame sanglant au pardon de Saint-Gildas à Tonquédec en 1707: Gwerz ar c'homt a Goat-Louri hag an otro Porz-Lann', *Annales de Bretagne et des Pays de l'Ouest*, 114 (2007), 58–88.

—— 'Gwerz sant Juluan. De la feuille volante à la tradition orale', in *Jean-Marie de Penguern (1807–1856): Collecteur et collectionneur breton* (Brest: Centre de recherche bretonne et celtique, 2008), pp. 139–67.

—— and Donatien Laurent, 'Gwerz an Aotrou Kergwezeg', *Planedenn*, 6 (1980–1), 13–43.

Glencross, Michael, *Reconstructing Camelot: French Romantic Medievalism and the Arthurian Tradition* (Cambridge: Brewer, 1995).

Gourvil, Francis, '"Voleur sans le savoir": Prosper Mérimée et Gwenc'hlan en 1835', *Nouvelle Revue de Bretagne* (1949/2), 104–15; (1949/3), 211–23; (1949/4), 299–306.

—— *Théodore-Claude-Henri Hersart de La Villemarqué (1815–1895) et le 'Barzaz-Breiz' (1839–1845–1867)* (Rennes: Oberthur, 1960).

Guillerm, Henri, *Recueil de chants populaires bretons du pays de Cornouailles* (Rennes: François Simon, 1905).

Guillevic, Augustin and Jean-Mathurin Cadic, *Chants et airs traditionnels du pays vannetais* (Pontivy and Vannes: Dastum Bro-Ereg, Archives départementales du Morbihan, 2007).

Guillorel, Éva, 'La *gwerz* de la tour de plomb', *ArMen*, 162 (2007), 6–13.

—— 'La complainte du marquis de Pontcallec, les *gwerzioù* bretonnes et l'histoire', in Joël Cornette, *Le Marquis et le Régent: Une conspiration bretonne à l'aube des Lumières* (Paris: Tallandier, 2008), pp. 297-338 + CD.

—— *La Complainte et la Plainte: Chanson, justice, cultures en Bretagne, XVIe–XVIIIe siècles* (Rennes and Brest: Presses universitaires de Rennes, Centre de recherche bretonne et celtique, Dastum, 2010).

—— *Barzaz Bro-Leon: Une expérience inédite de collecte en Bretagne* (Rennes and Brest: Presses universitaires de Rennes, Centre de recherche bretonne et celtique, 2012).

—— 'Folksongs, Conflicts and Social Protest in Early Modern France', in Dieuwke Van der Poel (ed.), *Identities, Intertextuality and Performance in Song Culture (1500–1800)* (Leiden: Brill, 2016), pp. 287–307.

Guilloux, Jean-Marie, 'Mort de Jean Jan et de l'Invincible', *Bulletin de la Société Polymathique du Morbihan* (1899), 54–77.

Guilloux, Philippe, *Qui a tué Le Ravallec?* (Carrément à l'Ouest, 2013). Film, 90 minutes.

Gunderloch, Anja, 'The Heroic Ballads of Gaelic Scotland', in Sarah Dunnigan and Suzanne Gilbert (eds), *The Edinburgh Companion to Scottish Traditional Literatures* (Edinburgh: Edinburgh University Press, 2013), pp. 74–84.

Hélias, Pierre-Jakez, *Le cheval d'orgueil* (Paris: Plon, 1975).

Herrieu, Loeiz, *Guerzenneu ha soñnenneu Bro-Guened. Chansons populaires du pays de Vannes* (Paris: Rouard, Lerolle, 1911).

Hobsbawm, Eric J., *Bandits* (London: Weidenfeld and Nicolson, 1969).

Hopkin, David, *Voices of the People in Nineteenth-Century France* (Cambridge: Cambridge University Press, 2012).

Jarman, A. O. H., 'Cerdd Ysgolan', *Ysgrifau Beirniadol*, 10 (1977), 51–78.

—— (ed.) *Llyfr Du Caerfyrddin* (Cardiff: Gwasg Prifysgol Cymru, 1982).

Jarnoux, Philippe, 'Pontcallec ou les métamorphoses de la mémoire', in Dominique Le Page (ed.), *11 questions d'Histoire qui ont fait la Bretagne* (Morlaix: Skol Vreizh, 2009), pp. 183–206.

Jones, Ffion Mair (ed.), *Welsh Ballads of the French Revolution* (Cardiff: University of Wales Press, 2012).

——'Welsh Balladry and Literacy', in David Atkinson and Steve Roud (eds), *Street Ballads in Nineteenth-Century Britain, Ireland, and North America: The Interface between Print and Oral Traditions* (Aldershot: Ashgate, 2014), pp. 105–26.

Kemener, Yann-Fañch, *Carnets de route. Kanaouennoù Kalon Vreizh, Chants profonds de Bretagne* (Morlaix: Skol Vreizh, 1996).

Kerenveyer, François-Nicolas Pascal de, *Ar farvel göapaër. Le bouffon moqueur*. Texte traduit et présenté par Ronan Calvez (Brest: Centre de recherche bretonne et celtique, 2005).

Keryell, Gaela, 'The *Kalevala* and the *Barzaz-Breiz*: The Relativity of the Concept of "Forgery"', in Anders Ahlqvist, Glyn Welden Banks, Riita Latvio, Harri Nyberg and Tom Sjöblom (eds), *Celtica Helsingiensia*, 107 (Helsinki: Societas Scientiarum Fennica, 1996), pp. 57–103.

La Villemarqué, Théodore Hersart de, *Barzas-Breiz: Chants populaires de la Bretagne* (Paris, 1839); 2nd ed. *Barzaz-Breiz* (1845); 3rd ed. (1867, repr. Paris: Perrin, 1963).

Lagadeuc, Jehan, *Le Catholicon armoricain* [1499] (Mayenne: J. Floch, 1977).

Larboulette, Jean-Louis, *Chants traditionnels vannetais* (1902–1905) (Pontivy: Dastum Bro-Ereg, 2005).

Lasbleiz, Bernard, 'Itron Varia ar Porzh-Gwenn', *Musique bretonne*, 163 (2000), 24–7.

——'Fontanella, un héros de chanson populaire', *Musique bretonne*, 172 (2002), 28–31.

——'Marc'harit Fulup: Les enregistrements de François Vallée', *Musique bretonne*, 173 (2002), 33–5.

——'Le timbre de Kêr Is: Un air populaire qui traverse les siècles', *Musique bretonne*, 188 (2005), 34–8.

—— *Ma'm bije bet kreion: Chroniques musicologiques du Trégor et autres pays de Bretagne* (Lannion: Dastum Bro Dreger, 2007).

——'War don… Les timbres des chansons et cantiques populaires en langue bretonne (17ᵉ–20ᵉ siècle)', unpublished doctoral thesis (Brest: 2012).

Laurent, Donatien, 'La gwerz de Louis Le Ravallec', *Arts et Traditions Populaires*, 15 (1967), 19–79.

——'La gwerz de Skolan et la légende de Merlin', *Ethnologie française*, 1 (1971, 3–4), 19–54.

——'Aymar de Blois (1760–1852) et les premières collectes de chants populaires bretons', *Cahiers de l'Iroise*, 93 (1977, January–March), 1–8.

——'Breton Orally Transmitted Folk Poetry', in Otto Holzapfel (ed.), *The European Medieval Ballad: A Symposium* (Odense: Odense University Press, 1978), pp. 16–25.

——'Brigitte, accoucheuse de la Vierge. Présentation d'un dossier', *Le monde alpin et rhodanien*, Croyances, récits et pratiques de tradition. Mélanges Charles Joisten (1982, 1–4), 73–9.

——'Enori et le roi de Brest', *Études sur la Bretagne et les pays celtiques: Mélanges offerts à Yves Le Gallo*, Cahiers de Bretagne Occidentale 6 (Brest: Centre de recherche bretonne et celtique, 1987), pp. 207–24.

——'La gwerz de Louis Le Ravallec: Enquête sur un crime de 1732', *ArMen*, 7 (1987), 16–35.

——'Histoire et poésie chantée: l'exemple de la Bretagne', *Historiens-Géographes*, 318 (1988), 111–14.

—— *Aux sources du Barzaz-Breiz: La mémoire d'un peuple* (Douarnenez: ArMen, 1989).

——'Tradition and Innovation in Breton Oral Literature', in Glanmor Williams and Robert Owen Jones (eds), *The Celts and the Renaissance: Tradition and Innovation* (Cardiff: University of Wales Press, 1990), pp. 91–9.

——'Aymar I de Blois (1760–1852) et "L'héritière de Keroulas"', in Gwennolé Le Menn and Jean-Yves Le Moign (eds), *Bretagne et pays celtiques. Langues, histoire, civilisation. Mélanges offerts à la mémoire de Léon Fleuriot* (Saint-Brieuc and Rennes: Skol, Presses universitaires de Rennes, 1992), pp. 415–43.

——'Mémoire et poésie chantée en Pays Bigouden: La gwerz de Penmarc'h', *Le pays bigouden à la croisée des chemins* (Brest: Centre de Recherche Bretonne et Celtique, 1993), pp. 179–87.

——'Le siège de Guingamp', *ArMen*, 143 (2004), 18–23.

——, Fañch Postic and Pierre Prat, *Les passeurs de mémoire* (Mellac: Association du manoir de Kernault, 1996).

—— *Parcours d'un ethnologue en Bretagne* (Brest: Emgleo Breiz, 2012).

Le Berre, Yves, *La littérature de langue bretonne. Livres et brochures entre 1790 et 1918* (Brest: Ar Skol Vrezoneg, Emgleo Breiz, 1994).

—— *Qu'est-ce que la littérature bretonne? Essais de critique littéraire XVe–XXe siècle* (Rennes: Presses universitaires de Rennes, 2006).

Le Braz, Anatole, *Rapport sur une enquête relative aux saints bretons, à leurs légendes, à leurs oratoires. (août-septembre 1894).* Rapport au Ministre de l'Instruction publique et des Beaux-Arts (Quimper: 1895).

—— 'L'origine d'une gwerz bretonne', in Joseph Loth (ed.), *Mélanges en l'honneur d'Arbois de Jubainville* (Paris: Fontemoing, 1906), pp. 111–28.

—— *La légende de la mort en Basse-Bretagne* (Paris: Champion, 1893).

Le Diberder, Yves, *Chansons traditionnelles du pays vannetais (1910–1915)*, 2 vols (Vannes: Archives départementales du Morbihan, 2010).

Le Disez, Jean-Yves, *Étrange Bretagne: Récits de voyageurs britanniques en Bretagne (1830–1900)* (Rennes: Presses universitaires de Rennes, 2002).

Le Duc, Gwenaël, 'Les lais de Marie de France', *Regards étonnés: De l'expression de l'altérité… à la construction de l'idéntité. Mélanges offerts au professeur Gaël Milin* (Brest: Centre de recherche bretonne et celtique, 2002), pp. 299–316.

Le Gonidec, Marie-Barbara, *Les archives de la Mission de folklore musical en Basse-Bretagne de 1939 du Musée national des arts et traditions populaires* (Rennes and Paris: Dastum, Comité des travaux scientifiques et historiques, 2009). Available at: http://www.bassebretagne-mnatp1939.com.

Le Guennec, Louis, '"L'élégie de Monsieur de Névet" et "Le Baron Huet"', *Bulletin de la Société Archéologique du Finistère*, 48 (1921), 112–21.

—— 'La légende du Marquis de Guerrand et la Famille Du Parc de Locmaria', *Bulletin de la Société Archéologique du Finistère*, 55 (1928), 15–41.

—— 'Un épilogue ignoré de l'histoire de La Fontenelle', *Bulletin de la Société Archéologique du Finistère*, 62 (1935), 103–14.

Le Menn, Gwennolé, *La femme au sein d'or* (Saint-Brieuc and Rennes: Skol, Dastum, 1985).

—— 'La prosodie des chants en moyen-breton (1350–1650)', in Jean Quéniart (ed.), *Le chant, acteur de l'histoire* (Rennes: Presses universitaires de Rennes, 1999), pp. 13–21.

—— 'Les femmes dans les dictions et proverbes en langue bretonne', *Mémoires de la Société d'Histoire et d'Archéologie de Bretagne*, 78 (2000), 311–35.

Le Mérer, Constance, *Une collecte de chants populaires dans le pays de Lannion*. Textes et musiques présentés par Bernard Lasbleiz & Daniel Giraudon (Lannion: Dastum Bro Dreger, 2015).

Le Prat, Youenn, '"*Vive la République!*". Ar Volonter, récit de combat naval et chant républicain', in Fañch Postic (ed.), *Bretagnes, du cœur aux lèvres: Mélanges offerts à Donatien Laurent* (Rennes: Presses universitaires de Rennes, 2008), pp. 69–90.

—— 'La mémoire chantée d'une frontière maritime au XVIIIe siècle: la menace britannique sur les côtes françaises vue d'en-bas', in Jean de Préneuf, Eric Grove and Andrew Lambert (eds), *Entre terre et mer: L'occupation militaire des espaces maritimes et littoraux* (Paris: Economica, 2014), pp. 279–86.

Le Rol, Yvon, 'La langue des 'gwerzioù' à travers l'étude des manuscrits inédits de Mme de Saint-Prix (1789–1869)', unpublished doctoral thesis, 5 vols (Université de Rennes, 2013). Available at: https://tel.archives-ouvertes.fr/tel-00854190.

Leerssen, Joep, 'Ossian and the Rise of Literary Historicism', in Howard Gaskill (ed.), *The Reception of Ossian in Europe* (London: Thoemmes Continuum, 2004), pp. 109–25.

—— *Encyclopedia of Romantic Nationalism in Europe* [online]. Available at: http://romanticnationalism.net.

Loth, Joseph, 'La chanson du marquis de Pontcallec', *Annales de Bretagne*, 8 (1892), 480–7.

Lucas, Désiré, 'La Lieue de grève en Trégor, un espace de légende', *ArMen*, 27 (1990), 20–9.

Luzel, François-Marie, *Gwerziou-Breiz Izel: Chants et chansons populaires de la Basse-Bretagne. Gwerziou*, 2 vols (Lorient: Corfmat 1868 and 1874; repr. Paris: Maisonneuve et Larose, 1971).

—— *De l'authenticité des chants du Barzaz-Breiz* (Saint-Brieuc: Guyon, 1872).

—— *Soniou Breiz-Izel: Chants et chansons populaires de la Basse-Bretagne*, 2 vols (Paris: Bouillon, 1890; repr. Paris: Maisonneuve et Larose, 1971).

—— *Journal de route et lettres de mission*. Texte établi et présenté par Françoise Morvan (Rennes: Presses universitaires de Rennes, Terre de Brume, 1994).

—— *Correspondance Luzel-Renan*. Texte établi et présenté par Françoise Morvan (Rennes: Presses universitaires de Rennes, Terre de Brume, 1995).

MacGregor, Martin, '"Surely one of the greatest poems ever made in Britain": The Lament for Griogair Ruadh MacGregor of Glen Strae and its Historical Background', in Edward J. Cowan and Douglas Gifford (eds), *The Polar Twins* (Edinburgh: John Donald, 1999), pp. 114–53.

Malrieu, Patrick, *Histoire de la chanson populaire bretonne* (Rennes: Dastum, Skol, 1983).

—— 'Les pèlerinages… dans la chanson de tradition orale en breton', *Musique bretonne*, 106 (1990), 3–7.

—— 'La chanson populaire de tradition orale en langue bretonne. Contribution à l'établissement d'un catalogue', unpublished doctoral thesis, 5 vols (Rennes: Université Rennes 2, 1998).

[no author] *Marie-Josèphe Bertrand, chanteuse du Centre-Bretagne* (Dastum: Rennes, 2008), CD + booklet.

Milin, Gabriel, 'Kloarek Lambaul: La mort du marquis de Guerrand', *Bulletin de la Société Académique de Brest*, 4 (1864–5), 98–110.

—— 'La tour de plomb de Quimper', *Bulletin de la Société Académique de Brest*, IV (1864–5), 90–7.

—— *Gwerin*, vols 1–3 (Lesneven: Hor Yezh, 1961–2).

—— 'De Saint-Jacques-de-Compostelle à Notre-Dame-du-Folgoët: les voies de l'acculturation', *Annales de Bretagne et des Pays de l'Ouest*, 101 (1994/3), 7–47.

Morvan, Françoise, *François-Marie Luzel: Enquête sur une expérience de collectage folklorique en Bretagne au XIXᵉ siècle* (Rennes: Terre de Brume, Presses universitaires de Rennes, 1999).

Nassiet, Michel, *La France du second XVIIᵉ siècle. 1661–1715* (Paris: Belin, 1997).

—— 'La littérature orale bretonne et l'histoire', *Annales de Bretagne et des Pays de l'Ouest,* 106/3 (1999), 35–64.

Oiry, Michel, 'L'école vannetaise (1825–1916) et les collectes d'Yves Le Diberder (1910–1916)', in Fañch Postic (ed.), *La Bretagne et la littérature orale en Europe* (Mellac and Brest: Centre de recherche bretonne et celtique, Centre de recherche et de documentation sur la littérature orale, Centre international de rencontres des cultures de tradition orale, 1995), pp. 177–89.

Ollivier, Joseph, *La chanson populaire sur feuilles volantes: Catalogue bibliographique* (Quimper: Le Goaziou, 1942).

Padel, Oliver, 'Evidence for Oral Tales in Medieval Cornwall', *Studia Celtica*, XL (2006), 127–53.

—— 'Legendary poetry in *englyn* metre', unpublished article.

Paris, Gaston, 'L'élégie de Monsieur de Névet', *Revue de l'Histoire de l'Ouest*, 4 (1888), 5–28.

Peaudecerf, Hervé, 'Alexandre-Louis-Marie Lédan (1777–1855): Un imprimeur breton au XIXᵉ siècle (1805–1855)', unpublished doctoral thesis, 3 vols (Rennes: Université de Rennes 2, 2002).

Penguern, Jean-Marie de, *Gwerin*, vols 4–6 and 8–10 (Lesneven: Hor Yezh, 1963–5 and 1997–8).

Pérennès, Henri, 'Chansons populaires de la Basse-Bretagne', *Annales de Bretagne*, 45 (1938/1–2), 40–71 and 212–17; 46 (1939/1–2), 88–113 and 263–303.

Perréon, Stéphane, *L'Armée en Bretagne au XVIIIᵉ siècle: Institution militaire et société civile au temps de l'intendance et des États* (Rennes: Presses Universitaires de Rennes, 2005).

Pichette, Jean-Pierre (ed.), *L'apport des prêtres et des religieux au patrimoine des minorités: Parcours comparés Bretagne/Canada français*, special issue of *Port-Acadie. Revue internationale en études acadiennes*, 24–25–26 (2014).

Piette, Gwenno, *Brittany: A Concise History* (Cardiff: University of Wales Press, 2008).

Piriou, Yann-Ber, 'La *gwerz* du "Siège de Guingamp" et la duchesse Anne dans la tradition orale', in Jean Kerhervé and Tanguy Daniel (eds), *1491. La Bretagne, terre d'Europe* (Brest and Quimper: Centre de recherche bretonne et celtique, Société archéologique du Finistère, 1992), pp. 489–99.

Porter, Gerald, '"Eaten with Merriment and Sport": Cannibalism and the Colonial Subject', *The Atlantic Literary Review Quarterly*, 3 (2002), 21–32.

Postic, Fañch, 'La peste d'Elliant', *ArMen*, 80 (1996), 18–29.

—— 'Premiers échanges interceltiques: Le voyage de La Villemarqué au pays de Galles', *ArMen*, 125 (2001), 34–43.

—— 'Le rôle d'Émile Souvestre dans le développement du mouvement d'intérêt pour les traditions orales', in Bärbel Plötner-Le Lay and Nelly Blanchard (eds), *Émile Souvestre: Écrivain breton porté par l'utopie sociale* (Brest: Centre de recherche bretonne et celtique, 2007), pp. 117–36.

—— 'Écrire "l'histoire de l'imagination": Cambry face au paysan breton' in Anne de Mathan (ed.), *Jacques Cambry (1749–1807): Un Breton des Lumières au service de la construction nationale* (Brest: Centre de recherche bretonne et celtique, 2008), pp. 73–83.

—— (ed.), *La Bretagne et la littérature orale en Europe* (Mellac and Brest: Centre de recherche bretonne et celtique, Centre de recherche et de documentation sur la littérature orale, Centre international de rencontres des cultures de tradition orale, 1995).

—— (ed.), *François Cadic (1864–1929), Un collecteur vannetais "recteur" des Bretons de Paris* (Brest: Centre de recherche bretonne et celtique, 2012).

[no author] *Révoltes, Résistances et Révolution en Bretagne* (Spézet: Coop Breizh, 2007), CD + booklet.

Rouaud, Thierry, 'Gwerz an Tour Plomb. L'incendie de la cathédrale de Quimper en 1620', *Musique Bretonne*, 163 (2000), 28–31. Available at: http://follenn.chez.com/tourplomb.html.

Rouz, Bernez, 'Ar Vosenn e Breizh-Izel. Studiadenn war Hengoun ar Bobl', *Hor Yezh*, 166 (1986).

Saintyves, Pierre, *En marge de la légende dorée: Songes, miracles et survivances. Essai sur la formation de quelques thèmes hagiographiques* (Paris: Émile Nourry, 1930).

Sand, George, 'Les visions de la nuit dans les campagnes', *L'Illustration*, 504 (1852), 267–8.

Scott, Walter, 'Reliques of Robert Burns', *Quarterly Review*, 1–2 (1810), 16–31.

Sharp, Cecil, *English Folk Carols* (London: Novello & Co., 1911).

Sims-Williams, Patrick, 'The visionary Celt: the construction of an "ethnic preconception"', *Cambrian Medieval Celtic Studies*, 11 (1986), 71–96.

—— 'Celtomania and Celtoscepticism', *Cambrian Medieval Celtic Studies*, 36 (1998), 1–36.

Souvestre, Émile, 'Poésies populaires de la Basse-Bretagne', *Revue des deux mondes* (1 December 1834), 489–537.

Tanguy, Alain, 'Anatole Le Braz (1859–1926) et la tradition populaire en Bretagne – analyse de quatre carnets d'enquêtes inédits – (1890–1895)', unpublished doctoral thesis, 5 vols (Brest: Université de Bretagne Occidentale, 1997).

Tanguy, Bernard, *Aux origines du nationalisme breton* (Paris: Union générale d'éditions, 1977).

Taylor, Tom, *Ballads and Songs of Brittany* (London: Macmillan and Co., 1865).

[no author] *Tradition familiale de chant en pays bigouden* (Rennes: Dastum, 1991), tape recording.

[no author] *Tradition chantée de Bretagne. Les sources du Barzaz Breiz aujourd'hui* (Douarnenez and Rennes: ArMen [Dastum, 1989], CD + booklet).

Trebitsch, Rudolf, *The Collections of Rudolf Trebitsch* (Vienna: Verlag der Österreichischen Akademie der Wissenschaften, 2003), CD + booklet.

Trévédy, Julien, 'Le dernier exploit de La Fontenelle', *Bulletin de la Société d'Émulation des Côtes-du-Nord*, 26 (1888), 4–16.

Troadeg, Ifig, *Carnets de route* (Lannion: Dastum Bro Dreger, 2005).

Trollope, Thomas Adolphus, *A Summer in Brittany* (London: H. Colburn, 1840).

Vallée, François, 'Une exploration musicale en Basse-Bretagne! Les airs des Gwerziou de Luzel retrouvés et phonographiés', *Annales de Bretagne*, 16 (1900), 130–5.

Van Dam, Raymond (ed.), *Glory of the Confessors* (Liverpool: Liverpool University Press, 1988).

Vasallo, Marthe, *Les Chants du livre bleu. À travers les* Musiques bretonnes *de Maurice Duhamel* (Guimaëc: Son an Ero, 2015).

Williams, Heather, *Postcolonial Brittany: Literature between Languages* (Bern: Peter Lang, 2007).

Williams, Jane, *The Literary Remains of the Rev. Thomas Price, Carnhuanawc*, 2 vols (Llandovery and London: W. Rees and Longman, 1855).

Glossary of Places in French and Breton

An index of places as they appear in their French form in the book, with their standardized Breton equivalents.

Audierne: Gwaien
Basse-Bretagne: Breizh-Izel
Basse-Cornouaille: Kerne-Izel
Baud: Baod
Berné: Berne
Bieuzy: Bihui
Brest: Brest
Bretagne: Breizh
Bubry: Bubri
Callac: Kallak
Carhaix: Karaez
Cavan: Kawan
Clohars-Carnoët: Kloar-Karnoed
Cornouaille: Bro Gerne
Croixanvec: Kroeshañveg
Duault: Duaod
Elliant: Eliant
Goëlo: Goelo
Goulven: Goulven
Guéméné: Ar Gemene
Guénin: Gwennin
Guimiliau: Gwimilio
Guingamp: Gwengamp
Haute-Bretagne: Breizh-Uhel
Haute-Cornouaille: Kerne-Uhel
Hengoat: Hengoad
Henvic: Henvig
Kernascléden: Kernaskledenn
Kerpert: Kerbêr
La Chapelle-Neuve: Ar Chapel-Nevez
Lamballe: Lambal
Landudec: Landudeg
Lanester: Lannarstêr

Langoélan: Lanwelan
Langonnet: Langoned
Lannion: Lannuon
Lanrivain: Larruen
Le Faouët: Ar Faoued
Le Folgoët: Ar Folgoad
Le Ponthou: Ar Pontoù
Le Yaudet: Ar Yeoded
Léon: Breo Leon
Lieue-de-Grève: Al Lev-Draezh
Lignol: Lignol
Locmaria-Quimper: Locmaria-Kemper
Locquirec: Lokireg
Loctudy: Loctudi
Lorient: An Oriant
Finistère: Penn-ar-Bed
Louannec: Louaneg
Melrand: Mêlrant
Minihy-Tréguier: Ar Vinic'hi
Moncontour: Monkontour
Monts d'Arrée: Menez Arre
Morlaix: Montroulez
Mûr: Mur
Nantes: An Naoned
Nizon: Nizon
Noyal-Pontivy: Noal-Pondi
Ouessant: Eusa
Pays bigouden: Bro Vigoudenn
Pays melenig: Bro Velenig
Penmarc'h: Penmarc'h
Penvénan: Penvenan
Perros-Guirec: Perroz-Gireg
Pleudaniel: Planiel

Ploemeur: Plañvour

Ploëzal: Pleuzal

Plouaret: Plouared

Ploubezre: Ploubêr

Plouégat-Guerrand: Plegad-Gwerann

Plouescat: Ploueskad

Plougrescant: Plougouskant

Plouguiel: Priel

Plouigneau: Plouigno

Ploumilliau: Plouilio

Plounéour-Ménez: Plouneour-Menez

Plounévez-du-Faou: Plonevez-ar-Faou

Plounévez-Quintin: Plounevez-Kintin

Plourac'h: Plourac'h

Plouvorn: Plouvorn

Plozévet: Plozeved

Plussulien: Plusulian

Pluvigner: Pleuwigner

Pluzunet: Plûned

Pont-Scorff: Pont-Skorf

Pontcallec: Pontkelleg

Pontivy: Pondi

Pontrieux: Pontrev

Port-Blanc: Porzh-Gwenn

Port-Louis: Porzh-Loeiz

Quimper: Kemper

Quimperlé: Kemperle

Rennes :   Roazhon

Riantec: Rianteg

Saint-Brieuc: Sant-Brieg

Saint-Jean-du-Doigt: Sant-Yann-ar-Biz

Saint-Nicodème: Sant-Nigouden

Saint-Nicolas-du-Pélem: Sant-Nikolaz-ar-Pelem

Saint-Rivoal: Sant-Riwal

Saint-Thuriau: Sant-Turiav

Saint-Vougay: Sant-Nouga

Sainte-Anne-d'Auray: Santez-Anna-Wened

Sept-Îles: Ar Jentilez

Taulé: Taole

Trébrivan: Trabrivan

Trédrez: Tredraezh

Treffrin: Trefin

Trégor: Bro Dreger

Tréguier: Landreger

Trémel: Tremael

Vannes: Gwened

Vannetais: Bro Wened

General Index

A List of Songs on the CD (and their Equivalents in the Book)